Advance Praise

A valuable addition to the biographical literature encompassing the crucial decades around Independence.

Professor Joachim Oesterheld
Historian and Specialist on South Asia,
Humboldt University of Berlin, Germany

Netaji's grandniece tells the story of the Bose Brothers' contribution to India's struggle for independence through the eyes of her father, Amiya. She relies on extensive conversations with her father over the years that have shaped her own view of the history of Indian independence. The result is an interesting insight into the experiences, perceptions and analyses from the inner circle of the Bose family.

Dr Jan Kuhlmann
Historian and a Netaji Scholar

The legend of the two shining stars of Indian patriotism, Subhas Chandra and Sarat Chandra is truer than truth itself. Madhuri Bose, a family insider, has chronicled it in a way, at once moving and charming. The inspiring legend has gained in the telling and is embellished by the first-person recollections from Amiya Nath Bose. The story unfolded in this beautiful narrative is indeed a priceless legacy of renascent India.

Justice M. N. Venkatachaliah
Former Chief Justice of India

Madhuri Bose has thrown new light on aspects of India's independence struggle. The story she tells—and the new material contained in it—will be invaluable to scholars both in India and elsewhere. It is also a reminder of the complexity of the independence movement and of the different perspectives of some of the main players.

John McCarthy
Former Australian High Commissioner
to India (2004–2009)
National President of Australian Institute
for International Affairs

The Bose Brothers

and Indian Independence

The Bose Brothers

and Indian Independence

An Insider's Account

Madhuri Bose

Los Angeles | London | New Delhi
Singapore | Washington DC | Melbourne

First published in 2016 by

 SAGE Publications India Pvt Ltd
B1/I-1 Mohan Cooperative Industrial Area
Mathura Road, New Delhi 110 044, India
www.sagepub.in

SAGE Publications Inc
2455 Teller Road
Thousand Oaks, California 91320, USA

SAGE Publications Ltd
1 Oliver's Yard, 55 City Road
London EC1Y 1SP, United Kingdom

SAGE Publications Asia-Pacific Pte Ltd
3 Church Street
#10-04 Samsung Hub
Singapore 049483

Published by Vivek Mehra for SAGE Publications India Pvt Ltd, typeset in 10/12pt Century Schoolbook by Diligent Typesetter, Delhi and printed at Sai Print-o-Pack, New Delhi.

Library of Congress Cataloging-in-Publication Data Available

ISBN: 978-93-515-0397-2 (HB)

The SAGE Team: Aditi Chopra, Saima Ghaffar, Neena Ganjoo, Rajib Chatterjee and Ritu Chopra

To My Father

Who remained a lifelong flag bearer of the Bose Brothers

Contents

List of Photographs and Letters

Photographs

Letters

Foreword

This illuminating book is an important addition to the literature on India's freedom movement and the roles in it of the formidable Bose Brothers, Sarat and Subhas. It is also extremely readable, not many will put it down midway.

The portraits on which this book sheds light are intimate ones, though the word 'interior' may be more apt. Here we are offered, among other things, the inner thoughts of Subhas Bose in his 20s, 30s and early 40s, communicated to a brother older by eight years and also to the brother's son Amiya Nath, 17 years junior to Subhas and devoted to his uncle.

Clearly Subhas nursed high expectations from Amiya Nath. In one significant letter written in 1933, he asks his nephew, then 18 years old, to seek 'the loftiest heights' and explains how he can do it. He should work hard but aim 'to serve others and die for others'. Arrogance, Subhas adds, was 'a great sin'; a really great person is self-confident but arrogance-free. Moreover, life's key principle 'is to give and not to take'. Those who are mean to us can be conquered by love.

This remarkable advice was also a challenge to which, it must be said, Amiya Nath rose manfully. Like father Sarat, and grandfather Janakinath Bose, Amiya Nath became a successful lawyer. Bold, self-confident and dedicated to his country's liberty, he spent most of the Second World War years in England, from where he remained in secret contact with Uncle Subhas, who was in Germany from April 1941 to February 1943.

Some years after independence, Amiya Nath entered the Lok Sabha (in opposition to the Congress) and later served as India's Ambassador to Rangoon, where the family members of Burma's hero Aung San were Netaji's warm admirers.

It is Amiya Nath's daughter Madhuri, who has created this valuable book. I say 'created' rather than 'authored' for two reasons. First, the book offers sentences from Amiya Nath, from his father Sarat, and from Subhas, not merely those from

Madhuri's pen. Second, the book follows a creator's design. Starting with a glimpse of Amiya Nath's relationships with his father and uncle, and concluding with the deaths of Subhas, Sarat and Amiya Nath, in the middle chapters, it provides the stirring story, often in Amiya Nath's words, of two extraordinary brothers who gave their joys, comforts and lives for the freedom and unity of their beloved land.

If in the end the goal of unity was not achieved, it was not for lack of trying by the Bose Brothers. Part of the book's merit is its ability to convey the spirit of Sarat Bose's earnest effort in 1947 to preserve a single Bengal in the subcontinent's east, even if partition in the west was unavoidable.

Quite a few will be startled to learn from these pages that Subhas's clandestine network in Kolkata included friends who were able to smuggle out, for his inspection, an entire dossier of files that the British-run police was keeping on him. For about seven successive nights in the summer of 1939, Subhas and his nephew Amiya Nath pored over files secretly brought to their Elgin Road home from intelligence headquarters on Elysium Row (now Lord Sinha Road) and returned discreetly to their shelves at dawn. Containing information on who in Subhas's circle were informers, the files were helpful to Subhas when in January 1941 he made his famous escape from house arrest in Kolkata all the way to Afghanistan and Germany.

Thus, while the imperial armour contained chinks, the empire's foe possessed resourceful agents.

The book also captures the family's shock and disbelief at the report in August 1945 of Subhas's death in an air crash, as well as the family's initial surprise and subsequent delight on learning that Subhas had married Emilie Schenkl of Austria and had a daughter from her called Anita. We discover, too, that Amiya Nath had met Emilie Schenkl in Europe in 1937, while she was assisting his uncle as interpreter and secretary.

Not surprisingly, the Bose Brothers' differences with Gandhi feature prominently in the book. Neither Gandhi nor the Bose Brothers could tolerate India's inferiority or subjugation, but Gandhi opposed the use of the gun or the bomb for liberty. He thought that while the British knew how to suppress a violent rising—they had done so in 1857—non-violent resistance would baffle them. Moreover, once violence was legitimised in India's struggle, armed Indians would bully their compatriots. Women, the lame, the blind and the downtrodden would go to the wall. Gandhi's non-cooperation call of 1920 galvanised Subhas who had gone to England to clear the ICS exam. This he did brilliantly but, renouncing the career he had earned, Subhas flung himself into the national struggle.

However, disagreeing in the 1920s with some of Gandhi's decisions as the struggle's commander, Subhas also conveyed his disagreement with non-violence as a principle. If suitable opportunities arose for armed action for independence, Subhas would take them.

All know of the Gandhi–Subhas break that occurred in 1939, which this book describes in detail. That split notwithstanding, in the 1940s Netaji would address Gandhi as the Father of the Nation in broadcasts from his Burmese battlefront.

Prior to that, in their last face-to-face meeting, which took place in June 1940, Subhas (to use Gandhi's own words) told the Mahatma, 'in the friendliest manner that he would do what the Working Committee had failed to do'. To this Gandhi evidently responded by saying, 'If at the end of his plan there was Swaraj during my lifetime, mine would be the first telegram of congratulation he would receive' (*Harijan*, 13 July 1940).

Thus conveying the texture of a partnership that transcended major differences, the book also underlines the Bose–Gandhi congruence on the secular character of the state in a free India and on the imperative of Hindu–Muslim friendship.

Not everyone cultivated or cultivates this plant. Sadly, even some who had fought together in the INA under Netaji, succumbed to the poison of 1947. We know that the frenzied killers of 1947 unfortunately included, on both sides of the communal divide, recent INA soldiers as well as demobilised soldiers from the Empire's Indian armies.

Madhuri Bose's book is a helpful reminder that today's India and South Asia can do with Subhas's—and Sarat's—concern for an inclusive state and society, which was the Mahatma's concern as well.

As mentioned before, Sarat Bose's gallant effort in and around May 1947 for a United Bengal unattached either to India or Pakistan is part of this book's story. Nehru and Patel were totally opposed to the bid, as were many in both parts of

Bengal; Shyama Prasad Mookerji, in particular, was championing Bengal's division; yet at one stage it seemed as if both Gandhi and Jinnah might support Sarat's proposal. Then, to Sarat's bitter disappointment, Gandhi apparently backed off.

If Gandhi had continued to support Sarat's bid, would we have seen a United Bengal in 1947? Natural though such a question may be, it cannot be clearly answered. That Gandhi's word was not exactly law with the Congress in 1947 was demonstrated in April of that year, when Gandhi's proposal of a Jinnah-led government in New Delhi to avoid partition was summarily rejected by the Congress.

More than once, the book cites Amiya Nath's appraisal that India's partition had become inevitable after the provincial elections of 1937, when the Congress refused to share power with the Muslim League in the UP ministry. While others have argued similarly, there are indications elsewhere that Jinnah may have chosen a religious or separatist path at least a year earlier than this—in 1936—after being snubbed in Punjab by the Unionist Party's leaders, Fazli Husain and Sikander Hayat Khan.

In May 1938, Subhas Bose, who was the Congress President at the time, held talks with Jinnah in an attempt to bridge the Congress–League divide. Noting that Subhas was 'a good listener', Gandhi, who had encouraged this dialogue, thought that Bose 'may succeed where others might have failed,' but the Bose–Jinnah talks also led to nowhere.

However, it is not to settle or resolve questions of Partition history that Madhuri Bose has created this book. Love for her father, mother, grandfather, grandmother and granduncle has impelled her to produce it, along with the legitimate conviction that her father, Amiya Nath's memories and appraisals of the Bose Brothers should find a permanent record and reach a wider public.

When Madhuri asked me to write a foreword for it, I was touched. I had had the good fortune, in the 1960s and 1970s, to meet Amiya Babu a few times. Much earlier, as an 11 year old in New Delhi, I had received a small prize for a short Sanskrit recitation from the hands of Sarat Babu. That was in end-1946, when, along with Nehru, Patel and a few others, Sarat Babu was a member of the Interim Government that preceded independence.

In his speech on the occasion, Sarat Babu spoke of a book called *Ideas Have Legs*. The phrase was unusual and I remembered it. More than a decade later, I would meet the author of that book, an unforgettable Englishman called Peter Howard.

Subhas Babu I never met. But he is in my mind and heart, as he is inside all who love India and want greatness for her.

May this book's glimpses of the Bose Brothers and Amiya Babu prod all of us to aspire for the 'lofty heights' that Subhas commended to his nephew.

Rajmohan Gandhi

Acknowledgements

This book about the legendary Bose Brothers of India, Sarat Chandra Bose and his beloved younger brother Subhas Chandra Bose, has been a long labour of love inspired by my father Amiya Nath Bose, son of Sarat and nephew of Subhas. As a young man, Amiya had at various key times in Indian history worked closely with both of them, and was thus a direct and compelling witness to the tumultuous lives of his father and uncle.

As an ardent collector and early custodian of the records of the Bose Brothers, Amiya was thus uniquely placed to act as a chronicler of their contributions to the long struggle for independence in the subcontinent. It is fortunate that he has left for all of us the Private Collection of Amiya Nath and Jyotsna Bose, a rich assembly of articles, lectures, notes and memoirs which forms the basis of this book. These will be made progressively available to both a national and global audience, primarily through a dedicated website www.TheBoseLegacy.com.

It may seem unusual as the author to be acknowledging and expressing appreciation for the writings of the Bose Brothers themselves. I found quite simply that this was unavoidable. To begin with, one of the best—if not the best—accounts of the political history of the independence struggle in the two decades leading up to the Second World War is *The Indian Struggle*. This was first written by Subhas in 1934 to cover the period 1920–1934, and updated in the early 1940s to cover the period 1934–1942. The reader will observe in this book that where he needed to, my father Amiya drew liberally on *The Indian Struggle* to place events in context. It is no coincidence that Amiya had initiated and overseen its translation and first publication in Bengali in book form, in 1948 and 1953 for the two sequential parts respectively.

Sarat for his part was just as prolific, with a wealth of written materials in the form of articles, speeches, manifestos, newspaper editorials, parliamentary interventions, letters and the like. Much of this material has been published by The Sarat Bose Academy established at Netaji Bhawan, Calcutta, in 1952, including the *Selected Speeches and Writings of Sarat Chandra Bose 1947–1950* (1954) and the *Sarat Chandra Bose Commemoration Volume* (1982). A third volume entitled *Interpreting a Nation* (2001) compiled and edited by well-known author and academic, Professor Anjan Bera for the Netaji Institute for Asian Studies in Kolkata, has also informed the preparation of this book.

In his lectures and commentaries about his father and uncle, Amiya made frequent reference to materials which he collected over time from the India Office Library and Records in London, including British India Government intelligence reports emanating from both the British Government in London and from colonial India.

These diverse source materials pertaining to both Sarat and Subhas have been drawn upon extensively, often in original form to illustrate to the reader the ways in which the brothers thought and expressed themselves, and what others thought of them. The source of such materials has been acknowledged in the text.

I recognise here with deep appreciation the role of the late Professor Prasanta Ghosh who did some earlier work with my father on an unfinished biography of Sarat Chandra Bose. In that context he translated from Bengali to English a key item of correspondence from 1930 which had been hand-carried by a teenage Amiya from Subhas to the revolutionary leader Barin Ghosh. A draft of that precious letter was preserved by Amiya Nath and the translation is included in full in the book.

I am indebted to a number of people for the preparatory work on this book, which goes back a number of years. It began with the digitisation and recording of voluminous collections of written materials and transcriptions from audio recordings. Kathakali Mukherjee was with me to initiate that painstaking process. My sincere thanks go to Somendra Narayan Ghosh and Jaya Mukherjee, who worked diligently over the years in pursuit of the task of digitisation. I must thank Madhumita Dasgupta for her work in summarising British Intelligence records. Jayanti Neogy very kindly volunteered to help me with the tedious task of doing the endnotes for which I am very grateful. My nephew Anirban Ray enhanced the quality of photographs used.

I am indebted to my long-time friend Raju Raman who not only translated Subhas's letters to Amiya from Bengali to English, but has readily provided advice and support whenever required. As an authority on Subhas, Chandrachur Ghose of Mission Netaji and www.subhaschandrabose.org in Delhi has been a valuable source of information and confirmation of many aspects of the life and work of Subhas and the volumes that have been written about him.

I am thankful to my 'readers' who carefully perused the manuscript and offered valuable suggestions and editorial comments: my favourite teachers at Modern High School in Kolkata, Chhanda Bose, who taught me the importance of history and Supriya Bhattacharya who imparted to me a love of the English language; my friends Toopsi Ray and Sara Adhikari; family friend Krishno Dey with whom father had shared many of his remarkable experiences.

From faraway Australia, friends John McCarthy (former High Commissioner to India), Peter and Charmaine Maccoll, Alan and Cheryl Swan and Elizabeth Hattie and Colin. McLellan read the final manuscript, and were a collective source of interested, objective and thoughtful commentary.

My friends from across the globe have never ceased to ask through the years about 'The Book' and when it will appear! From London, Trisha Ambris-Dening (in whose home I once spent hours scanning my documents while she went out so as not to disturb me!) and Tracy Ulltveit-Moe in particular have persistently expressed their high expectations of what is to come. I trust that they will not be disappointed.

My brothers Surya and Chandra have been particularly close to the process and have been a constant source of encouragement and support. On many occasions they were able to confirm for me key events in the panorama of our father Amiya's life as it pertained to the vision of the Bose Brothers. Surya was by our father's side during a call on Lord Mountbatten in London in October 1976, a meeting which led to an exchange of correspondence reflected in the book. Chandra has in recent years been very much in the public eye, as part of a collective and ongoing movement to address distortions in the historical record where the Brothers are concerned, and to declassify documents about Subhas, stubbornly held in secret to this day by successive Governments of India.

My mother Jyotsna has throughout been a pillar of strength for me. When my father passed away suddenly on 27 January 1996, she assumed direct responsibility for the care and protection of the priceless archive assembled by her husband. At the same time, she never ceased to remind me of my own inherited responsibility to put together the book that my father had always intended to write and to which he had already devoted much time and energy. Partly due to my own career path and peripatetic ways, that book has been some time in the making. My mother passed away on 1 March 2015, and was thus not able to see the final published product. That she was able to see and thoroughly approve of the completed manuscript, is of some consolation.

Introduction

My very first history lessons on the epic struggle for Indian independence were from my father Amiya Nath Bose, who grew up in colonial India in the tumultuous decades leading to independence in 1947. As a child, these lessons were for me enthralling *tales from the Raj* with a distinct twist, accounts of momentous events in our history from the perspectives of many of the most prominent Indian nationalist leaders, freedom fighters and revolutionaries. That the narratives were often first-hand and graphic, made the events and the personalities come truly alive for me, born as I was in a different era of independent, though sadly divided India.

I grew up in the extended family home at 1 Woodburn Park in south Calcutta, the three-storied imposing house of my grandfather Sarat Chandra Bose built in 1928 as his family residence, just a stone's throw from the ancestral house at 38/2 Elgin Road (now Netaji Bhawan). It was here at 1 Woodburn Park (now called Sarat Bose Bhawan and run under government auspices as the Netaji Institute for Asian Studies), where Sarat and Subhas, the famed Bose Brothers, lived and worked together during the critical phases of the struggle for Indian independence.

During the working week, my father would be busy with his legal cases at the Calcutta High Court, followed by evening consultations with his clients at home. His continuing engagement with politics and public affairs also took much of his time. So it was usually in the quiet evenings at weekends when he would find time to relax, read (he was a voracious reader) and spend time talking to his children, my two brothers Surya and Chandra, and myself.

Father had a remarkable skill for storytelling or rather 'talking history'. He had a phenomenal memory and cited dates and events with precision and accuracy, which never failed to impress us. He also had a wonderful sense of humour and would delight us with anecdotes from his childhood, whether about an eccentric, sleep-walking uncle, or a comical incident at a family wedding.

Often these journeys into great moments of our freedom struggle, followed by episodes of stalemate and even regression, and then the catastrophic descent into the tragedy of partition, would carry on through dinner, which was always punctually at 9 p.m., when our mother Jyotsna (née Ghosh) would take her place at the head of the table. Mother's own family originally came from the eastern part of Bengal, and she was thus well aware of the misery and heartache which partition had wrought. She would at times recall happier days of travel with her father as a senior public servant, mother and siblings across Bengal, and holidays spent in their house on the banks of the Buriganga river (Old Ganges) on the edge of Dhaka city.

My parents were married on 7 March 1948. Their wedding was a most joyous occasion, with festivities spreading over one week, planned and overseen by Sarat and wife Bivabati. The house at 1 Woodburn Park was resplendent with lights and flowers, and the auspicious sound of the shenai (a traditional wind instrument) wafted in the air. The gloom that had descended on Sarat's household with the disappearance of Subhas and the tragedy of partition was lifted for a while. The march of national events would quickly take centre stage again.

It did not take much time for my mother to adjust to the rhythms of life in a large and very busy household headed by Sarat and Bivabati, where their private home was also the centre of a very active public life. Mother saw at close hand the unyielding efforts of Sarat to deal with the aftermath of partition including the flood of refugees from over the new border with what was now East Pakistan, and to bring peace and harmony in divided Bengal. Mother also witnessed Sarat's last desperate attempt to undo the partition of Bengal, just hours before he passed away on 20 February 1950, with a public call for its reunification.

For my mother, her father-in-law Sarat was at once a deeply revered public figure and national leader who could have changed the course of Indian history, and a loving family man and doting grandfather. In her eyes, her mother-in-law Bivabati, petite and gentle as she was, embodied enormous strength and stoicism which were put to the test often in her life.

Growing up under the strong influence of his father Sarat and uncle Subhas, Amiya was from a very young age a keen observer of the ongoing national movement. The Woodburn Park house itself was the venue for key meetings of the Indian National Congress during the late 1920s and 1930s, where Mahatma Gandhi and Jawaharlal Nehru, among others, stayed as guests. Gandhiji had written to my grandmother Bivabati on 29 July 1942.

Dear Sister

I hope you got my message sent thro [sic] Manoranjan Babu. You will believe me when I say that political differences do not alter affection. I became a member of the family when you placed your whole house at my disposal & you and all the family showered unforgettable affection on me.

I hope you have good news from Sarat Babu.

Love to you all,

M K Gandhi

Through the formative years of his political apprenticeship to the Bose Brothers, my father came into direct contact with Congress stalwarts including Gandhi, Nehru and Vallabhbhai Patel, and in time came to know them well. This early acquaintance with the principal players on the national stage would stand him in good stead in the future, in his own role in politics and diplomacy, both before and after independence.

Father would speak about a host of subjects but often the focus would turn to the dramatic changes that took place in the Indian Nationalist Movement from the early 1920s with the emergence of Gandhi and Deshbandhu Chittaranjan Das (C. R. Das). It was also the time when Sarat and Subhas actively joined the groundswell of nationalist aspirations with the launch of the Non-Cooperation Movement by Gandhi. About the Bose Brothers father could speak with intimacy and deep personal knowledge which came from not only being a son and nephew, but also from his later adult experience as their confidant, political ally and personal envoy.

In speaking about his illustrious father and iconic uncle, my father would always point to their life-long commitment to communal harmony in a free, united and socialist India. He would emphasise that neither Sarat nor Subhas could be understood or studied alone—their principles, vision and goals converged, complemented and reinforced each other.

Commenting on the overall significance of the extraordinary relationship between the brothers, father said at a lecture in Netaji Bhawan in Calcutta on the occasion of the birth anniversary of Subhas on 23 January 1976:

> [T]he life and work of Subhas Chandra Bose cannot be fully appreciated without an understanding of Sarat Chandra Bose. They shared a common vision of a free and united India, took an uncompromising stand on majority or minority-based communalism, and believed passionately in the principles of socialism.

> As my father Sarat's friend and fellow barrister Kali Prasad Khaitan once observed in a memorial lecture at Netaji Bhawan on 6 September 1953 organised by the Sarat Bose Academy: 'Sarat was coeur-de-lion. He made Subhas what he was; Subhas made Sarat what he is. Alive in the heart of Bengal, of India, the India that the proud and sturdy Bose Brothers helped to be free ...'

Father would trace the beginnings of India's freedom struggle to the armed uprising of 1857 as the first mass revolt by force of arms against British power, put down by the British through a reign of terror. He would describe the genesis of the Congress in 1885 and its gradual transformation from being simply a platform for civic and political dialogue between educated Indians on the one hand, and members of the British Raj on the other, into a pivotal mass-based organisation which brought together nationalists—both moderates and extremists (radicals)—claiming increasingly more constitutional change and greater autonomy in governance. Father never failed to mention Lokmanya Bal Gangadhar Tilak who was one of the first advocates of Swaraj (full independence) by the turn of the nineteenth century and had famously declared, 'Swaraj is my birthright, and I shall have it!'

Father would also talk about the role of the Indian revolutionaries active from the last decade of the ninteenth century, many of them from Bengal, and their attempts to foment a revolutionary movement during the First World War which was quickly crushed by the superior force of the British. He would recall his own childhood memories of those revolutionaries who came to meet Sarat and Subhas at their Woodburn Park home. Of Surya Sen who led the Chittagong Armoury Raid in 1930, he would reminisce that he appeared to be 'a very quiet and simple man and who could have possibly known of the fire that was inside him!'. He would relate too, his excitement when he was sent off by his Uncle Subhas sometime in 1930 to deliver by hand a long, intimate letter (reproduced in Chapter 3) to Barin Ghosh, younger brother and fellow revolutionary of Aurobindo Ghosh.

Father was only a child when C. R. Das gained prominence as a Congress leader and later as the founder of the Swaraj Party, which split from the mainstream Congress in January 1923 and rapidly gained in popularity and strength. C. R. Das was of course the acknowledged political guru of the Bose Brothers, and on his premature death Subhas had lamented, 'Deshabandhu's public career was meteoric and he died in the plenitude of his powers.'

Father related his earliest memories of the Deshabandhu at Swaraj Party meetings which were held at the then Sarat Bose residence at 38/1 Elgin Road, next door to the ancestral house. At one such meeting of the Swaraj Party, Motilal Nehru, Hakim Ajmal Khan, J. M. Sengupta, all leading lights of the new Party and a few others had gathered in the room. Sengupta was reclining in his chair smoking a cigar, taking no notice of Motilal Nehru and the others present. Shortly, Sarat came up the stairs and announced, 'Karta (the boss) is here!' Deshabandhu entered the room. Sengupta immediately got up from his chair and quickly disposed of his cigar. Everyone in the room was all attention and the meeting promptly began.

From 1933 father was an undergraduate at the Scottish Churches College, University of Calcutta, where he was instrumental in the establishment of the Calcutta University Students Union. As its first president, he had invited Mohammad Ali Jinnah to speak on the subject of Hindu–Muslim unity in the historic Darbhanga Hall of the University, sometime in early 1937. Father recalled that on that occasion Jinnah spoke passionately in support of understanding and harmony between the two communities, with no hint from him of the cataclysm to come.

In March 1937, my father left for England to study for the Economics Tripos at the University of Cambridge, and also to qualify as a Barrister-at-Law. There too, he became active in support of the independence movement back home. For more than seven years until his final return to India in December 1944, he was to spend much time and effort in propagating the Indian cause among British Members of Parliament, artistic and cultural circles, various celebrities and the general public of Great Britain.

For the last three years of his stay in England and after his return to India, Amiya also campaigned ceaselessly for the release of his father Sarat from isolated detention in southern India. After Sarat was finally released in September 1945, he was always by his father's side, through the trials and tribulations of returned Indian National Army (INA) personnel and consequent upheavals, critical negotiations on independence and partition, and against the background of the heart-rending disappearance of Subhas in August 1945.

My father often spoke with deep emotion of the agony of Sarat in not having been able to prevent the partition of India and of Bengal in particular, despite all of his efforts, unwavering commitment and foresight. He also spoke of Sarat's life-long fight against the scourge of communalism and of his fearless voice against the corruption, nepotism and favouritism which had accompanied the Congress Party into power from 1947.

Following the sudden and untimely death of Sarat in February 1950, father with the active help of friends, family and associates took over the task of consolidating the Bose legacy, in the hope that India could be reshaped in line with the vision of the Bose Brothers and their dream of Asian regional solidarity and cooperation. Sarat, after his release from detention, had taken steps to acquire from his other brothers the Bose ancestral house at 38/2 Elgin Road in order to establish a museum, research and community centre, and had called it Netaji Bhawan after his beloved brother.

As part of the efforts to implement the plans of Sarat, The Sarat Bose Academy was established in 1952 as the principal functional arm at Netaji Bhawan. My father assumed the office of General Secretary of the Academy. He immediately began an earnest and assiduous global search and collection of documents from the United Kingdom, Germany, Italy, Japan, as well as from India itself, of both state and private archives, correspondence, photographs and films related to the work of the brothers. These substantial and valuable collections were housed at Netaji Bhawan.

At the same time, the Academy launched a programme for publishing the writings, speeches and correspondence of both Sarat and Subhas. Photographic exhibitions depicting the life and work of the Bose Brothers were also undertaken by the Academy.

Father lectured extensively both in India and overseas on the role of the Bose Brothers in the struggle for Indian independence. He also covered many topics of contemporary Indian interest, including challenges to national integrity, the inherent problems with a quasi-federal system as was established in India and the ideal of South Asian solidarity.

The contents of this book are drawn essentially from my father's many writings, both published and unpublished, his numerous lectures in India and abroad, private correspondence, personal diaries, memoirs, as well as official records and documentation preserved by him in his Private Collection of Amiya Nath and Jyotsna Bose.

My extensive conversations with father over the years have also informed my own understanding of the history of Indian independence, and thus the writing of this book. I have sought to recount that history as my father saw it at close hand, his own involvement in the process and how he analysed and interpreted events after independence was won.

The task of compiling and editing has been challenging, made more difficult by inaccessibility to the bulk of my father's personal and archival collections stored by him in the archives at Netaji Bhawan, which have for many decades not been readily accessible.

This book is not a biography of the Bose Brothers. Rather, it is based entirely on my father's perceptions, insights and analyses of the roles of key personalities, with a focus on Sarat and Subhas, over three decades from the early 1920s. As such I hope that this commentary on the Bose Brothers and the road they travelled, as seen through my father's eyes, will make its own unique contribution to a resurgence of interest in them, and all that they stood for. Theirs was above all a story of commitment, selflessness and sacrifice, a beacon for the young and for the generations to come. My father sought in his own characteristic way to keep the flame alive and to inspire others to do the same.

Readers may ask: Why this book now? Part of the answer is the continuing—even enhanced—relevance of the Bose Brothers and all that they believed in and fought for throughout their lives. There is also the imperative of ensuring that their legacy does not fade or become distorted by the ever-present threats posed by time and misinterpretation.

In Chapter 1—The Bose Brothers and 'Ami'—we catch a glimpse of Amiya's passage from childhood to responsible adulthood, and of the love, support and guidance which enveloped him. His father Sarat and uncle Subhas were central to this evolution, despite their physical distance for long periods of enforced absence. When his father and/or uncle were in jail or under detention away from Calcutta, it did not interrupt their careful nurturing of the boy, and later the young man. In one of many eulogies upon his death, the then Acting Chief Justice of the Calcutta High Court was to say of Amiya, 'Coming from the illustrious family of the late Sarat Chandra Bose and Netaji Subhas Chandra Bose, he really matched his seniors in the family not only in his patriotism but also as a man of outstanding qualities of head and heart.' Amiya was truly inspired by his father and uncle, and throughout his life sought to live up to their ideals and aspirations.

Chapter 2—The Road to Mandalay—invites the reader to join Sarat and Subhas as they embark on the long road to freedom for India. As the older brother by eight years, Sarat is the first in 1918 to join the swelling Congress movement inspired by Gandhi, followed by Subhas upon the latter's return from England in 1921. At that time it was the charismatic leader from Bengal, C. R. Das, to whom they looked for leadership and inspiration. The train of events sees the younger brother incarcerated in faraway Mandalay Jail in Burma from January 1925 to May 1927. In this chapter, the reader will be given the opportunity to look inside the mind of young Subhas who, while in Mandalay Jail, wrote what he called *Pebbles on the Seashore*, a collection of 'stray thoughts'. The chapter also includes a series of reflections which he jotted down in a notebook while held in Berhampore Jail, prior to being moved to Mandalay.

Chapter 3—Swaraj Beckons, Swaraj Denied—as the title graphically suggests, tracks the ebb and flow of the independence movement in its many manifestations, particularly through the 1920s and the 1930s. The reader will readily identify the beginnings of the rupture between Gandhi and his followers of the Satyagraha movement on the one hand, and the Bose Brothers and their left-wing supporters with a much more robust and revolutionary approach to the ending of imperial rule, on the other hand. The reader might also discern in this chapter the emerging signs of fundamental communal rupture between Hindus and Muslims, leading eventually to the partition of the subcontinent.

Chapter 4—Bose Brothers and Gandhi: Parting of the Ways— lifts the veil on the growing political and ideological rift between Gandhi and the Bose Brothers, leading Sarat to refer to an inevitable 'parting of the ways' and Gandhi himself to say, 'We must sail in different boats.' In this chapter, Amiya highlights a central tenet of this book which is that the spectre of partition can be traced back to events of the 1930s, with particular reference to the circumstances of 1937 and national and provincial elections held at that time under the reconstituted Government of India Act 1935. The reader is informed that Gandhi and his Congress High Command missed a strategic opportunity to win the loyalty and commitment of Jinnah and the emerging Muslim League to a united India, through Congress refusal to countenance both the principle and potential of coalition government.

Chapter 5—Partition: A Bitter Pill—opens a window for the reader into the campaigns for and against partition, and the increasingly desperate efforts of Sarat in particular to turn the tide. We see Sarat over and over again warning his countrymen and women of the catastrophe that partition would bring and encouraging them to stay firm and united. A similar message was being broadcast by Subhas from the jungles of Southeast Asia, but a message which remained largely unheard and certainly unheeded.

In Chapter 6—A Free and United Bengal—the battle against partition of the subcontinent has been irretrievably lost, and Sarat without his beloved younger brother turns to a last-ditch effort to save Bengal. It is alas too little too late. Bengal had already suffered the mass killings in Calcutta in 1946, and while this did not recur (in Calcutta) at the time of independence and partition as glumly predicted by many, trust between Hindu and Muslim communities in Bengal had been fatally damaged. Even apparent support for a united Bengal from Jinnah was not enough to prevent the cleavage of a people of one language, one culture and a shared history. Until the moment of his death on 20 February 1950, Sarat pursued his quest to reunite the Bengalis, but it was not to be.

Finally, in the Epilogue, the reader is invited to reflect upon the legacy of the Bose Brothers, and the life-long commitment of their protégé Amiya to realise the visions and aspirations of his father and uncle and ensure that the flame was not extinguished. This final chapter seeks to briefly capture the herculean efforts of Subhas in both Europe and Asia, to harness the apocalypse of world war in favour of independence for India; and to convey the mystery and sense of loss around his disappearance as the war came to an end. The reader will be reminded too of the determination of Sarat in the absence of Subhas to continue the campaign for the independent, socialist India of their dreams, and of the sadness and emptiness left by the untimely death of Sarat. As the passage of time was to show, and sadly for India, Sarat and Subhas were to be the last in what had been a long tradition of pre-eminent visionaries and national leaders from Bengal, until this day.

1

The Bose Brothers and 'Ami'

Ry Train,
5. 2. 32

My dear Ami,

Khuro must have told you about yesterday's happenings. Don't get unnerved in the least. Be a good boy & attend diligently to your studies and at the same time look to the comforts of your grandparents & your mother. My blessings to you, Mira, Neru, Gita, Bui & Putul.[1]

Yours very affly (affectionately)
S. C. Bose

Through this brief and unexpected missive from Sarat on an otherwise uneventful day in early February 1932, Amiya, or 'Ami' to his close family, learned of the sudden arrest and imminent incarceration of his father by the British colonial authorities. Ami was then barely 16 years old and preparing to sit for his matriculation examination.

Sarat had been away from Calcutta at the time appearing in a legal case in the coal mining town of Jharia, Bihar, now in the state of Jharkhand. Instead of returning home to Calcutta, Sarat was on a train bound for a British jail. He had been arrested on the grounds of alleged connections with revolutionaries under Regulation III of the Bengal Ordinance promulgated more than 100 years earlier in 1818, which provided for preventive detention without trial.

Sarat Chandra Bose, an eminent barrister, a leading member of the Indian National Congress, head of a large family with then pregnant wife Bivabati and their seven children, as well as responsible for his aging parents and many dependents within the extended family, was arrested for the first time in what seemed a sudden and surprise move by the British. The personal and political consequences of Sarat's arrest would have been

---

[1] Siblings of Amiya.

known to the British. Whether Sarat himself was prepared for such an eventuality or not, his letter to his son Ami expressed no anguish. It was simply a call to duty and equanimity in the face of an impending crisis.

For young Ami, his father's arrest could not have come at a more inopportune time, but he sought to follow his father's words and set his mind to do well in his first major examination. At the same time, he did his best to provide comfort and support in every way possible to his mother and grandparents.

From a very early age, father Sarat would turn to Ami, relying on him to carry out responsibilities and tasks far beyond those expected of his contemporaries. Such an early expression of trust bestowed from father to son would mature over the years into a relationship which featured Amiya as confidant, interlocutor, personal envoy and political ally.

Just a little over a month before Sarat's arrest, his younger brother Subhas, Ami's uncle or *Rangakakababu,* had been similarly detained from Calcutta on 2 January 1932 on the same charge under the same Act. Thus, Sarat and Subhas, the Bose Brothers, were to spend the next few months together in Seoni and Jubbulpore jails in central India. Sadly, separation of the brothers to different jails was to follow by the middle of the year. Sarat would remain in detention for three and a half years until 26 July 1935, with the last two years spent under house arrest at his own bungalow in Giddapahar, Kurseong, near Darjeeling in the foothills of the Himalayas.

Subhas for his part would be transferred first to Madras Penitentiary in southern India in mid-July 1932, then to continued detention at the King Edward Sanatorium at Bhowali in Uttar Pradesh, northern India on 8 October 1932, after suffering from prolonged and persistent illness. By the end of the year, it appeared that an unlikely 'alliance' of Bengali medical doctors including Subhas's elder brother and eminent cardiologist Dr Sunil Bose, and the British colonial medical authorities, was sufficiently alarmed to recommend further treatment for suspected tuberculosis and recuperation in the more temperate climate of Europe. Advanced medical facilities were also more readily available there.

With no improvement in his condition and no hope for release from detention while in India, Subhas accepted exile to Europe.

This of course was to be at personal expense. Close friends of the family came forward with financial support for both Subhas's journey to Europe and for Sarat's wife Bivabati left behind in the 1 Woodburn Park residence to take care of her family and other dependents. After his release from detention, Sarat repaid all the debts to his friends, including the loans for Subhas.

For their part, the colonial authorities adamantly refused to allow Subhas a family visit to Calcutta prior to his departure, including to see his now-ailing father Janakinath and mother Prabhavati. His travel documents were purportedly rendered invalid for entry to Britain. Clearly, the British did not want Subhas to carry his struggle for *Purna Swaraj* (Complete Independence) to the soil of Britain. Thus, it transpired that after a brief stay at Lucknow Jail (in Uttar Pradesh), Subhas found himself back in Jubbalpore to board the train on 22 February 1933, for the long overnight journey to Bombay, and then by sea and land to Vienna in Europe.

To his delight Subhas found that his request to have his nephew Ami accompany him on the train journey from Jubbalpore to Bombay had been granted by the authorities. Recalling that train journey with his Uncle Subhas, which would have been both exciting and at the same time rather poignant for young Ami, he later wrote:

> Before his departure for Europe for treatment, Uncle Subhas was brought back to Jubbalpore Central Jail. A large number of the members of the Bose family, including my mother Bivabati and myself, as well as Mrs Basanti Devi (widow of Deshabandhu Chittaranjan Das) went to Jubbalpore Jail to visit him. During one of those prison visits, Uncle Subhas told me that he wanted me to travel with him on the train which would take him from Jubbalpore to Bombay from where he would sail for Europe.
>
> On 22 February 1933, Uncle, still a prisoner, accompanied by the Superintendent of Police of the Central Provinces, boarded the Bombay Mail which left Jubbalpore at about three in the afternoon. As previously planned, I boarded the same train but took a berth in another compartment.
>
> A little after midnight when the train had stopped at a station, the Superintendent of Police accompanying Uncle suddenly appeared in my compartment and told me that I could go to my Uncle's compartment and travel with him during the night. He

said that he would occupy my berth for the overnight journey but that I must return to my own compartment at day break. Thus it transpired that I joined Uncle Subhas in his compartment and travelled with him as the train made its way to Bombay. I gathered from Uncle that the Superintendent was an Irishman and that he had been able to persuade him to let me travel with him if only for the night.

During this unforgettable overnight train journey together, Uncle Subhas showed me a copy of his thesis entitled 'Hindustani Samyavadi Sangha' (Indian Socialist Organisation) which he had written during his detention in the Madras Penitentiary (latter half of 1932). He told me that he intended to have consultations on the basis of his thesis with the Communist International (Comintern) during his stay in Europe. I came to know later that Uncle Subhas did indeed have discussions with three representatives of the Comintern in Switzerland but they did not come to any agreement. One of the representatives of the Comintern at that meeting was Clemens Dutt.[2] Uncle Subhas wanted to establish a Socialist Party and to work for an armed revolution inside India for which he desired assistance from the Comintern. He however made it clear that he did not wish to be under the control of the Comintern in any way.

Subhas left Bombay for Venice on 23 February 1933 on the Italian ship S. S. Gange. His detention order was lifted as the ship sailed out of the harbour. On the following day, the Indian news agency Free Press of India carried a farewell message from Subhas to the Indian people:

> On the eve of my departure for Europe, I desire to convey my cordial and affectionate thanks to my friends and well-wishers all over the country for the kind interest they have taken in me.... Acutely sensitive though I am, I have not hesitated to accept the help offered by my friends and well-wishers, because I have always felt that my family is not confined to my blood relations but is coterminous with my country and when I have once and for all dedicated my humble life to the service of my country, my countrymen have as much right to look after my welfare as my nearest relatives have.... I only hope and pray that God in his

[2] Born in England 1893, Clemens Palme Dutt worked as a journalist in London, writing in particular on the independence struggle in India. Founded the Communist Party of Great Britain together with his brother Rajni Palme Dutt.

infinite mercy may make me worthy in the same measure of love and affection that has been showered on me by all sections of the Indian community.

At the time of the arrests of Sarat and Subhas in early 1932, Sarat and wife Bivabati lived in their family home at 1 Woodburn Park (built in 1928, only a few minutes walk from father Janakinath's house at 38/2 Elgin Road), with six of their seven children born until then. The household included Subhas as a much-loved younger brother of Sarat and favourite uncle to the children. The oldest of the children Asoke, born just four years earlier than Amiya on 13 December 1911, had by this time left for Munich, Germany, to further his studies in chemical engineering. He was on hand on 6 March 1933 at the docks in Venice to receive his Uncle Subhas as the latter began his exile in Europe. Subrata the youngest of the children was born on 25 February 1932, only weeks after Sarat had been taken prisoner. Remaining at home from the time of the arrests were thus Amiya (Ami) and his five other siblings Mira, Sisir (Neru), Gita, Roma (Bui) and Chitra (Putul).

Janakinath and Prabhabati often came to stay at 1 Woodburn Park. Sarat always sought to ensure his parents' well-being and comfort, and they looked to him for advice and support at all times. When Janakinath's failing health made it difficult for him to continue with his law practice, Sarat took over the full responsibility of care for his parents and also of the many charities supported by Janakinath.

During Sarat's detention, Janakinath wrote to him from Cuttack on 29 July 1933:

> I am looking forward to the day when your presence will restore peace, harmony and good feeling where there is not much at present. It is always profitable in every sense to forgive and forget, and he who does not do so, is a loser. It is needless for me to tell you that we are bound to work for that end.

Amiya was close to his grandparents. As a child he was deeply influenced and inspired by the strong determination and perseverance of grandfather Janakinath in the face of many hardships that the latter had faced early in life. Due to financial stringency at home, Janakinath had to make his way by foot every day from his ancestral village of Kodalia (in the district of 24 Parganas, West Bengal) to the Albert School in Garia (Calcutta) and return, a journey of many miles. He nevertheless completed his education with distinction, and later achieved notable success in his career as a lawyer at the High Court in Cuttack, Orissa. Most importantly, Janakinath's kind heart and generous spirit made a deep impression on Ami, qualities which he also saw reflected in full measure in his father Sarat. As a successful lawyer in Cuttack, Janakinath supported many poor students and the needy, and in Kodalia he set up a library and dispensary, the former surviving to this day in service to the villagers.

Grandmother Prabhavati was outwardly of a rather stern temperament, and according to family folklore ruled over her extended household as a strict matriarch. She was held in awe by her many grandchildren but is known to have shown special affection towards young Ami, who would be often summoned by his *Ma-janani* (grandmother) to have an afternoon 'chit chat' perched on her bed.

From stories recounted through the generations, there were many that spoke of the everyday joys and sorrows in the large Bose household. A tale that always brought forth much laughter was that of the sleep-walker uncle who used to take off in the middle of the night with a pillow under his arm, declaring that he was on his way to give lessons. Another humorous tale was that of one domestic staff member who when challenged about some missing item would always insist, somewhat indignantly, that he would only 'borrow' from the matriarch of the house (Prabhavati), and nobody else!

Thus Amiya's early years were spent under the care and guidance of his grandparents and parents, living within a large extended family with many adults—aunts and uncles, siblings and numerous cousins—at the ancestral house at 38/2 Elgin Road. After Sarat moved with his immediate family to 1 Woodburn Park, Ami became especially close to his Uncle Subhas, who came to live with them. In speaking about those years, Amiya observed[3]:

> From 1928 until his arrest in early 1932 and subsequent departure for Europe, my Uncle Subhas and I shared the same room

---

[3] Amiya Nath Bose's final lecture delivered at Presidency College on 23 January 1996.

on the second floor of our 1 Woodburn Park house. He used to come back home very late after his days of hectic political work at about mid-night or even later. He would first take a bath and then eat the food that was kept for him on the table in the room. He would then wake me up. It was not the most pleasant experience for me to be woken up in the middle of the night but of course I would get up.

He would talk to me about many events—about Gandhi, Nehru, Patel and others. I did not know them personally then but I came to know them well in later years. He would also talk to me about the revolutionary leaders of our country. He told me about Nikunja Sen who later became the editor of a paper published by my father Sarat, a Bengali weekly called Mahajati.... So a good deal of my knowledge of politics, about personalities and the political scenario came from Uncle Subhas.... In 1928 the Congress Annual Session was held in Calcutta and a uniformed Congress Volunteer Corps was organised on that occasion. My Uncle became the General Officer Commanding. I remember when Uncle Subhas in uniform was coming down the stairs from the second floor to the first floor, his father Janakinath, my grandfather, came out of his room and said: 'Subhas, I hope you will be the Garibaldi of India!' This wish proved to be rather prophetic.

With the rapid rise of the Bose Brothers, Sarat and Subhas, as leaders of the left-wing in the Congress, 1 Woodburn Park quickly became a centre of frenetic political activity. The brothers hosted key Congress meetings and the house bustled with the presence of nationalist leaders and freedom fighters of every hue, even Bengal's revolutionaries.

The arrest and enforced departure of the brothers into detention in the early months of 1932 transformed Woodburn Park from an active hub of Bengal and national politics into a quieter family home which sorely missed their charismatic presence. In their absence, it was left to Bivabati to continue to care for and run her household under severe financial constraints, which she did with her characteristic determination and stoicism.

With Sarat in prison, Janakinath decided to return to his law practice to provide for the family, but alas the strain proved too much for the frail patriarch. The intransigence of the British authorities would not allow either Sarat or Subhas to see their father alive again as Janakinath passed away on 2 December 1934. Subhas did return briefly to Calcutta from Europe, without the permission of the British authorities, in early December 1934 on hearing that his father was seriously ill. He arrived in Calcutta a day too late. Immediately on arrival Subhas was served with an order for home internment, and was thus confined to the parental home at 38/2 Elgin Road for the duration of what was to be an all too brief stay. From his detention in Kurseong, Sarat was also allowed only a short stay to join Subhas and his other brothers to perform the *Sradh* ceremony (last rites) for their father.

The loss of a much-loved and revered husband of Prabhavati, father and grandfather, cast a 'shadow of grief' on a family already persecuted for their nationalist vision and ideals. Subhas was compelled by the British to return to Europe in early January 1935. Sarat had been earlier forced to return to house arrest in Kurseong on 10 December 1934, to be finally released after three and a half years of internment in July 1935.

For Sarat this was the first of his two long periods of detention, the second coming in December 1941, until September 1945 after the end of the Second World War. Subhas was already a veteran of political imprisonment, having been locked up in Presidency, Alipore and Berhampore Jails in Bengal for shorter periods between 1921 and 1924, before being transferred in January 1925 from Berhampore Jail to Mandalay Jail in far-away northern Burma. He remained there until May 1927 when he was released on health grounds and allowed to return home to his brother Sarat's then residence in Calcutta at 38/1 Elgin Road, next door to their parents' house.

Altogether Subhas spent no less than 11 separate periods in detention by the colonial authorities, and both brothers were to suffer life-long serious health problems as a direct result of the rigours of imprisonment. The attitude of the colonial authorities can at best be described as politically cautious where the health of the brothers was concerned, but they showed little or no sympathy for the emotional and financial well-being of the Bose family, including at times of crisis and even bereavement.

* * *

When Amiya was born on 20 November 1915 in Calcutta, Sarat had just begun his legal practice at the Calcutta High Court on his return home from London the previous year, where he had qualified as a Barrister-at-Law. Sarat had married Bivabati, daughter of Akshoy Kumar and Subala Dey from a renowned family of north Calcutta, on 9 December 1909. This was a close and remarkable partnership which was destined to weather many storms through Sarat's hectic professional and political life and his two long imprisonments. Meanwhile, the close rapport between Sarat and Subhas carried over into a profound familial bond between Subhas and his sister-in-law Bivabati.

In 1915, Subhas, born on 23 January 1897 and eight years junior to Sarat, was an undergraduate student at the elite Presidency College of the University of Calcutta, studying Philosophy Honours. His student life would be abruptly interrupted in the following year by his expulsion from the College as a consequence of the well-chronicled 'Oaten incident'.[4]

Subhas would later, in July 1917, resume his studies, this time at the Scottish Churches College, also the Alma Mater of Swami Vivekananda. On successful graduation and on the initiative of his father Janakinath and brother Sarat, Subhas left for England, the imperial heartland, in September 1919, to study and compete for the famously rigorous and prestigious Indian Civil Service Examination (ICS) scheduled for August 1920. He was also to pursue at the same time further studies in philosophy at the University of Cambridge.

Born on 6 September 1889, Sarat received his early primary and secondary education in Cuttack where his parents had established themselves, before being admitted to Presidency College in Calcutta in 1905. Over the following politically volatile years until 1911, he obtained a Bachelor of Arts Degree (1907) and then a Master's Degree (1909) from Presidency College, followed by a further Bachelor's Degree in Law from Ripon College University of Calcutta in 1911.

Sarat's student years in Calcutta over the six-year period from 1905 to 1911 coincided with the nationalist or Swadeshi movement sparked by the partition of Bengal in 1905 (ostensibly for reasons of administrative efficiency but in reality to stem the tide of growing Indian nationalism of which Bengal was the nerve

---

[4] In February 1916, a group of Indian students at Presidency College were accused of assaulting the History Professor, Englishman Edward Oaten. Subhas acted as a spokesman for the students and was among those expelled.

centre), and with its ultimate annulment and reunification of Bengal in 1911. Sarat was greatly influenced by this Swadeshi movement led by Surendra Nath Banerjee, Ananda Mohan Bose and Bepin Chandra Pal.[5]

As narrated by Amiya in an unfinished biography of his father:

> Father told me that he regularly attended the meetings addressed by Surendra Nath Banerjee in College Square (not far from Presidency College) and that he drew much inspiration from his eloquent speeches. Surendra Nath would end his speeches with the words from Byron:

> > *For freedom's battle once begun*
> > *Bequeathed from bleeding sire to son*
> > *Though baffled oft is ever won*

Amiya would often allude to his father's love of the English classical writers and poets, not only Byron, but also Milton, Browning and Shelley. Amiya would marvel at his father's phenomenal memory and how he would keep them spell-bound with his recitations by heart from Milton's *Prometheus Unbound* and entire scenes from Shakespeare!

Upon the conclusion of his studies in Calcutta in 1911, Sarat returned to Cuttack where his father Janakinath was at that time one of the prominent lawyers in the District Court and had been appointed government pleader and public prosecutor. Sarat began his legal apprenticeship and law practice, and his special aptitude as a lawyer was soon evident in court. As reflected in his personal diaries (a habit which Sarat maintained especially while in prison, and which provide a window into his thinking and the impact of notable events in his life), an ambition to qualify as a barrister-at-law soon emerged:

> On 22 February 1912: Proposed to mother about going to England to qualify myself for English Bar.

> On 23 February 1912: Mother proposed to father about my going to England—father reserved his opinion.

---

[5] Indian nationalist and Congress leaders at the turn of the nineteenth and into the early twentieth century.

On 24 February 1912: Father opened the subject of my going to England during breakfast—he is agreeable. It was settled that I should join the Michaelmas Term.

Thus in September 1912, Sarat left for London, where in less than two years he completed both formal law studies and an apprenticeship in the chambers of a London barrister. During his stay in Britain, Sarat also enjoyed some of the attractions of life in London. He went to the theatre, and noted in his diary on 4 April 1913:

After dinner went to the Drury Lane Theatre to see the performance of 'Hamlet' (Forbes-Robertson). Enjoyed it immensely. This is my first night at a theatre. Came home at about 12 p.m. Went to bed at 1 a.m.

In London, Sarat also took the opportunity to witness cases heard in the Royal Courts of Justice and observe some of the leading members of the English Bar arguing and cross-examining in court. He was especially impressed with the powers of cross-examination of well-known barrister and Irish Unionist politician Sir Edward Carson. He attended the House of Lords to listen to the appeals that were being heard there, and also took an interest in the processes and proceedings of the House of Commons.

On 24 June 1914, Sarat was called to the Bar by Lincoln's Inn, arriving back in Calcutta on 22 July 1914. On return, he enrolled as an advocate of the High Court of Judicature at Fort William in Calcutta on 20 August 1914. He began his legal practice at the Calcutta High Court and joined the chambers of Sir Nripendra Nath Sircar, a then leading legal luminary.

Within a short time, Sarat was reported to have built up an extensive practice, and soon became an outstanding leader of the Calcutta Bar. He came to be considered as a master in the art of cross-examination, and to be widely admired and respected by members of the Bar and Bench alike. To this day his name stands for one who brought dignity and honour to the court and to the cause of justice.

From this time for the following several years, Sarat concentrated on building his legal practice and meeting the needs and responsibilities of his growing family. However, after the comparative lull in nationalist activity during most of the period of the Great War, the fires of independence and self-determination were again being lit in India, and crucial and exciting political dynamics were again on the horizon. Gandhi had in 1915 returned from his 20-year sojourn in South Africa, where he had honed his resistance skills.

An equally iconic and much revered fellow barrister, Deshbandhu Chittaranjan Das (C. R. Das) from Bengal, was becoming more and more prominent in the burgeoning Congress movement now spreading through the masses under the inspirational drive of Gandhi. It is thus no surprise to find the politically aware Sarat being drawn into the flow of more nationalistic politics, and in 1918 to see him taking up active membership of the Congress under the leadership of C. R. Das.

While Sarat was busy at home in Calcutta pursuing his legal career and at the same time becoming increasingly involved in the political scene, Subhas pursued further studies at Fitzwilliam College at the University of Cambridge. During the same period, he sat for and passed the ICS examination in August 1920, standing fourth in the order of merit, and was accepted on probation. But the call of momentous events back home and an increasing conviction that he could not 'serve two masters' was too much for the young firebrand. To the consternation of many he declined this 'heaven sent' opportunity, and in July 1921 returned home to India to work alongside C. R. Das and brother Sarat in support of the Gandhi-inspired Non-Cooperation Movement.

Subhas had written to Sarat on 26 January 1921:

I am now at the cross-ways and no compromise is possible. I must either chuck this rotten service and dedicate myself wholeheartedly to the country's cause—or I must bid adieu to all my ideals and aspirations and enter the service.... I am sure many of our relatives will howl when they hear of such a rash and dangerous proposal.... But I do not care for their opinions, their cheers or their taunts. But I have faith in your idealism and that is why I am appealing to you. About this time five years ago I had your moral support in an endeavour which was fraught with disastrous consequences for myself. For a year my future was dark and blank, but I bore the consequences bravely, I never complained to myself, and today I am proud that I had the strength to make that sacrifice. The memory of that event strengthens my belief that if any demands for sacrifice are made upon me in the future I shall respond with equal fortitude, courage and calmness. And in this new endeavour can I not expect the same moral support which you so willingly and so nobly lent me five years ago?

In a longer and more reflective letter of 23 April 1921 to Sarat before leaving Cambridge, and well aware of his older brother's unstinting support for the fateful choice that he had made, Subhas agonised about the effects on his close family of his decision, perhaps the first major step towards the realisation of his destiny:

> I have always felt that it is unfair from our point of view to place such a huge financial burden on your shoulders—though I could never effect any other practical solution of our financial problem...I need not make it a secret that I felt I was responsible more to father, mother and yourself for what I did, than to anyone else.... My position therefore is that in entering upon a new career I am acting against the express wishes of father and mother and against your advice though you have sent me your warmest felicitations in whatever course I choose.... My greatest objection to joining the service was based on the fact that I would have to sign the Covenant and thereby own the allegiance of a foreign bureaucracy which I feel rightly or wrongly has no moral right to be there. I have come to believe that compromise is a bad thing—it degrades the man and injures his cause.... The best way to end a government is to withdraw from it. I say this not because that was Tolstoy's doctrine nor because Gandhi preaches it—but because I have come to believe in it.... I received a letter from mother saying that in spite of what father and others think she prefers the ideal for which Mahatma stands. I cannot tell you how happy I have been to receive such a letter...
>
> How is Ami? Does he still remember me? He will be a big boy by the time I return.

Years later the adult Amiya would observe that the personality of Subhas Chandra Bose reflected the union of a philosophical and pragmatic intellect, and that these aspects of his personality blended into 'Subhas the man as we know him'. For Amiya, his uncle was someone who never acted on impulse—rather all his actions were based on careful consideration, serious deliberation and detailed planning. At certain times, his spiritual and ascetic qualities were in the ascendant.

Amiya would explain that Subhas's student years in Calcutta from 1913 to 1919 featured the gradual maturing of the meditative or contemplative aspects of his character. Subhas particularly enjoyed his studies in philosophy and psychology, and paid special attention to the works of Kant, Hegel and other European philosophers. Earlier, at barely 15 years of age, he had come under the profound influence of the teachings of Ramakrishna and his disciple Swami Vivekananda, which instilled in the young Subhas a conviction in the essential unity of all religions and the equality of man. This in turn encouraged a keen sense of social service, which remained with him throughout his adult life and which he sought to put into practice whenever he could.

Amiya further recorded that the years immediately following, which Subhas spent in England between 1919 and 1921, saw the development of a broader and even pragmatic side to his personality. When he arrived in England, Europe had recently emerged from the First World War (1914–1918). It was a time of great change in the political, economic and social landscape of Europe, and from Cambridge Subhas had the opportunity to study and observe at close hand the Irish revolutionary movement, which clearly left a lasting impression on him. He also took a keen interest in the unfolding history of the Russian Revolution, and what it might all mean for the rest of the world including colonial India.

His letters of those days give some indication of the tenor of his thinking. Amiya would refer in particular to a letter written in Bengali by Subhas on 12 May 1920 from Cambridge, to his friend and contemporary in Calcutta, Priya Ranjan Sen. Excerpts from that letter (which was published in the 23 January 1971 issue of the Calcutta Desh Magazine) provide some flavour of the early evolution of Subhas's thoughts on the shape and content of an Indian form of socialism:

> Anyway, I approve of what you have written about Russian thought. Just as France towards the end of the eighteenth century had inspired the world with her ideals, thought and action, Russia will inspire the world during the twentieth century. But

the fact remains that no modern problem can be comprehended without a knowledge of economics and politics. The novels of Sarat Chatterjee are masterpieces in many ways—in their analysis of human character, in their portrayal of the family and domestic life etc. But it appears to me that there is nothing in the nature of the solution of political and social problems that one finds in Ibsen's plays. Perhaps if he (Sarat Chatterjee) had studied economics and politics, his range of vision would have been broader and his books would have offered solutions to many other problems...

Could you write a book on Socialism? There is, I believe, a book in the Peoples' Book Series on this subject. There is, of course, one written by Ramsay Macdonald in the Home University Library Series—I feel that India's progress can be brought about by her people alone, as has been the case in Russia. Socialism teaches people what their rights are and how society has deprived them of these rights. Within our own society we have a great enemy—the landed and commercial aristocracy—particularly the former. Having studied the histories of several countries of the world, I am convinced that everywhere they have stood in the way of progress. If they had not opposed change so vigorously, neither the French revolution nor Bolshevism would have been necessary.

It is because the landed aristocracy in England did not stand in the way of progress to that extent that they still exist (here)—(as they do not in France or Russia) and there has been no (violent) revolution in this country. With every passing day you will realize the terrible extent of harm that can be caused by this enemy within the country. We have to be prepared for this; and it is futile to expect anything from the Labour Party here. All parties in England are the same—the differences among them are really on minor points. 'Nations by themselves are made'—only this can be our motto.

So much for today. I shall not be able to write again; my examination begins on 2 August. I shall of course be very happy to hear from you. We await the Indian mail here like thirsty birds (the Chataka) looking for water.

Subhas returned to India from England as a firm believer in revolutionary struggle against all forms of oppression, and at the same time with a clear understanding and faith in western philosophical thought. This evolution in his thinking was of course built on the foundations of a strong background in Hindu philosophy and beliefs, and his early education back home in India. Subhas wrote in *An Indian Pilgrim*, his unfinished auto-biography: 'Education in the lower stages must be "national," it must have its roots in the soil. We must draw our mental pabulum from the culture of our own country.'[6]

* * *

With the enforced physical separation of the brothers from their family and loved ones over the period from 1932, there ensued a sustained exchange of correspondence with members of the family, close friends and political associates. Most of this correspondence has been published over time, with the exception of a collection of letters to Amiya from Sarat and Subhas. A small selection of these letters, in whole or in part, is appearing here for the first time.

Subhas's earlier internment in Mandalay from 1925 to 1927 had also given rise to an intensive, albeit censored, exchange of letters between the brothers, on matters ranging from the philosophical to the political to the family. Letters from Subhas to Sarat and philosophical reflections of Subhas during his time in Mandalay and earlier in Berhampore Jails will be dealt with in the following chapter.

From behind prison bars, first in Seoni and then other jails and detention centres, father Sarat and uncle Subhas each persisted in long-distance endeavours to prepare an obviously willing and committed son and nephew for the many challenges ahead of him in life. They saw him as a future cohort in the realisation of their vision of an independent, united and socialist India. They also considered young Ami a confidante with whom they could share many personal details, including about their health and the treatment of their respective medical conditions under the watchful eye of the detention authorities.

From Seoni Jail on 20 March 1932, some six weeks after his arrest and incarceration and when it was probably becoming increasingly clear that no release was in sight, Sarat wrote in

---

[6] Subhas Chandra Bose, *An Indian Pilgrim* (Kolkata: Jayasree Patrika Trust, 2013), 131.

what was to be the first of many intimate and supportive letters to Amiya:

My dear Ami,

Your telegram was handed to me at about midday on Friday last (18th). I was happy to learn that you had done fairly well in your examination and that all are keeping well at home. Your letter (referred to in your telegram) has not come in yet; but I received yesterday (19th), two letters written by your mother and bearing date the 8th and 11th March respectively. I learnt from your mother's letter of the 11th March that you had done well in English & Mathematics but not quite so well in Sanskrit. I do not blame you at all for not doing well in the Sanskrit paper. Knowing as I do there have been numerous hindrances and distractions in the way of your studies since December last, I shall feel quite happy if you get pass marks in the Sanskrit paper; and this I am told by your mother, you expect to get.

As you will have plenty of spare time now, I have no doubt you will attend to the comforts of your grandparents, your mother and others in the house. During my absence, most of my responsibilities in the direction indicated above fall naturally on your shoulders and I feel sure you are quite alive to them. You will also have time to think about your future studies. Now is the time for you to come to a decision whether you will take up the Arts Course or the Science Course. Of course, you needn't be in a hurry to arrive at a decision. Take your own time over it, consult your grandparents and your mother about it, disclose to them *fully* all that passes through your mind regarding your future studies; and after you have had the opportunity of a full discussion with them, write to me on the subject. I have plenty of time here to think about your future career and after I hear from you about your ideas, I shall assist you in coming to a right decision.

Now one word as to how you should spend your holidays. I think you should devote part of your spare time to reading good literature both Bengali & English. As regards Bengali begin with Michael Madhusudan Dutt's Meghnad Badh Kavya. As regards English, I suggest two books at the start viz. Washington Irving's Rip Van Winkle and Prof. Blackie's Self Culture. I think you will find both those books in our old bookcase at 38/2 Elgin Road. But in case you don't find them there, please buy them from the Book Co or some other shop. This will be enough to begin with.

At the same time you must not neglect your health. In fact, you should be far more attentive to your health than to your studies for the next three months. I hope you are continuing to take the physical exercises you have been accustomed to take under the guidance of Dipen Babu. Please give my love & compliments to Dipen Babu.

I was happy to learn from your mother's letters that your Dadabhai is able to walk about a little and that your Mejomami is better than before. Please try to make them as cheerful as possible. You know how fond they are of you.

Your grandparents may go to Puri in the beginning of Baisakh next. If you wish, you can spend a few weeks with them by the seaside at Puri. If however you would like to go out of Calcutta for a change immediately, do so by all means. Your mother informs me that your Jethababu has asked you to come to Patna and that you desire to go to Jamshedpur. Your mother will gladly send you to whichever place you prefer.

Pravas's letter to me dated the 15th which was to hand this morning conveyed to us the sad news that dear Rabi was no more. I have first written to your Mami. I am sure you had been to College Square after the cruel bereavement. Your maternal grandmother will feel somewhat comforted if you go and talk to her.

There is nothing particular to write about ourselves. Your Rangakakababu is practically in the same state. His digestion has not improved at all. For the last few days he has been living on milk and sago, as that is the only thing that is agreeing with him. However, you needn't be anxious for him, so long as we are together. I am fairly well.

I hope Mira, Neru & Gita are attending to their studies diligently and that Bui is as fussy as before. I am told that Putul has taken very kindly to her auntie. Please tell Mira, Neru & Gita that I shall write to them after a week or so.

Please write to your Rangakakababu from time to time & ask your brothers & sisters to do the same. My love & blessings to you all.

Yours very affly
S. C. Bose

P.S. Please hand over this letter to your mother after you have done with it.
S.C.B.

Again from Seoni Jail on 8 May 1932, Sarat wrote to his son:

I was extremely delighted to learn that you had passed your examination in the first division and I offer you my heartiest congratulations. That you may steadily progress in every direction and develop physically, intellectually and spiritually, is the heart's desire of your very affectionate father.

Both your letter of the 4th May and Pravas's letter of the 3rd came in at the same time on the 6th. I learnt from the latter that the news of your success was communicated by Mr Promatha Nath Banerjee Barrister-at-Law, to both of you. Please convey my thanks to Banerjee for sharing of the information.

I have received the letters of the 11th, 16th, 22nd and 27th April. I approve of your decision to take the Science Course for the Intermediate Examination. Which college would you like to join? There are really two colleges to be considered—the Scottish Churches College and the Ashutosh College. I believe the former is good for the Science Course, but it is rather at a distance from our house. If however Ashutosh College be equally good for the Science Course (information regarding which you can obtain from Mr Promatha Banerjee), you can join that College. There is one advantage—and that is, the Ashutosh College is near our house. Please apply to the better of the two Colleges without delay. I am ruling out St Xavier's as I have very little confidence in the authorities there.

As regards Bengali literature, I think you should begin with a close study of Madhusudan's works and end up with living writers. If you want grounding in English literature you shouldn't confine yourself to modern writers, however brilliant they may be, ignoring Shakespeare and Milton. The same is true in the case of Bengali literature.

I have nothing new to communicate regarding our life and our health here. I wrote to your mother in detail three days ago. Your Rangakakababu does not wish to give to Dr B. C. Roy the trouble of coming to Seoni. We are waiting for some orders of the C.P. (i.e. Central Provinces) Government regarding x-ray exam of Subhas. The best thing undoubtedly would be if the C.P. Government send him to Calcutta for thorough medical examination. He could then have the advice of eminent physicians like Sir Nilratan Sarkar and Dr B.C. Roy who have treated him in the past and who know his constitution. However it is idle on our parts to express our wishes. Government will act as they are advised.

Will you please buy from Swadeshi Silpa Bandhar (College Street) a few cakes of Blanco for white shoes and send them with your mother. Also please ask Subodh Brothers to send us five lbs of Darjeeling tea (Flowery Orange Pekoe of the best quality) as they sent last time.

I hope the Government of Bengal have granted permission to your maternal uncle to see us here. Please send us a telegramme mentioning the date on which your mother will arrive here. The dates of interviews with us will have to be fixed with reference to that.

Have the Diocesan and South Suburban Schools closed for the summer? I trust Mira, Neru and Gita are alright. I haven't heard from them for sometime. I was glad to learn from Haren Babu's letter that they are making good progress in drawing and painting. How did Neru fare in his quarterly examination? Please ask all of them to read Rabindranath's Galpaguchha during the holidays.

I understand Bui and Putul are coming here with their mother. I am afraid that the latter has almost forgotten me. I think both of them will be pleased to see our collection of birds here. We now have five parrots, two green pigeons, two ordinary pigeons (milk white), and one bird called 'Nilkantha'. The last one was caught yesterday inside the jail and we have kept it. I haven't seen Nilkanthas in Bengal. They are supposed to be very auspicious birds but they are difficult to domesticate.

Yours very affly
S. C. Bose

Meanwhile Subhas, who after a few months in Seoni had been moved with Sarat to Jubbulpore Central Jail, was clearly preoccupied with their deteriorating health as well as the continuing uncertainties of their detention. In a letter of 13 June 1932, he sought to share his worries with young nephew Ami:

My dear Ami

I am sorry I have not been able to write to you for some time past. Your last letter to me has remained unanswered.

Your application for interview with us has been sanctioned and the intimation has arrived here. But there is no news about Chotodada's application. Apparently the matter is being considered by Govt.

I am very sorry that for some time past, our letters have not been reaching their destination and I therefore do not know if this letter will reach you either. I am nevertheless writing.

The medical examination began on the 4th June and continued till the 6th. Mejdada was examined for diabetes and besides the usual tests, the blood sugar test was applied. It was a rather painful process as several injections had to be given.

I was x-rayed after being given bismuth meal. Several photos had to be taken after regular intervals. There were other forms of examination as is usual in such cases.

We were examined by a medical board of 3 medical men attached to the military here. Their report has gone up to Government but we have no idea as to what they have reported. We are still in the dark as to the correct diagnosis in my case—and in the absence of a diagnosis, no treatment can be resorted to. I wish we had been acquainted with the diagnosis made by the Board—because we could then start scientific treatment and I also would realise what I should do and what diet I should take up.

I am rather disappointed with the examination because the most important item had to be omitted, viz. x-ray examination of the gall-bladder. I think in medical parlance they call this cholecystography. The necessary materials for cholecystography were not available at the British Military Hospital here. I feel more and more convinced that the gall-bladder is the source of all my troubles and the first step towards verifying this diagnosis is to have recourse to cholecystography viz. x-ray examination of the gall-bladder. It was the Civil Surgeon of Chindwara, Capt. Scott J. M. S. who first said that the gall-bladder was misbehaving and he recommended x-ray exam for the purpose of testing the correctness of his theory. Capt Scott examined me as early as April last but until the gall-bladder is x-rayed—we cannot proceed any further towards verifying his diagnosis. And without a diagnosis there can be no treatment.

We have no idea as to our future movements. We are simply awaiting further orders.

I am somewhat better now, the acute stage of my recent illness being over. But the pain is persisting in the region of the liver and gall-bladder—and there is a rise in temperature along with it. The old symptoms like sciatica are, of course, present. There has been a big drop in my weight recently—the total loss being 41 lbs. up till now.

Your letter of the 7th inst. reached Mejdada on the 11th inst. He may not be able to write to you this week.

I am writing to Akhoy along with this letter. I find that he has not received my last 2 letters. I have got his letter dated the 7th June.

How are you all keeping? I am glad that you have got into the Scottish Churches College—it will be better than St Xavier's, I hope.

Please tell all the kiddies that I duly received all of their loving notes—but I am sorry that I cannot write to them—though I would love to do so, if there had not been any restrictions regarding number. I am glad they liked my pantua [a Bengali sweet].

I am writing in English purposely in order to expedite censoring. Please tell the kiddies that they may write to me more often than they have done.

Your very affly
Subhas

P.S. Has the parrot learnt to talk?

In mid-July 1932, the brothers were separated, with Sarat remaining for the time being in Jubbulpore Central Jail and Subhas transferred to Madras Penitentiary some 500 odd miles away by road and rail. On 18 July 1932, the day after his arrival in Madras, Subhas wrote to Ami still clearly preoccupied with the poor health of Sarat and himself:

I arrived from Jubbulpore last night. I left Jubbulpore by car on the morning of the 16th. I reached Nagpur by car in the evening of the same day and went straight to the bungalow of the Jail Superintendent. After some rest I boarded the train at Anjni, three miles from Nagpur, where the train was made to halt. I reached Madras last night and alighted from the train at Basin Bridge two miles from the Madras Station. From there I drove straight to the Madras Penitentiary. I thought at first that the Penitentiary was a Borstal Institution but it is the ordinary jail.

The journey was a long one & very fatiguing. Madras, I find, is quite hot—and I don't know why they brought me all the way to Madras from Jubbulpore. The rest of India is now cool because of the monsoon—but at Madras the rains set in as late as October—this is what I have been told. This probably accounts for the heat. I am going to the hospital presently for examination.

At Jubbulpore I was informed that I would be transferred to Madras Penitentiary *for examination and treatment in a hospital.* I therefore expected to be admitted into the local general Hospital as an in-patient. But after arrival here, I find that I am not at all sure about admission into hospital. However, if I am admitted into hospital, I shall inform you. Please wire me Rs. 50/- C/o the Superintendent, Madras Penitentiary for my use. Also wire Rs. 50/- to Jubbulpore to Mejdada's account.

If Mr. P. C. Basu goes to Jubbulpore, he must see that Mejdada does not cut down his diet. The allowance of Rs. 3/8/- is too inadequate for him and he must spend from his private account to make up for the deficiency. If there is delay about Mr Basu's going to Jubbulpore, please write to Mejdada or ask Mejobowdidi to write to Mejdada to say that he should not cut down his diet but should spend his private cash. At present our private cash is almost exhausted.

I had fever last night on my arrival—as usual. I had also internal pain at night. Other complaints are the same.

Hope all well there,

Yours very affly
Subhas

P.S. I shall write to the Govt. again from here asking them that Sir Nilratan Sircar, Dr. B. C. Roy and Dr. Sunil Bose should be permitted to examine me.
S. C. B.

As was becoming increasingly clear in these letters from both Sarat and Subhas, the health of the latter in particular was a matter of growing concern to family and supporters—perhaps most of all to Sarat, who was obviously much constrained in what he could do to help from prison. The fact that after a few short months together in Seoni Sub-Jail and Jubbulpore Central Jail, they were now again very much separated, would have been an additional worry for both of them.

It was also starting to become clear that the medical condition of Subhas was not improving, as reflected in further letters to Amiya of 28 July and 8 August 1932. His frustration with the inadequacy of his medical examinations and treatment is manifest, as is his continuing concern for Sarat back in Jubbulpore. He still finds time to advise his nephew (8 August 1932):

For the next two years you will have to devote yourself to your studies very closely. You will then be able to discover your own aptitude. I have already told you that if the science subjects do not interest you, you may revert to the Arts Course in your 3rd year—or if they interest you, you may take up Medicine or Higher Science. It does not matter very much if mathematics does not interest you. During the next two years, the only thing you will have to be careful about is not to neglect the study of Bengali and English which is necessary for your own culture and education.

As the months dragged on and with no sign of release from detention, Sarat in a letter of 4 October 1932 which seems to have been smuggled out of Jubbulpore Jail, perhaps by his wife Bivabati during a visit, wrote movingly and reassuringly to Ami:

Your letter of the 20th September last reached me on the 30th (along with your mother's letters of the 16th and 19th September) and I was happy to learn you were all keeping well.

You will have all information about me from your Jethababu so it is unnecessary to write in detail.

I was glad to learn that your 'Mam' was proposing to take you all to the holy city of Kashi [Varanasi]. I hope the proposal will materialize and that you will have the opportunity of seeing the 'arati' [offering of worship] of Lord Biswanath, the magnificent ghats of Kashi, the Manmandir and other places of interest as also the remains of Buddhistic glory at Sarnath. Kashi is a place of special interest and attraction to Hindus and I hope you will profit both intellectually and spiritually by your stay there.

You and your brothers and sisters must not feel depressed on account of my indefinite detention. You should always call to mind the burning words of the late Balgangadhar Tilak when he was sentenced to a long term of imprisonment by the Bombay High Court—'There are higher powers that rule the destinies of men and nations, and it is perhaps the Will of Providence that the cause which I represent will prosper more by my suffering than by my remaining free.' You should also remember that you have your own duties to perform viz, devotion to superiors (both near and dear relations and friends of the family), love for those who are younger than you and kindness and sympathy for all who are less fortunately placed than yourself. It is by cultivating the qualities mentioned above that you can develop your intellect and elevate your soul. Try to realize every moment of your waking life that 'Man does not live by bread alone'.

I shall probably be late in sending you my Bijoya asirbad (blessings), having regard to my limitations. I am therefore sending you in anticipation, my warmest love and blessings for the Bijoya day.

Yours very affly
S. C. Bose

P.S. *Don't make any reference* to this letter in the letters you may write to me in future.
S.C.B

On 9 October 1932, due to a continuing and worrying deterioration in his health, Subhas was transferred to the King Edward Sanatorium at Bhowali in north-western India. On 1 December 1932 he wrote briefly to Ami in Calcutta, beginning with an apology for not having been able to write for some time and expressing best wishes for his nephew's studies.

Meanwhile Sarat remained behind in Jubbulpore Central Jail from where he continued his long distance efforts to inspire and guide the academic, intellectual and spiritual development of his son, now in his first year at the Scottish Churches College in Calcutta. On 1 February 1933 Sarat wrote:

I received your letter of the 8th ultimo on the 11th. I was glad to learn you were getting on well with your studies and were looking forward with great interest to laboratory work. I hope you are finding it as interesting as you anticipated.

Please tell your mother and your uncle that I received the telegrams they respectively sent and was happy to learn that they had a comfortable journey home and that all were well there.

I was interested to read what you had written about Poet Michael Madhusudan Dutt's works. Readers will no doubt differ as to their merits and demerits. But all agree that his greatest contribution to his mother tongue was that he gave to it a form of verse which was practically unknown before. Before his works were published, I do not think it was realized that the Bengali language was capable of scattering grandeur and magnificence with such generous profusion. A galaxy of talent followed him; and we find today that pinnacle after pinnacle of poetic heights have lifted themselves before the eyes of an admiring world. Those giddy poetic heights have radiated unspeakable joy and unquenchable hope all round; and who but a Philistine will say that he has not felt their touch?

I do not quite agree with you that the delineation of Ravana's character after the passing away of Meghnad seriously detracts from the force or grandeur of Michael's epic. I may not be right; but I do think that the poet deliberately gave a *human* touch to Ravana in order to captivate the minds of his readers. One has also to remember that Ravana was an 'Asuric' force and not a 'Sattwic' one and could not therefore be represented to be impervious to pleasure and pain (Sama Dukha Sukham).

Do not hurry through Shakespeare's works. Read them slowly and critically and you will then appreciate his masterly, almost merciless, analysis of human character. In that respect, there is only one other English poet whose works deserve close study—and that is Robert Browning. But you needn't take him up just yet.

Please send me two books from our library viz. Romain Rolland's 'Vivekananda' and 'Trial of Roger Casement' and remind the Book Co. Ltd. about sending me Arthur Avalon's 'Serpent Power'.

It was around this time that Subhas left on his involuntary exile in Europe departing India on 23 February 1933. After his arrival in Vienna in early March 1933 he had undergone treatment for his intestinal ailments at the Sanatorium Dr Fuerth in Schmidgasse 14. His continuing indisposition did not stop him from embarking on a whirlwind tour of European cities as India's 'unofficial ambassador'. His travels took him to Prague, Warsaw, Berlin, Geneva, Marseilles, Nice, Rome, Milan, Florence, Budapest, Belgrade, Zagreb, over the period 1933–1934.

His special interest was of course to promote better understanding of India in Europe and the cause of Indian independence. He attended an Indian Students' Conference in Rome on 22 December 1933, and was also present at the inauguration of the Indian Society in Prague in March 1934. In view of his interest in municipal affairs he met with the Mayor of Vienna, and also visited industrial facilities in various European countries.

In the course of his European missions and a hectic schedule, Subhas still made time to advise and inspire his nephew from afar. In a letter written largely in Bengali from Nice on 30 November 1933, Uncle Subhas encouraged nephew Ami to believe that he had 'been born at an auspicious time':

Glad to receive your letter of 26th October. What shall I write? I feel like writing many things but cannot.

You have been born at an auspicious time. The environment all around is favourable for growing up. The situation of the family that you are born into is also quite good. We had to struggle and work hard. You all are reaping the rewards. Hence your responsibility is much more. If we can't succeed, you must. You have to build the monument of your success on our failures.

You must endeavour to reach the heights of the greatest people. A very difficult exercise, I know. But you must achieve success through hard work. Have the highest ambition in life—but not a selfish ambition. The ambition should be to serve others and to die for others. If you nurture such unselfish ambition, then you will never become arrogant. Arrogance is a great sin. Really great men are never arrogant. They are certainly self-confident, but self-confident cannot be equated with arrogance.

Don't get angry at the meanness and narrow-mindedness of others. Meanness has to be conquered with love. If anyone harms or insults you, don't despise him. Continue loving him—one day he will realize your greatness and learn to love you.

The world is very crooked, very mean. But one has to love and serve it selflessly and turn it into a paradise. One who loves and serves the country does not always get love and praise. He often gets crucified like Christ. That's why Christ said of his attackers 'Father, forgive them—for they know not what they do'.

Transform your inner self into a paradise, and then you will never suffer. Remember, the essential principle in life is to give and not to take.

Have you read Bankimchandra's Kapalkundala? At the beginning, there is the example of Nabakumar. One has to be a selfless worker like Nabakumar.

That's all for today. God bless you! You must rise to the loftiest heights.

Ever your well-wisher
Your Rangakakababu

In another letter a month or two later, this time from Geneva dated 21 February 1934, Subhas sought to guide Ami on the development of strength of character, the importance of rising above narrowness and hate, and the imperative of love and openness in countering these.

Learning Science makes one's habits exact. The fault with our clan is that we are very casual and lackadaisical—there is no exactness and discipline in our character. For this our education system has to be scientific. If it was possible for me I could begin learning Bengali from the beginning again. But I grew up studying Philosophy—when I realised the significance (relevance) of Science, it was already too late. In this country every child learns higher science at school—we have no such infrastructure—so we start on higher science from the College level.

To build the correct base for our character we have to fall back on Vivekananda. Our main fault in character lies in lack of concentration. To gain this we had to resort to meditation earlier. With this there must be 'tenacity'—to stick to it. We have to embrace one ideal and spend our whole life trying to achieve it. If Bengalis gain concentration and tenacity, if his character is built on idealism, nobody can beat him. Because he has every other commendable quality of character.

Always remember, to overcome narrowness and connivance in this world—it is possible to do so with love only. There is no other greater truth than this. If you have to hate anything—hate narrowness and connivance. You cannot return narrowness with narrowness, you have to counter it with love and openness. That is why Christ, when he was being nailed on the Cross, said: 'Father forgive them for they know not what they do...'—and Gauranga Mahaprabhu had said: 'You hit me with the corner of the vessel, but that doesn't mean I cannot love you....'

The Man of God's idealism is not for show—it is deep inside him. The saffron dress does not make one a sadhu (priest). To be the ideal worker—you have to be a sanyasi (or a man of god). Every age has witnessed sanyas in a different image. This age has identified a 'sanyasi' as one who gives his life for work—the Karma Yogi.

Meaning one has to give his or her life for a greater idealism, forget about all pettiness and small needs. This is called selfless work.

You know that I left home once. There was an urge to look for the ideal Guru. I didn't find the right Guru. So I came back. I realised at that time that life (reality) is not outside us, it is inside all of us. Even in the most remote forest he will think of his desires if they remained in him. But I believe it is good to visit a lonely, silent place—it is sometimes necessary.

After this, the woman. Brahmacharya is of two kinds—the first is keeping the body healthy. The next stage in Brahmacharya means lack of lust towards a woman. The first kind is not very tough but to be adept at the second needs many years of effort and discipline.

Speaking from my experience I can say to be a true Brahmachari two things are essential:

1. One has to love a great ideal and one has to put in maximum effort towards that ideal. Automatically then your mind will move away from other yearnings.

2. One has to think of the woman in the form of the mother. In fact, one must worship her in the form of Durga or Kali. Meditating on these forms for a long time will create a mental state whereby thinking or even seeing a woman will make one think of the mother. To concentrate on this our culture has several puja provisions—like Kumari Puja. This means making a young girl sit before you and thinking only of your mother or the Mother Goddess.

Do not lose hope even if you cannot achieve this in a short time. Whether you get married later or not, you have to follow Brahmacharya from now on.

Meditating in front of the image of Mother Durga every morning and night will definitely help. Chandi's text elaborates: 'All education is in your varied images and all womankind is also in your image...O Mother Goddess.'

If there is any good in me hope you emulate it and discard whatever is bad.

Yours,
Rangakakababu

Meanwhile in April 1933 Sarat had been transferred from Jubbulpore Central Jail to effective house arrest at his family bungalow in Kurseong, where he remained under detention until July 1935. Sarat was joined there some of the time by his wife Bivabati and Amiya's younger siblings, while Amiya himself remained at college in Calcutta. From Kurseong Sarat continued to guide young Amiya through correspondence, often, as reflected in two letters of 14 October 1933 and 28 January 1934, from a philosophical and spiritual as well as from an educational and methodological stand-point.

In his letter of 14 October 1933, Sarat advises Amiya to undertake an intensive study of the essence of Hinduism as enunciated in the *Srimad Bhagavad Gita*—'Thy right is to work only; but never to the fruits thereof...by performing action without attachment one attains to the highest'. He further asks Amiya 'to try to *realise* in your daily life what is taught therein.'

Also in this letter, Sarat not only prescribes what Amiya might usefully read but also impresses upon him that 'serious literature must not be read with break-neck speed. Acquisition of knowledge depends upon the amount of concentration you bring to bear upon what you are reading and not on the extensity of your reading. Voracious readers are more often than not superficial. One can derive more from a careful study of one good book than from a rapid skipping over of dozens'.

In the letter of 28 January 1934, Sarat informs Amiya that he had 'read your article in your College magazine with interest. The idea you have sought to give expression to is right'. Sarat allows that reforms of the educational system introduced by an eminent Bengali educationalist the late Sir Ashutosh Mookerji, had revived a 'cultural outlook more in keeping with our Indian traditions'. Sarat quipped that before then, 'education that was being imparted was merely giving the majority of us the intellectual equipment necessary for high grade clerkships'.

* * *

As a child of the new mass-based phase of the freedom struggle which began under the leadership of Gandhi in the early 1920s, Amiya was both a witness to and deeply influenced by, the resurgent nationalism of the years that followed. His own early education, understanding and knowledge of 'men and events' were greatly influenced by Sarat and Subhas. Both father and uncle instilled in him very early on, their vision of the world and the high principles by which they thought one should live.

After completing his school and undergraduate years in Calcutta, Amiya went for further studies to Cambridge University. Following in the footsteps of his father Sarat, he studied law and was called to the Bar by Lincoln's Inn in 1941. Sarat had been called to the Bar also by Lincoln's Inn almost three decades earlier, in June 1914. Amiya then joined the Chambers of one of the leading lawyers in London Sir Norman Birkett. Meanwhile he had obtained his Bachelor's and Master's Degrees in Economics Tripos from the University of Cambridge. Amiya had in fact completed his studies by June 1941 and had intended to return to India, but was told firmly by the British authorities in London that he would not be permitted to return home at that time.

With the Second World War raging first in Europe and then Asia-Pacific, Amiya was thus compelled to remain in England. He turned his attention to political activism and in particular began an active campaign in support of Indian independence. Meanwhile his Uncle Subhas had escaped from Calcutta in January 1941 and arrived in Berlin in April of the same year, from where he had sent a secret message to Amiya asking him to join him there via Ireland. This did not prove feasible in the circumstances prevailing at the time.

As a member of the Congress since 1937, Amiya was instrumental in the formation in Britain of a Committee of Indian Congressmen in August 1942, and was elected as its General Secretary. In its efforts to promote the cause of Indian independence, and in particular to support Gandhi's Quit India movement launched around the same time on 8 August 1942, the Committee received widespread support from the Indian community in Britain (both Muslim and Hindu), as well as from—in spite of the war setting—a range of British Members of Parliament from both House of Lords and House of Commons.

Amiya was also centrally involved in the establishment in London in October 1942 of a Council for International Recognition of Indian independence, and became Vice-President and Secretary of this organisation.

Over the remaining months of 1942, the Quit India movement was quickly and violently suppressed by the British colonial authorities, with virtually all of the important Congress leaders, including Gandhi, rounded up and imprisoned on 9 August 1942, the day after the Quit India Resolution was approved by Congress. When some months later on 9 February 1943, Gandhi himself once again invoked from his continued imprisonment in

Poona the non-violent weapon of the fast to maintain pressure on the British Government and its imperial authorities, the London-based Congress Committee under the guidance of Amiya as General Secretary, decided to send the following telegram on 13 February 1943 to United States President F. D. Roosevelt at the White House.[7]

THE PRESIDENT

ON BEHALF OF 45 INDIAN MEMBERS OF THE COMMITTEE OF INDIAN CONGRESSMEN AND OTHER INDIAN SUPPORTERS WE URGE YOU STRONGLY TO INTERVENE IN THE GANDHI FAST CRISIS STOP WE SUBMIT THAT ON THE PRINCIPLE OF THE GOVERNMENT WITH THE CONSENT OF THE GOVERNED THE INDIAN PROBLEM CAN BE IMMEDIATELY SOLVED BY THE HANDING OVER OF ALL POLITICAL POWER TO THE INDIAN NATIONAL CONGRESS STOP

AMIYA BOSE, AMIR SHAH, DEV MOGUNDER, KARTAR SINGH, PULIN SEAL, 70 OXFORD STREET, LONDON W1

While we do not know the precise impact of this particular item of correspondence, we do know now of American uneasiness at the time at what they saw as British intransigence on the question of Indian independence. This may even have extended to an American perception of a preoccupation on the part of Churchill and some of his Ministers towards the retention of India at the expense of prosecution of the Pacific War against the Japanese.

For his part Amiya had come to be recognised as a driving force in Britain for the cause of Indian independence. In its edition of 31 October 1942, the Chicago Defender wrote of him:

Within a stone's throw of the British Ministry of Information, anti-British Indian nationalists, ardent supporters of Mahatma Gandhi and fanatical members of Congress, have organised a Committee of Congressmen under the leadership of Amiya Nath Bose. Young Bose is the nephew of the famous Subhas

---

[7] This telegram was found by the author, then based in New York, during a visit in July 2007 to the United States National Archives in Maryland, where her father Amiya Nath Bose featured as the very first item under 'B' in the card catalogue brought out for perusal.

Chandra Bose, ex-President of the Indian National Congress, who escaped from India and is now allegedly helping the Japs organise an army made up of Indian soldiers captured in Hong Kong, Malaya, Singapore and Burma as well as Burmese nationalists and Siamese to drive the British from India. 'The decisive phase of our freedom movement has begun', declared the young Bose, when I called on him at the New Oxford Street headquarters of the Indian Congressmen. Surrounded by members of his 'Brains Trust' or Working Committee as the High Command of the Congress Party in India is called, Mr Bose who has all the cultivated mannerisms of a matured statesman, expressed his pleasure in granting an interview to the representative of the colored American press. 'The colored peoples everywhere are our allies. India is fighting not only for her own freedom but for the freedom of Africans and peoples of African descent all over the world' asserted Bose.

In the following year 1943 when a disastrous famine struck Bengal killing several millions, Amiya became active in organising relief and raising funds in England. 'It was largely due to his personal dedication and effort that a much acclaimed Exhibition of Indian Art was mounted in London in June that year (1943), displaying paintings, textiles and a large collection of Indian sculpture—no mean achievement in the war-torn Britain of that time,' commented his co-worker Ms Sehri Saklatvala.[8] Amiya also worked in conjunction with the Tagore Society in London organising public readings of Rabindranath Tagore's works. All the monies raised from these events were sent to the Mayor of Calcutta's Relief Fund.

From the other side of the world, Amiya's Uncle Subhas in Burma through repeated radio broadcasts offered to send rice for his starving people, an appeal which remained unheeded by the British authorities.

In early December 1944, after more than seven years away from home, during which time he returned just once to India from June to October 1939, Amiya left England and returned to the political fray in India. His father had been writing for some time from his place of detention in Coonoor imploring his son

---

[8] Sehri Saklatvala, a daughter of Communist politician and Member of the UK Parliament Shapurji Saklatvala, became a life-long friend of Amiya and his family.

to find some way to get back; but he was effectively prevented from doing so by the British authorities who clearly felt that it was better for them that Amiya be in London than Calcutta. Thus, it was that at the time when Amiya did manage to make his way home, his Uncle Subhas was based in Rangoon Burma as the head of the Provisional Government of India and the Indian National Army, and his father remained in detention inside India.

On arrival at Howrah Station in Calcutta on 9 December 1944, by train from Bombay where he landed in India from Europe, Amiya was welcomed back home by members of the Bose family who were there to receive him. Amiya sorely felt the absence of his father, whom he had not seen now for more than five years.

In his lonely detention in Coonoor, Sarat's heart was heavy as he could not be there to receive the son he had missed so much and had not seen for so long. Sarat had written from Coonoor in a letter of 8 December 1944:

> This morning at about 10.30 am the Special Officer in Charge of this detention camp delivered into my hands what he said was a copy of the telegram you sent me from Bombay on the 5th inst. I do not know whether it was a copy or a paraphrase of your telegram. Be that as it may, I was very happy to learn that you had safely arrived at Bombay and you would be reaching Calcutta tomorrow.... I cannot help feeling sad that I cannot run up to Calcutta to welcome you home after an absence of more than five years.... For sometime past I have been anxiously awaiting your return. I asked Sisir to forward you extracts from my letter to him of the 10th September last and he informed me that he had done so. I wrote to you on the 8th October last but I doubt if the letter reached your hands. I need hardly say that I felt somewhat relieved when I read in the 'Hindu' (of Madras) in the beginning of last month that you had sailed for home.

In a long interview covered by the Hindustan Standard on 10 December 1944, Amiya emerged as a strong advocate of the Congress and initiator of its activities in Britain from the time of the Gandhi-inspired Quit India movement in 1942. As noted in the article, one of his first acts upon landing in Bombay was to ask for an early meeting with Gandhi to brief him on developments in London as the heartland of the imperial power. Gandhi subsequently received Amiya a number of times, on one occasion asking the newly trained Cambridge economist to prepare an outline plan for the electrification of rural India, a request with which Amiya complied.

It was during these several meetings with Gandhi that Amiya agreed to carry the message from Gandhi to Sarat, that the latter should return to an active role in the resurgent Congress movement, with its Gandhian emphasis on constitutional rather than revolutionary change.

Amiya's immediate concern and challenge was to effect the release of his father from detention (as well as his younger brother Sisir and two cousins who had been arrested earlier in 1944). Through his political activities in Britain for the cause of Indian independence and active campaign in support of the Quit India movement, Amiya as we have seen had developed wide-ranging contacts among the British public, Members of Parliament especially from the leftist parties and had prominent and influential friends. Now from India, he again sought their assistance and canvassed ceaselessly for Sarat's release.

In the event it was not until after the surrender of Japan and the end of the War in the Pacific in mid-August 1945, that Sarat was eventually released on 14 September 1945. He arrived home in Calcutta to a tumultuous welcome at Howrah Station.

2

The Road to Mandalay

The national goal is to me at least as clear as daylight. It is an independent republic free from British control.... An independent India has been the dream of my life and I believe it shall be a fact in Indian history

—Subhas Chandra Bose,
Notes from Berhampore Jail, December 1924

On his way back to Calcutta from Cambridge University in England in 1921, the young 24-year-old Subhas was very keen to meet in Bombay with the now prominent Indian nationalist leader Mohandas Karamchand Gandhi, to learn more of his ideals and activities as represented by the non-violent Non-Cooperation Movement and to join the struggle which had now reached epic proportions.

At their meeting, Gandhi encouraged Subhas on his return to Calcutta to join with the charismatic Congress leader in Bengal C. R. Das, who had risen to prominence over the period of Subhas's absence in Britain and with whom his older brother Sarat was already in league. Subhas himself had from Cambridge initiated an exchange of letters with C. R. Das, in which the latter had told Subhas about the work that was already being done and bemoaned the 'dearth of sincere workers'.

Back in Calcutta, Subhas wasted no time in meeting with and joining the Congress and C. R. Das, for whom he quickly developed profound admiration and adopted him as his political guru. With older brother Sarat, Subhas launched headlong into national, provincial and municipal politics, the beginning of a life-long symbiotic relationship between the brothers. This would deepen through the many trials and tribulations which were to ensue over the following decades.

By 1923, the Bose Brothers were fully engaged under the leadership of C. R. Das in the programme of the Swaraj Party within the Indian National Congress. The Swaraj Party with C. R. Das in the lead had come into existence at the Gaya Annual

Session of the Congress in December 1922, with a proposed plan of action which challenged that of the Congress mainstream represented by Gandhi and his followers, termed the 'no-changers'. The essence of the position of the Congress 'no-changers', following the suspension by Gandhi of the Non-Cooperation Movement earlier in February 1922 (see further discussion in Chapter 3), was that Congress members should continue their 'constructive' work in promotion of inter-communal harmony, humanitarian relief assistance, hand-spinning and weaving, extension of national education and the like. At the same time, they would maintain the boycott of the national and provincial legislatures which had been in place since the Calcutta Annual Session of the Congress in 1920.

The contrary view, as represented by C. R. Das and his legion of followers and nurtured in animated discussion groups convened during contemporary spells in jail, was to compete for representation in the legislatures and once elected run a unified campaign of opposition from within them. As related by Subhas in *The Indian Struggle*, C. R. Das had found himself in an untenable position as Congress President at the Gaya Session, when the Gandhi-supported 'no-changers' won a majority and carried the day on the key issue.[1]

At the same time support for the position of C. R. Das and his followers had been strong and across the provinces. He, thus, felt compelled to resign and form the Swaraj Party with a plan of action at odds with that of the majority of the Congress session. Political stalwarts Pandit Motilal Nehru (father of Jawaharlal) and Vithalbhai Patel, along with the Bose brothers, joined C. R. Das in this new Swaraj party and its commitment to a more activist stance.

In a tumultuous national and political agenda over this period, Sarat was appointed by C. R. Das as Managing Director of Forward Publishing Ltd. This company oversaw the publication from 25 October 1923 of a new English daily newspaper *Forward* (which effectively became *Liberty* from 1929 as the result of a successful defamation case brought by the state-owned East India Railway Company) as the official organ of the

---

[1] Subhas Chandra Bose, *The Indian Struggle* (Natyachinta Foundation Kolkata, 2005), 110.

Swaraj Party. C. R. Das was the first editor of the newspaper, and Subhas helped out in organisation and production for a time when others were in jail.

For both Sarat and Subhas, this was an opportunity to bring into play and give expression to a nationalist political vision which dovetailed with that of C. R. Das and the Swaraj Party. Each of the brothers was able to bring to bear a combination of a remarkable grasp of the English language and power of the pen, employed to great effect in all of their writings, journalistic and otherwise. Sarat had as early as 14 March 1912 written an article for the *Star of Utkal*, seeking to expose corruption among the political leadership of Bihar. The close association with *Forward* and then *Liberty*' provided a vehicle to showcase and further refine those skills, as well as lessons for the future on using the news media to optimum effect.

For Sarat in particular, the importance of an independent and fearless press to inform and influence public opinion, especially in a subject nation, was to be a feature of his entire public life. Much later in September 1948, in what was to be the penultimate year of his life, Sarat founded his own national newspaper called *The Nation*, when he realised that the broad discourse in national politics was not being fully and properly treated by the then existing news media.

Also during this period of the first half of the 1920s, Subhas was appointed Publicity Officer of the Bengal Provincial Congress Committee (BPCC), and became a Captain in the recently formed National Volunteer Corps. He is credited with the successful organisation of a boycott in Calcutta on 17 November 1921 against the visit to India of the Prince of Wales (who later became King Edward VIII in 1936 and abdicated in 1938), leading directly to his first arrest and subsequent imprisonment from 10 December 1921 to 14 February 1922. (Subhas quipped on this short stint in jail—Did I steal chickens?) On release from prison he demonstrated his powers of organisation and capacity for selfless work as the Secretary of the North Bengal Flood Relief Committee, in a successful and acclaimed response to catastrophic floods in Bengal at the time.

On 24 April 1924, Subhas was appointed as the Chief Executive Officer (CEO) of the newly reconstituted Corporation of Calcutta by C. R. Das in his capacity as the first Mayor of Calcutta. (Prior to this, the position of Chairman of the Corporation fulfilled both mayoral and chief executive officer functions.) Subhas was just 27 and decided to accept just half the salary attached to the post, an example followed by colleagues. Sarat was at the same time voted in as an Alderman of the Corporation in April 1924, a position he continued to hold until 1932.

Unfettered tenure and effective work as CEO of the Corporation were short-lived for Subhas. Just six months after his appointment, he was again arrested on 25 October 1924 along with a number of other Congressmen for alleged revolutionary conspiracy, under a combination of an emergency ordinance enacted by the Viceroy the night before, and the pernicious Regulation III of the Bengal Ordinance of 1818. The charges against Subhas and his co-prisoners were that they were in touch with Russian Bolshevik agents in the Far East, and were attempting to smuggle arms into India for revolutionary struggle.

Subhas was first held briefly in Alipore Central Jail in Calcutta, followed by Berhampore Jail some 200 kilometres north of Calcutta, and finally removed to Mandalay Jail in Burma from 25 January 1925. The British colonial authorities were not in a position to prove the charges in a court of law, so Subhas and the others were simply detained and no trials were ever held.

Nor was there to be any early release. It was not until 16 May 1927, and even then only on health grounds, that Subhas regained his freedom and rejoined brother Sarat and his immediate family living at 38/1 Elgin Road in Calcutta, the house from where he had been arrested and detained more than two and a half years earlier.

The British had clearly wanted to remove the fire-brand lieutenant of C. R. Das from Bengal's political scene and even deter him through harassment and punishment; but as Amiya observed, the outcome could not have been more different and certainly not as hoped for by the British.[2]

Subhas emerged from Mandalay jail as a mature, radical thinker, ready to play a central role in Congress politics of the Left. Uncle

[2] *Memoirs of Amiya Nath Bose* (unpublished, from the Private Collection Amiya Nath and Jyostna Bose).

Subhas took advantage of his involuntary confinement to read and study widely, taking meticulous notes while at the same time seeking to keep abreast of developments back home through regular correspondence with family and friends, on subjects ranging from day to day family matters to the larger social, civic and political issues of vital concern to him.

The Mandalay years gave him an opportunity to reflect on, and to further develop his vision of what should be the nature and direction of the struggle for Indian independence, his own role in it, and also of the future social and economic development of India.

These habits of reflection arising from involuntary confinement, and for Subhas what proved to be a process of incubation for his ideas, had probably first taken root in Berhampore Jail, where Subhas spent some two months immediately prior to being moved to Mandalay. It was at Berhampore where he began to tease out and develop his embryonic ideas on what he had seen and experienced so far of the Indian struggle against modern imperialism.

In a series of observations in a jail notebook which he left in the custody of Amiya, his thoughts began to crystallise on the preferred nature of Indian society, on the goals of the Indian National Congress, and on the meaning of a national movement in an Indian context. Also in these brief notes from Berhampore, his later well-known allegiance to and faith in the youth of India and his aspirations for them began to take shape in testaments to the courage and sacrifice of Bengali youth.

On Society

It requires no small courage to broach heresies which militate against the beliefs, customs, laws and ideas prevailing in the family, society or state. And when heretic opinions are translated into action the vested interests or conservative elements in our family, society or state are up in arms in self-defence. There is in many cases no end to the relentless persecution to which the poor heretic is subjected. In dealing with the adult heretic both the family and society resort usually to non-violent means and by boycott, collective denunciation & similar methods pressure is sought to be exerted on the heretic. In the case of the State which is based on organised violence, force is usually applied in arresting or imprisoning and in hanging him if capital sentence is passed on him. It is therefore not easy for the individual to brave such odds and incur the displeasure of society & the state simply for the sake of giving expression to one's opinions and acting up to them.

In a class-ridden society or a subject state...

We have reached a stage in our national life when it is necessary for us to think clearly and to act boldly. Clear thinking and bold action presuppose a correct perception of the facts of life. What with the 'idols' of which Bacon complains, what with the intellectual and moral inertia to which we Indians have well nigh become habitual victims, what with the terror which the sword of Damocles—Law and Order—incessantly awakens in our hearts—correct perception is not so easy as it might appear at first.

In spite of the fact that we as a nation are fast overcoming the fear and cowardice born of age long servitude, there is no gain-saying the fact that if we had the courage of our convictions, the people of Great Britain and of the world at large would have heard a different account of the innermost desires and aspirations of our heart, honest opinions are not always uttered and rarely acted upon when the stronger party is likely to take vindictive action by way of persecution. This is particularly true in the sphere of politics. But the advancement of a social group depends primarily on clear thinking and bold action and it is not possible to think clearly or to act boldly without a correct perception of the facts of life.

Fearlessness in thought and action is to me the supreme virtue in life.

Correct perception is therefore what we want most of all. We must face facts—the facts not only of our inner life but of our outer life as well. The facts of human nature have to be studied, the lessons of world history have to be culled and the purpose of Indian history has to be discovered.

I have long wondered what was the secret of the influence of Sriyut Arabindo Ghosh on the youth of Bengal when he was in the political arena. I have come to the conclusion that the secret lay in the clarity of his perception and the boldness of his thought when he declared in the columns of his paper 'Bande Mataram'—'we want complete autonomy free from British control' he sent a thrill into the hearts of all young men in the province. The sheer grandeur of his conception was enough to capture the imagination of young Bengal—if not of young India. In him his countrymen found a man who thought boldly and saw clearly and who knew what he was talking about. Arabindo was a political visionary no doubt but his vision was to him more than reality. The vision of a free India was to him as real as any of the contemporary facts of life.

On the Congress

The Indian National Congress is at present groping in an intellectual mist. As Congressmen we are agitating—we do not know for what. I cannot say the same of the Liberal Party. The Liberal Party in India has set before itself a definite goal viz. Self government within the Empire. The Liberal Party may not have the courage or the capacity to dream of a free India and aspire after it. But their goal is clear and definite beyond doubt. The Congress has gone a step further. It has refused to accept the limitations of an imperial connection but it has not so far defined what is meant by Swaraj—and has left individual Congressmen free to put their own interpretation on the word.

The national Goal is to me at least as clear as daylight. It is an independent republic free from British control. Subjective feeling, study of human psychology and of the lessons of history appear to me to point clearly to this goal. An independent India has been the dream of my life and I believe it shall be a fact in Indian history.

A National Movement

What Bengal needs today is a real national movement. By 'national' I do not mean 'political'—for a political movement is already in existence. Neither do I mean a Jingoist movement, for such a thing is foreign to the Indian temperament. By national movement I mean a movement affecting all the spheres of our social and collective life and all the sections of our community. We want a renaissance in our collective life or rather a neo-renaissance. The creative spirit must set to work in the spheres of poetry, music, literature, painting, sculpture, history as also in our social, religious and commercial life. Society must be purged of narrowness and inequality. Religion must be freed from bigotry and superstition. The Indian business community must grow into a healthy self-conscious and public-spirited body corporate. In the domain of culture we want genuine poets, painters, sculptors, historians, philosophers, economists imbued with the spirit of scientific research and endowed with a real creative talent. Then alone will India be able (to hold) her own in the sphere of culture and science among the savants of the world.

On the Bengali Youth

There is no creature on the face of the earth who is so much maligned as the Bengali Youth. By the government he is looked upon as a potential anarchist and by his own guardians he is not infrequently looked upon as a mere child though he might be in his thirties. In the eyes of his European professors he is a good-for-nothing fellow, fit only for perpetual tutelage. Yet the Bengali youth in spite of his many failings possesses, in embryo at least, some of the noblest traits in human character. My own faith in the capacity and future of the Bengali youth is unbounded. The Bengali youth has, since the beginning of the renaissance in this province, worked under considerable disadvantages and several handicaps. When he has attempted to throw himself heart and soul into any altruistic organization he has had to incur the terrors of social and political persecution. The young enthusiasts who joined the Brahmo Samaj were penalized in several ways by their contemporaries. The young Sannyasis who flocked to the banner of Ramakrishna-Vivekananda were persecuted by their own people in more ways than one. Coming nearer to the present day we find that young men taking an active part in any philanthropic or political organization have constantly been under police surveillance and have sometimes been clapped into jail for no earthly offence. A comparison of the status of the Bengali student in his own country with that of the Cambridge undergraduate in his country will clearly illustrate the point.

Yet few are probably aware that beneath the pressure of social and governmental persecution the Bengali youth is developing nerves of steel. The phenomenon of thousands of students laying down their books one fine morning in the early months of the famous year 1921, is an indication that the young men of Bengal can develop a common will when they do so desire.

Like an avalanche the non-cooperation movement came and went. Students in thousands came out and went in again. But few are probably aware that there are still hundreds of young men who in 1921 silently took the vow of service and poverty, who are still sticking to their pledge and mean to do so in future. They now toil unnoticed in obscure corners of the province and may even die unwept and unsung. But on their solid sacrifice will be built the edifice of Indian nationalism.

The Bengali youth is not infrequently condemned as emotional. Yes he is emotional and in his emotion lies his salvation. The man who is devoid of emotion may be a saint but he may also be a brute. It is because the Bengali youth is emotional that he has so many noble impulses and is capable of responding so warmly to the call of duty, love and sacrifice. It is easy to condemn as misguided the young man who can snap his fingers in the face of death but it is difficult not to admire his heroism.

The heart of the Bengali youth is a peculiar one. Strike at the right place and he will be your slave. Strike wrongly and the response will be as cold as that of death. How is it that some organizations social, religious and political get hundreds of recruits while others fail to get any? The secret lies in the manner of striking at the heart of the Bengali youth. Vivekananda knew the secret and that is why he was and is still idolised by the youth of his province.

On 25 January 1925, Subhas was suddenly and with little or no warning moved from Berhampore to Calcutta for an overnight stay at the Lalbazar Police Station. He was then taken the next morning by ship to Rangoon, and from there a tiring and uncomfortable overland journey to Mandalay in northern Burma. While taken by surprise, Subhas seems not to have been unduly perturbed by this turn of events, perhaps seeing it as an inevitable chapter in his own history of struggle against British imperialism.

In *The Indian Struggle,* he observes that while he knew little of Mandalay, except as an ancient Burmese kingdom, he and his fellow transportees were very much alive to the fact that the fabled Indian revolutionary leaders Lokamanya Tilak and Lala Lajpat Rai had been imprisoned there at different times by the British colonial overlords. 'It gave us therefore some consolidation and pride to feel we were following in their footsteps,' he reflected.[3]

Health problems were to prove the most serious outcome and impediment from incarceration in Mandalay Jail, and these problems were to plague Subhas not only for the duration of his time in Mandalay, but virtually for the rest of his life, particularly on the multiple occasions that he was sent to jail by the British. Not long after arrival in Mandalay Jail around the end of the month of January 1925, Subhas wrote a long, partly-censored letter to Sarat on 12 February 1925 covering a range of issues including outstanding Calcutta Corporation matters, the

---

[3] Bose, *The Indian Struggle*, 169.

possibility of standing for elections, his 'establishment expenses' back home in Calcutta, and his probably already deteriorating health. On the latter, with a plea to Sarat not to tell his father or mother that he was not well, he wrote[4]:

> Regarding my health, for the first time since my confinement I have been feeling unwell. Since the day of my arrival I have been feeling seedy and out of sorts and have been suffering from indigestion without a break. This is the case with most of us here. It does not appear that the climate of this place will ever agree with me.... Mandalay Jail is supposed to be one of the healthiest jails in Burma and Mandalay is a place which, I understand has a heavy mortality in plague and small pox and particularly in plague. Last year there were as many as thirty thousand deaths from plague—if my information is correct...Subhas

His health was not to improve in Mandalay, and repeated attempts to have him transferred by the authorities back to Bengal on medical grounds, including in an early letter of 13 June 1925, were basically ignored for more than two long years. His trials and tribulations notwithstanding, it seems that he did not lose his sharp and ironic sense of humour. In a letter to Sarat dated 2 July 1925, which seems to have survived the censor, he wrote:

> The Inspector General of Prisons was down here a few days ago. He asked me if I was sure that my dyspepsia was not due to over-eating. I remarked that it was a pertinent question to ask after reducing the diet-allowance by 50%. Whatever one may think of him, he is quite consistent in his views for he has remarked in his annual administrative report which has just been published that prolonged stay in jail improves a man's health! I rubbed my eyes when I read it. Is any comment necessary?
>
> The I.G. suggested further that I should try fasting as a cure (so there are disciples of Mahatma Gandhi even in Government service!)

In another earlier letter to Sarat of 6 March 1925, Subhas was clearly reticent—at least at that early stage—to write in too

---

[4] One of a number of hitherto unpublished letters from Subhas to Sarat, from the Private Collection of Amiya Nath and Jyotsna Bose.

much critical detail in letters home about the prison and his conditions of imprisonment. He clearly suspected that it would prompt the censors to find any excuse to withhold them.

> You have asked me to write about the arrangements that have been made here. I dare not do so—as I am sure that my letter will be withheld in that case. You may feel surprised, but some of my letters were withheld because I referred therein to the arrangements that had been made for my journey from Berhampur [sic] to Mandalay—on the ground that my letters contained criticism of the action of Government...

His more reflective thoughts on the Mandalay imprisonment itself and the accompanying conditions would have to wait until much later to be publicly aired, including in *The Indian Struggle* which devotes a chapter (In Burmese Prisons) to the episode. A collection of more philosophical reflections appears publicly for the first time in the following pages of this particular chapter, as excerpts from *Pebbles on the Seashore.*

True to his character and spirit, Subhas refused to allow his ailments and general discomfort to hold him back in any way, and he plunged into a busy agenda which featured a dogged commitment to the Calcutta Municipal Corporation and its programme of work, and competing for election to the Bengal Legislative Council.

With the Corporation, Subhas had sought to continue to fulfil his functions as CEO in the first few months of incarceration in Alipore and Berhampore Jails. Documentation would be brought to him in the cells for consideration, action and approval as appropriate, apparently with the approval of the jail authorities. Faraway Mandalay in the remote regions of northern Burma was however a different story, and even Subhas was unable to bridge the geographic divide and maintain an effective role. In his aforementioned letter to Sarat of 12 February 1925, he laments that he has '...lost all touch with the Corporation since my arrival here. I have not received either copies of the Corporation Minutes or of the Municipal Gazette'.

That did not stop Subhas from pursuing, through his letters to his brother Sarat, Corporation matters close to his heart. One of these was compulsory primary education, where he was a pioneer in recognising its critical importance to effective nation-building and which was to prove a lifetime preoccupation. Subhas was later to translate this Corporation commitment to a national commitment through his Haripura Address in 1938 as Congress President. Meanwhile, he wrote from jail to Sarat on 5 September 1925, with a fundamental message for the Corporation and the Deputy Mayor.

> I think it is desirable to start compulsory primary education in a limited area—say one or two wards—in Calcutta in 1926. This will not only place us definitely on the road to primary education for Calcutta but will also afford sufficient experience, in the light of which further advances may be made...

And again on 9 October 1925:

> The Act will have to be amended, in the first place, in order to confer the necessary powers on the Corporation.... In the meantime the scheme should be made ready by the Corporation Education Department to be in time for the next budget. It may be desirable to commence work in the area which is at present the most literate, if there is financial stringency—for the most literate area could be made fully literate at a minimum cost.

Also during this Mandalay Jail period, in late 1925 the national and provincial legislatures in India were dissolved, and Subhas was nominated by the Bengal Congress Party, apparently with some prodding from Sarat, to contest the North Calcutta Constituency in an election for the Bengal Legislative Council. He won, defeating the sitting member Jatindra Nath Basu, who was the leader of the Liberal—or Moderate—Party in Bengal.[5] Sarat himself competed as a 'Swarajist' from the Calcutta University Constituency and joined his absent brother as a member of the Council.

In a handsome electoral victory against a formidable opponent, Subhas was generous to his campaign team and the voters, who were encouraged to adopt the Irish Sinn Fein revolutionary political slogan: 'Put him in to get him out.' (Subhas noted wryly in *The Indian Struggle* that the Government of India was less

---

[5] Jatindra Nath Basu was also a distinguished and popular figure, widely known for his integrity and commitment to the nationalist cause.

responsive to public opinion than the Government of Ireland, as his incarceration continued.)[6]

At the same time, and in the closest possible collaboration with brother Sarat given the vicissitudes of distance, Subhas planned and conducted his campaign from behind distant prison walls with meticulous care and considerable attention to detail, leaving as little as possible to chance. He summarised his nine-point election strategy in a letter of 23 November 1925 to Sarat.

> I am sorry that there has been so much delay in coming to a decision regarding my candidature, one way or the other. I am afraid there is hardly any time left for canvassing and I cannot say that I am not at all nervous about the issue. However superhuman eleventh-hour efforts will have to be put in—if we are not to fail.
>
> I do not think there is any harm if I repeat some of the salient points which strike me at the moment:
>
> 1. The principal point is to get a strong and energetic organizer at the centre to take charge of the entire campaign. I have suggested the name of Babu Nalini Ranjan Sarkar to uncle (who had visited Subhas in jail). I hope Nalini Babu will afford to spare 3 weeks or so for the work.
> 2. The electoral roll will have to be studied carefully and our efforts will have to be directed accordingly. If the majority of votes are in Calcutta, that will be the main field of action. If however, the mofussil votes outnumber the Calcutta votes, more attention will have to be directed towards mofussil organization.
> 3. From our point of view, we should be able to score better in the Mofussil than the other candidates. Our Congress organization being extensive, we should be at an advantage in canvassing the Mofussil votes. On the other hand, as we can command a large number of voluntary workers, we can carry on an intensive campaign in Calcutta during a short period more effectively than any other candidate.
> 4. The whole area (West Bengal) will have to be divided into several groups for election purposes, each group to be in charge of some responsible man or men. Whoever approaches the voter first after his ballot-paper arrives, stands a better chance of getting his vote than a belated canvasser.

---

[6] Bose, *The Indian Struggle*, 179.

5. I am sure there will be no dearth of voluntary workers if an appeal is published in the papers. As to whether any organization is possible with so little time at our disposal, is more than I can say.

6. It will be desirable to publish a manifesto signed by prominent men supporting my candidature in the different papers.

7. Please consider the desirability of inserting an appeal in the important papers on my behalf to the voters of the West Bengal Constituency. The appeal may be signed by you or by Mr Sengupta. The insertion may be repeated for a week or so.

8. If a prominent man is available, he should pay flying visits to the district centres.

9. We have written to the following gentlemen from here. You may hear from them. In case you do so, you may send them some money for the work if it is required by them.

Subhas identified particular individuals by name for election work in each district and pinpointed the names of a number of key individuals whose support should be enlisted. Essentially, he had to rely in the first instance on his brother Sarat, and also on a cohort of key individuals whom he could trust and to whom he could assign key responsibilities.

During this first year of imprisonment in Mandalay, Subhas—and for that matter Bengal and India—suffered a catastrophic bereavement. The sudden and unexpected death of C. R. Das on 16 June 1925 meant not only the loss of a political lion and mentor, it was also a personal tragedy for Subhas, Sarat and their families. They had not only been political allies with a common, noble purpose, but genuine friends who empathised with, protected and fought for each other. In what was to have become a biography of C. R. Das but not completed, Subhas on 16 June 1936 began to write from detention in Sarat's hill cottage at Giddapahar in Kurseong[7]:

Few public men anywhere in the world have had such a phenomenal rise as the Deshbandhu. His public career was meteoric and he died in the plenitude of his powers 'in a blaze of glory', as one

---

[7] Introduction to unfinished book on C. R. Das by Subhas Chandra Bose, included in *Outline Scheme of Swaraj* published by the Government of West Bengal, 5 November 1973, 73.

of his countrymen put it. He entered the political arena rather late in life, but from the first moment he was in the first rank of his country's leadership. To the superficial observer it appeared as if he had been suddenly foisted on his countrymen and did not have to work his way up the inevitable slope. In some quarters this impression fathered the thought that his wealth had served as his passport to national leadership, and caused considerable heart-burning in those who felt that they had been elbowed out by the obtrusive late-comer.

There might have been some justification for this impression, if prior to 1920, the Deshbandhu had been nothing more than a successful advocate and had not played any part in public affairs. But such was not the case. Though he represented a type that matures slowly and somewhat late in life—his qualities as well as his pursuits were manifold, and he brought to the service of public cause a rich and versatile genius and character which constituted the key to his success as a politician.

There have been many distinguished advocates in India in recent times, but it is difficult to find another lawyer who won so much popularity through his professional work. This was due to the large number of political cases in which he appeared for the defence. As a matter of fact, his professional career practically began with the defence of Aurobindo Ghosh in the Alipore Bomb Conspiracy Case in 1909. Aurobindo was then the outstanding left-wing nationalist leader in Bengal and among the left-wingers in the whole of India, his position was second only to that of Lokamanya B. G. Tilak. The trial aroused unprecedented interest throughout the country and the cynosure of all eyes was the young, passionate and enthusiastic advocate, C. R. Das. Aurobindo was acquitted and simultaneously C. R. Das leapt into fame as a lawyer. After that he was repeatedly briefed in political cases and he proved to be uniformly lucky in his defence. Each New Year's Day found him higher in the professional ladder, and by 1920 he was at the top of his profession with an unsurpassed reputation as both a civil and a criminal lawyer.

The Deshbandhu was a thoroughly self-made man for 'chill penury' haunted his footsteps at the threshold of his professional career. His father had died in the midst of heavy debts and the struggling barrister had to be judged an insolvent; but no sooner did he make his first pile than he repaid voluntarily all his father's debts to the very last copper. As his income went up by leaps and bounds—so also did his expenditure, for he was lavish in his charity to the point of recklessness. On the occasion of public calamities like floods and famines, which, by the way, are not infrequent in India, he would open his purse-strings wide. His munificence soon became a by-word in many an Indian home. But neither his literary attainments nor his professional eminence nor his manifold benefactions paved the way to his subsequent leadership so much as his own apprenticeship in public affairs.

It is true that prior to 1920, he was seldom in the limelight but that was due to the fact that during this period like so many other political leaders, he combined professional work with politics. After the split at the Surat Session of the Indian National Congress in 1907, as a result of which the Extremists (or left-wingers) led by Lokamanya B. G. Tilak were expelled from that body, the extremist movement in Bengal was conducted by Aurobindo Ghosh and the late Bepin Chandra Pal and with both of them, the Deshbandhu was intimately associated.

The introduction of the Constitutional Reforms of 1909, which were welcomed by the official Congress Party, the retirement of Aurobindo from politics in 1909, followed by a change of front on the part of B. C. Pal and the incarceration of B. G. Tilak, caused a setback to the extremist movement. The political stage was monopolised by the leaders of the official Congress Party (also called 'moderates' as contrasted with the 'extremists' who formed the left-wing opposition) like the late Sir Surendranath Banerji—and the Deshbandhu considered it advisable to divert his attention from politics to literature for the time being. But by 1916, the scene changed once again. The return of B. G. Tilak from prison and the advent of the late Mrs Annie Besant in Indian politics gave a fillip to the extremist movement and led to a rapprochement between the extremists and the moderates at the Benares Session of the Indian National Congress in 1916.

In 1917 the extremists again became active, and in Bengal their group was led by the late B. Chakravarti and C. R. Das. From 1917 onwards, the latter was an active figure in extremist circles. At the Amritsar Session of the Congress in 1919, along with B. Chakravarti, he led the left-wing opposition to the proposal to work the Reforms of 1919 which was advocated by no less a man than Mahatma Gandhi himself, and which was ultimately adopted by the Congress.

Much later on 16 June 1940 came an anguished cry from the heart of Sarat on the death anniversary of C. R. Das—by which time the Second World War was consuming Europe and threatening Asia—seeking to galvanise the nationalist but still as he saw them, subservient leaders of India into action[8]:

> Would Deshbandhu have approved of this inactivity, this passivity, had he been alive? Did he not shatter with his hands the inertia of the Congress in 1923, when he formed the Swarajya Party? Did not the super-human energy and strength of this Bengali hero turn the political life of India into new channels? Friends, remember today we are gathered here where his ashes are resting, to recall his message and memory.

During the course of his second year in Mandalay Jail, Subhas wrote what he himself termed his first (unpublished) book, which he called *Pebbles on the Seashore.* As Subhas noted, it was conceived as a collection of stray thoughts, but might rightly be seen as a further milestone in the evolution of his philosophical and socio-political thinking.

Subhas had on various occasions given Amiya handwritten manuscripts, letters, notes and other documents for safe-keeping and future publication. Among such documents was the handwritten draft of *Pebbles* in a small exercise book containing his thoughts and reflections on topics as widely diverse as: what should be the basis for a new ethical code for man and the nature of patriotism; the paramount importance of reason to combat fanaticism; the myth of the Teutonic race supremacy and the gradual fall and resurgence of Asia.

In the preface to the handwritten draft Subhas wrote: 'This is a suitable name for this book—ocean of knowledge lying unexplored in front—a few pebbles here and there have been picked up by me. The stray thoughts are as disconnected as pebbles lying on the seashore.'

In *Pebbles,* Subhas developed what he suggested could be the basis for a new ethical code.

1. Honour and self-respect above everything—die if you cannot live with honour and with self-respect.
2. While enriching your life to the fullest extent—be prepared to give it up at a moment's notice.

---

[8] *Sarat Chandra Bose Commemoration Volume* (Calcutta: The Sarat Bose Academy, 1982), 382.

3. Love your family more than yourself, your community more than your family, your country more than your community.
4. He who says that he loves humanity but does not love his country—is a liar. Serve your nation and your nation's culture and you will serve humanity.
5. Embracing Sannyasa when your country needs you—is only a refined form of betrayal.
6. By discarding life—you cannot attain the Life Divine.
7. Truth is beauty—beauty is truth.
8. Look upon woman as thy mother—wherever you may meet her.
9. The ethical value of a man's life depends largely on the performance of civic and national duty.

* * *

On the nature of patriotism and Indian nationalism, he postulated:

The nature of patriotism—there must be the identification of one's life with the mainstream of India's history. The realms of national life and of individual life must be merged completely. Any suffering of any nationality in India must be felt as one's own suffering, any glory as one's own glory. Every single invasion of India must be looked upon as an event in one's own life. All those who have accepted India as their motherland or all those who have made India their permanent home are my brothers. The temple of Lord Jagannath in Puri and the Taj Mahal are equally objects of my pride. The internecine disputes and quarrels that have taken place between different nationalities and religions in India have been like quarrels within a family—quarrels that come to an end with maturity. Toleration is not a characteristic of childhood; children frequently quarrel. The new nation of India is now in the phase of its childhood—we do not therefore practise toleration. The day will come when conflicts between the Hindus and Muslims will end much in the same way as conflicts between the Roman Catholics and Protestants have ended. (Translated from Bengali)

Nationalism is after all based on a sentiment—and sentiment can be cultured as much as physique can.

* * *

The Government of India should have a Department of Culture attached to the Education Department. The task of this should be to translate into all the important modern languages (e.g., French, English, German, Russian, Italian, Chinese and Japanese) the important books written in or about India either in Sanskrit or in any Indian language or in any other language. These books should be advertised in all countries and thereby India should propagate her own culture.

* * *

The Turks conquered Europe when feudalism reigned supreme there. There was no national feeling worth the name—and the predominant feeling in European society was class consciousness. The Turks formed a militant democracy and they possessed what might be regarded as the nearest approach to a national army. The conquest of India by Britain was possible because here too class consciousness in the form of caste consciousness predominated over national consciousness. The Turks had to retreat before the rising tide of nationalism in Europe—so also will the British have to retreat before the rising tide of Indian nationalism.

Musing on the differences in historical development between Asia and Europe, and the stages which each has reached at the time of writing, Subhas seemed to foresee the modern-day rise of Asia and the relative decline of Europe.

Asia conquered Europe and she was conquered by her. The conquest endured where it was backed by organisation and culture. The Moors who conquered Spain were cultured but they lacked organisation. Turkish sovereignty in Eastern and Central Europe lasted for a long period because it was backed by organisation and culture. European domination over Asia will last for a comparatively longer period because it is based on a splendid organisation buttressed by modern science.

The failure of the Turks was an intellectual & moral failure. If Turkey had kept pace with the onward march of science, her domination could have easily been prolonged by a few centuries. But she had lost the thirst for knowledge and as a result of religious fanaticism, intellectual hunger had disappeared. 'What is outside the Koran is superfluous or mischievous' mentality is not a proper soil for the growth and development of modern science. This hunger will not appear anywhere in Islam as long as religious fanaticism is not brushed aside. This is what Mustapha Kemal is now trying to do with a vengeance. Further, if Turkey had only recognised the influence of democratic principles and had granted local autonomy to the races residing within her Empire—the life of the Empire could have been prolonged.

The failure of Europe will also be a moral failure though not necessarily an intellectual failure. Internal adjustment within European society will not easily be established and some kind of class war is bound to take place. This is bound to affect the strength and prestige of Europe in Asia, Africa, etc. Further, jealousy and economic rivalry is bound to give rise to frequent fratricidal and internecine wars in Europe. Thirdly, if all the European nations do not practise birth control after the fashion of France, each of them will need colonisation outside Europe. This will be a further cause of strife among the European nations. Fourthly the increase of wealth in Europe will be accompanied by a gradually-increasing disregard of moral principles in international relations. What, for instance, is Europe's policy in Africa? Organised exploitation, the more powerful nation getting the lion's share after the partition. This policy of peaceful penetration and exploitation is from the point of view of higher ethics as mean, disgusting and selfish as a fight among wolves for a piece of carrion flesh and is in addition 'utterly immoral'. This selfish policy is bound to give rise to mutual war among the exploiting nations at some stage or other. Last but not least, Europe is systematically and deliberately engendering race prejudice between white and coloured races by proclaiming in season and out of season the supremacy of the whites. This, more than anything else will help to consolidate the whole of Asia against the onslaught of Europe.

And on race relations—Europe and Asia:

The supremacy of the Teutonic race expounded by Gobineau and supported by Wagner, Nietzsche and H. S. Chamberlain was a myth deliberately propagated with the object of bolstering the pride and self-confidence of the newly-awakened Germans. Likewise the Nordic myth has been deliberately propagated by Anglo-Saxons in Europe and America with the object of giving scientific support to the race-dogmatism of the Anglo-Saxons. Other races of northern Europe who have been included among the Nordic people have been tempted to give the theory their support. It was the habit of the German race-dogmatists to discover some traces of physical qualities such as tall stature, blue eyes, long heads or fair hair among whatever people achieved any noteworthy work and to take this as evidence of some infusion of Germanic blood. The Nordic-maniacs are also following in the same track.

The fundamental fallacy of the Nordic-maniacs seems to be that they have forgotten the element of time. They scarcely look back and ahead. Time was when the Anglo-Saxons, Teutons and in fact Europeans were steeped in ignorance and barbarism while the East was full of light and culture. No one would then have dreamt of laying down a theory like the Teutonic or Nordic supremacy. As a matter of fact, the peoples of the East, Jews, Hindus, Chinese and Japanese, as well as the Muslims, regarded themselves (and still do so) as the chosen people of God with the same sincerity, zeal and enthusiasm as the most extreme Nordic-maniacs today possess in regard to the supremacy of the Nordic race. The civilisations of the East have survived the onslaughts of time, their people still believe in their own supremacy and they cannot help indulging in a smile when they find that the tables have been turned on them and the peoples of the West hitherto regarded by them as barbarians (mlechhas) proclaiming themselves as civilised with the aid of gunpowder and with one sweep of the pen condemning the entire East as barbarous or semi-barbarous. Has Europe with all her culture and civilisation produced one single religion? How is it that barbarous Asia has been the mother of all the religions Judaism, Zoroastrianism, Islam, Christianity, Buddhism and Hinduism? The problem of race supremacy is one for the future to decide. Which of the many civilisations is going to survive? The immemorial East or the ever-changing West? Which is the stronger and more enduring factor, intellect or morality?

Asia says that she has witnessed the rise and fall of many civilisations which she has survived by dint of her moral and spiritual power. European civilisation is her last experience and who can say that Asia will not out-live Europe? No doubt at the present moment Europe seems to be the more powerful of the two by virtue of her discovery of steam, electricity etc, and of her armaments and economic development. But is not the top heavy civilisation of Europe sinking under its own weight? Is not the incessant pursuit of wealth engendering selfishness and increasing criminality? Is not the USA, the most advanced of modern countries, alarmed at the rapid increase of crime within her borders? Does not European civilisation contain within itself the seeds of its own downfall? Is not the accumulation of wealth in the hands of a few capitalists the source of social and economic problems of an alarming nature? And does not the solution of these problems threaten the very destruction of modern civilisation?

You say that the Nordic race is more intellectual than the other races. Granted. But will intellect alone save a people? Will not the accumulation of wealth give rise to selfishness and immorality and ultimately undermine intellect. Will not a more intelligent and ease-loving people be beaten in the struggle of life by a less-intelligent people possessing more moral stamina? When intellectual culture and comfort is once attained will not the absence of struggle unconsciously sap a nation's vital powers. Will not another nation less favourably situated by virtue of a keen struggle develop vital power and stamina of so high a degree as to beat the more intellectual race? Lastly are the resources of the intellect inexhaustible? It is not in the case of the individual and there is no possibility that it will be so in the case of the nation. Selective breeding might keep up the quality of the stock for some time but exhaustion is bound to appear at some stage. The race will then sink to a mediocre level and take rest for some centuries before it can once again re-appear in its former glory.

Further is not variation an important factor in heredity. Is it quite certain that the off-spring of x and y who are both of a particular quality will be of the same quality. Asia is waking up after a long sleep. Intermixture of blood, impact of the West and other factors both physiological and phsychological have been responsible for this renaissance. Who knows that this renaissance will not coincide with the decadence of Europe? Rome has been re-born in modern Italy and history has a habit of repeating itself.

We may suppose also that the greater curiosity of the Nordic race contributes to give the Briton that restless wandering habit which has spread him over all the surface of the earth, so that no matter to what remote region one may penetrate it is likely that some solitary Briton will presently appear and casually borrow a copy of the London Times. (McDougall in National Welfare and National Decay) This is the foundation of the British Empire.

On national character and national consciousness, Subhas wrote:

We are lacking in a sense of responsibility for the welfare of the village or city or district or province. Our ken is restricted by the four walls of our house. A violent reaction is bound to follow— people will give up their homes for the sake of the city or district or country. When this storm passes over an equilibrium will be established between domestic duty and civic and national duty.

This lack of the sense of responsibility is the result of age-long dependence and servility no doubt. But it is also true that our servility is due to this defect in our character. We have been too much inclined to transfer the burden of social and political welfare to certain castes (e.g., Brahman and Khstariya) or individuals. Social welfare was the special function of the Brahman and political welfare that of the Khstariyas. Society, including the lowest classes, had hardly any responsibility—the lower classes being Sudras. This was the weak point in Hindu social and political organisation. When the Brahmans and the Khstariyas ceased to be alive to their duties or ceased to be efficient (in the broadest sense) in their work—both society and the state fell to pieces. Society has now to be reconstructed on an entirely new basis. Brahmanical autocracy is to be replaced by an aristocracy of intellect and character and the state has to be reorganised on the basis of universal suffrage.

National consciousness to be real should be based on practical social service. Work for the village—for the city—for the district—for the province should gradually widen a man's national consciousness. Consciousness that is not based on service of some kind is airy and unreal. Pride in the progress of one's village, one's city, one's district, one's province should be coexistent with a feeling of pride in the progress made by one's country.

* * *

The two most hopeful signs of the present day are the Physical Culture movement and the awakening of class consciousness among the so-called lower classes. In the revival of physical culture and the interest evinced in it by the rising generation we have a foretaste of the new nation that is rising in Bengal before our eyes. Cycle trips to Cashmere and back, journey on foot from one corner of the Indian peninsula to another, long distance swimming and rowing, boxing, wrestling, soccer, hockey and similar sports will make the Bengal of the future, more than moral lectures or intellectual disquisitions. Those of us who are debarred by our physical constitution from taking an active part in these patriotic movements can at least encourage, by all the means within our power, all those who are in them. Words cannot sufficiently praise Sj. Parag Ranjan Dey who braved the horrors of the jungles and encountered wild and hostile tribes in his foot journey from Calcutta to Rangoon over hills and dales.

Those of us who belong to the so-called higher castes should by all possible means foster a growth of consciousness among the so-called lower castes. After all what is the percentage of the former? .....% - is it not? If Bengal is to rise, she will have to depend mainly on the remaining .....% of her population.

National consciousness in its infancy is in many cases antagonistic to internationalism. So also class consciousness in its early stages is often anti-national. But narrowness of vision is in both cases only a passing phase—and should neither frighten us nor deter us in our onward march. It may be undesirable from an ideal point of view—it may be that we would rather do without it even as a passing phase—but it is unfortunately a necessary stage in social evolution. Consciousness like heat has a tendency to expand—just as ignorance, like cold, contracts. As soon as class consciousness is ripe, it is bound to pass on to the next stages in an ever-widening circle. Consciousness is like the quiet and placid surface of a lake. When it is struck, it produces an eddy which goes on widening until it reaches the farthest limits of the lake. Progress is unfortunately not always unilinear. It advances then recedes for a while and advances again. Let us not be afraid of its crooked course or its temporary regressions but welcome it in all cases.

* * *

Why do we suffer, why is it that we can suffer with equanimity? It is because in present suffering we have a prevision of the future, glorious and radiant. We have hope and hope gives courage. We have un-bounded optimism and optimism lends vigour and strength.

We are in the mood of springtime and dawn such as inspired Uhland when he exclaimed: 'Die welt wird schoener mit yedem tag—nun muss sich alles, alles werden! (the world becomes more beautiful every day—now everything must change)' This youthfulness of hope, this delight in this outlook into the future is the tonic which steels our nerves.

The consciousness or the foretaste of the coming joy of the Life Divine that is to come—makes us oblivious of the darkness of the present hour and the misery that surrounds us. We are too dazzled with the light that has pierced its way through a rent in the storm clouds of the present from the farthest confines of the future to take any note of the over-hanging gloom. Yes, we can suffer because we believe in the future—because we know that a glorious destiny awaits us and our people. The trials of the hour, the suffering, the persecution—are but the price of the dawn. We are the nation's hostages who shall redeem the nation's honour and liberty. Those of you who shrink from persecution, who accept the present because you dare not stand up and welcome the crown of thorns—Know not your destiny, your glorious future and your heritage.

Is the cup of suffering altogether bitter? Is it not sweet, though sad. Are not the sweetest tears those that tell of saddest thoughts? Why then do you fear.... Liberty is only for the brave.

* * *

Unless you can stir the historic consciousness of a people, you cannot produce or create a national literature. A nation's soul has to be stirred to its very depths before you can expect a national literature. It is only when individuals plunge themselves into the stream of historic consciousness that the mainsprings of literature in the human soul are released and bubble forth into the light of day. The Swadeshi Movement produced a literature because it linked together the individual consciousness with the historic consciousness of the race. The Non-Cooperation Movement did not—because it was not a cultural movement. It was a purely political movement with 'Punjab, Khilifat and Swaraj' as its slogan. A study of the past literature of a nation and of its varied achievements in the different spheres of national life, together with a contemplation of its ancient glory and greatness—can alone afford that inspiration which creates a lasting literature and an abiding art.

We want more and more of reason in our individual and social life. Reason alone can sweep away superstition and prepare the soil for the growth of science.... Reason is the sworn enemy of fanaticism and to accept one is to reject the other.

As noted by Amiya, there is one powerful undercurrent of thought in these jottings and indeed throughout the life of Subhas, and that is the critical importance that he attached to 'character' in the way that people should lead their lives. As reflected in *Pebbles*: 'We do not want more brains—we have enough—at least potentially. We want more of character—strong will-power, self-assertiveness, unbending doggedness and a keen sense of honour and self-respect.'

On his release from Mandalay Jail in May 1927 and now still just 30 years old, Subhas returned to Calcutta to live with Sarat and his family at 38/1 Elgin Road, next door to father Janakinath's house. The Bose Brothers were again together after a physical separation of almost three years and preparing to face the myriad political and other challenges awaiting them, but now in a world without C. R. Das and with Subhas never to fully regain his health from the rigours of the Mandalay imprisonment.

Nevertheless by this time the way forward in the Indian struggle both for independence from the imperial power and for the shape of the optimum socio-economic system for independent India had effectively crystallised in the minds of the brothers.

That vision featured a now uncompromising struggle for complete independence from Britain as the imperial power, and a form of socialist governance adapted to the particular needs and demands of the vast population which would constitute independent India and which would be enabled to live in freedom, harmony and dignity.

3

Swaraj Beckons, Swaraj Denied

We cannot sing our way to Swaraj, nor spin our way to Swaraj.
We must fight our way to Swaraj. Purna Swaraj is our goal.

—Subhas in FORWARD BLOC,
A Political Weekly, 2 March 1940

The years after the Great War (First World War) in Europe ended in 1918 saw a resurgence of country-wide political activity in British India, including the introduction in 1919 by the British imperial authorities of a new constitution under the auspices of the Government of India Act of 1919. By this time, Gandhi had been back in India since January 1915 from his 20-year sojourn in South Africa. He had already by the beginning of 1919 emerged as a strong nationalist voice and a leading figure in Congress politics, although at this juncture still loyal to the Empire and the concept of dominion status for India inside the Empire.

The year 1919 in India also saw the introduction by the imperial power of the regressive Rowlatt Act of 18 March 1919, which inter alia conferred extraordinary powers of arrest and detention without trial. The infamous massacre of peaceful demonstrators—men, women and children—at Jallianwala Bagh in Amritsar followed shortly after on 18 April 1919.

In the shadow of the Jallianwala Bagh atrocity, the annual session of the Congress met in Amritsar in December of the same year. Despite all that had transpired, a still compliant Congress passed a resolution in favour of working with the new imposed Constitution. In this, Gandhi and his followers were instrumental in spite of strong opposition from C. R. Das and other Bengal leaders, in persuading a majority that new constitutional reforms should be given a chance. In doing so Gandhi and his supporters clearly understood or assumed that the perpetrators of the Jallianwala Bagh massacre would be brought to justice.

The failure of the imperial power to do so and indeed the failure to effect any measure of justice, together with its active prosecution of the more restrictive and odious provisions of the Rowlatt Act, gave rise to deep public revulsion, the setting aside by Congress of its cooperative Amritsar resolution and profound disillusionment on the part of Gandhi himself. As noted by Subhas in *The Indian Struggle*, '...on the rock of Jallianwala Bagh was wrecked the ship of co-operation built by the Secretary of State for India Mr Montagu' and 'The Punjab atrocities and their sequel made a rebel of the once-loyal Mr Gandhi'.[1]

Under the guidance and leadership of the now rebellious Gandhi, the 'progressive, non-violent, non-cooperation' movement took shape at a Special Session of the Congress in September 1920 in Calcutta, and was confirmed at the annual Congress Session of December 1920 held at Nagpur in central India. This Session also called for Swaraj (i.e., independence) within one year, either within or outside the Empire.

It was against this background of resurgent national feeling and political activity that the Bose Brothers began to emerge on the national scene. Sarat had in fact committed himself fully to the Indian National Congress in 1918, becoming increasingly active as the influence of C. R. Das began to take hold in the years following. By this time Sarat had also established himself at the Calcutta High Court Bar and was doing very well as a successful and prosperous barrister.

By the time of the return of Subhas in July 1921 from England, the Gandhian Non-Cooperation Movement—featuring renunciation of titles bestowed by the imperial power, boycott of legislatures, law courts and educational institutions, and non-payment of taxes—was gathering momentum. As previously noted in an earlier chapter, Subhas himself had in his own way supported the call for renunciation with his final refusal on 23 April 1921 to take up an offer to join the prestigious Indian Civil Service.

Now back in India, Subhas was also to witness at first-hand the totally unexpected suspension by Gandhi on 12 February

---

[1] Subhas Chandra Bose, *The Indian Struggle* (Natyachinta Foundation Kolkata, 2005), 56.

1922 of what had been up to that moment an increasingly effective Non-Cooperation Movement which was beginning to cause consternation within and for the Raj. Gandhi had taken this step in the wake of the killing of Indian policemen on 4 February 1922 by the enraged inhabitants of the village of Chauri Chaura in Uttar Pradesh, northern India, reportedly in response to provocations by the police. Gandhi's decision provoked much angst and unhappiness among many Indian resistance leaders, including C. R. Das and the Bose Brothers. Subhas later wrote in *The Indian Struggle*[2]:

> No one could understand why the Mahatma should have used the isolated incident at Chauri Chaura for strangling the movement over the country. Popular resentment was all the greater because the Mahatma had not cared to consult representatives from the different provinces and because the situation in the country as a whole was exceedingly favourable for the success of the civil disobedience campaign. To sound the order of retreat just when public enthusiasm was reaching the boiling point was nothing short of a national calamity.

When Gandhi had captured the Congress in 1920 with the presentation and approbation of his proposed non-cooperation programme, he had temporarily silenced the advocates of alternative strategies. C. R. Das's idea was that non-cooperation should be extended to the Legislative Councils in the provinces, but in the sense that Congress should first contest and win seats in the Councils, and then bring those bodies to a halt by negative action.

The followers of Gandhi—the 'No-Changers'—adhered to a non-cooperation policy which meant boycott of the Councils in the first place, and were thus directly opposed to C. R. Das and his supporters. A struggle within the Congress between the 'No-Changers' and the followers of C. R. Das took place at the Gaya Session of the Indian National Congress in December 1922, ironically with C. R. Das as Congress President at the time. The Gandhi faction emerged triumphant.

The 'victory' was a hollow one, with the immediate, principled resignation of C. R. Das as Congress President. The suspension earlier in the year by Gandhi of the Non-Cooperation

---

[2] Ibid., 99.

Movement and its consequent withering away for a time, and the formation and nurturing of the Swaraj Party out of the ashes of the Movement by Congress stalwarts C. R. Das, Motilal Nehru and Vithalbai Patel, saw a tectonic shift in the national political focus, back towards the urgency of *Swaraj*, of independence from the British imperial power.

As C. R. Das noted in the introduction to his *Outline Scheme of Swaraj* of 30 January 1923, the formation of the Swaraj Party arose initially as a consequence of a division of opinion over the question of contesting elections for the official Legislative Councils. It was at the same time a response to the perceived need for 'stating the fundamental principles and formulating the broad outlines of a scheme of self-government which should form the basis of Indian Swaraj'.[3]

The *Outline Scheme* thus constituted an important step forward in the long journey to freedom, as the Indian nationalists of every persuasion began to dare to think of what independent India might look like. Reflecting the platform and ideals of the Swaraj Party itself, the *Outline Scheme* avoided the still thorny question of dominion status within a British commonwealth of nations as against the severance of all constitutional links with Britain by a totally independent India. C. R. Das and the other leaders of the Party were content for the time being to leave resolution of that matter until later (although the Bose Brothers themselves were clearly for the latter option). For the time being the Swaraj Party and the *Outline Scheme* focussed on what they saw as the more immediate imperative of how Indians might rule themselves on a day-to-day basis, and what representative arrangements might be put in place to reflect the will of the people.

Thus, the *Outline Scheme* called for universal suffrage, but with a qualification that astonishes to this day. Females over the age of 21 would be allowed the vote, but for men the minimum age would be set at 25, the age at which they were presumably judged to have become mature enough to vote! Universal suffrage would be accompanied by 'provision of appropriate education of all educable children and youth of both sexes'.

---

[3] Chittaranjan Das, *Outline Scheme of Swaraj* (Kolkata: Government of West Bengal, November 1973).

The *Outline Scheme* called for a separation of powers among the executive, the legislature and the judiciary. It envisaged a heavily federal system where

> The residuary power of control must remain in the Central Government, but the exercise of such power should be exceptional, and for that purpose proper safeguards should be provided, so that the practical autonomy of the local centres may be maintained and at the same time, the growth of the central government into a really unifying state may be possible. The ordinary work of such Central Government should be mainly advisory.

Drawing on the 'time-honoured traditions of the country' where the village and the village communities of the rural 90 per cent of the population had traditionally been 'the natural basis of our special type of culture and civilisation, and of all wise adminis-tration', the *Outline Scheme* sought to delegate the constitutional responsibility for the administration of their lives to the people themselves.

In an appendix where some of the fundamental principles which underpinned the *Outline Scheme* are examined, the frus-tration of C. R. Das and his contemporaries with the prevailing system of government rises to the surface.

> Excessive centralisation, and the concentration of all power in the hands of a bureaucratic clique, mindful of its own prestige and emoluments, careless of the public weal, walling itself off more and more thickly from touch with public opinion, in fact arrogant and disdainful towards the public—regarding itself as public *master* rather than public *servant*—this is the bane, in consequence of which the public servant waxes and the public wanes, more and more every day, in India. Genuine decentrali-sation of administration, substantial distribution of power, and real responsibility of the public servants to the People's trusted representatives—this is the only remedy. Hence the formulation of practical local autonomy as a fundamental principle.

As described at some length in *The Indian Struggle,* and as referred to in the previous chapter of this book, C. R. Das and his *Swarajist* followers including the Bose Brothers moved immedi-ately into a period of proactive and frantic political activity both in Bengal and nationally. As has also been noted, on 25 October

1923 the new daily newspaper *Forward* began publication as the mouthpiece of the Swaraj Party, with C. R. Das as Editor and Chairman of a Board of Directors, and under the watchful eye of Sarat as Managing Director and Chief Financier.

The maiden issue of this new English language daily was welcomed into the public eye by none other than Rabindranath Tagore, who wrote a special poem for the occasion.

> *Freedom from fear is the freedom I claim for you,*
> *My Motherland*

> *Fear, the phantom demon.*
>   *shaped by your own distorted dreams:*
> *Freedom from the burden of ages*
>   *bending your head, breaking your back*
>   *blinding your eyes to the beckoning call of future:*
> *Freedom from shackles of slumber*
>   *with which you fasten yourself to night's stillness*
>   *mistrusting the star that speaks*
>   *of Truth's adventurous path:*
> *Freedom from the anarchy of a destiny*
>   *whose sails are weakly yielded*
>   *to blind uncertain winds.*
>   *And the helm to a hand*
>   *ever rigid and cold as death:*
> *Freedom from the insult*
>   *of dwelling in a doll's world,*
>   *where movements are started*
>   *through brainless wires.*
>   *Repeated through mindless habits*
>   *Where figures wait in patient obedience,*
>   *for a master of show*
>   *To be stirred into a moment's*
>   *mimicry of life.*

Rabindranath Tagore
27 September 1923

In elections to a newly constituted Corporation of Calcutta in March 1924, the Swaraj Party captured a safe majority of seats in the new administration of the Corporation, with a significant number of Muslim members. The Swaraj Party members in turn elected C. R. Das as the first Mayor (replacing the previous position of Chairman), with Muslim leader Saheed Suhrawardy as Deputy Mayor. C. R. Das in turn appointed Subhas as Chief Executive Officer of the Corporation, also a new position whose functions had previously been the responsibility of the Chairman.

The *Swarajists* also achieved representation in both provincial and national legislatures, where they energetically pursued their programme of 'wrecking from within' and generally making life extremely difficult for the ruling colonial authorities. They were particularly successful in the United Provinces and Bengal where the Swaraj Party held absolute majorities, and where the diarchical system as prescribed under the system was simply not allowed to function.

In the National Assembly, the Party was also well represented under the leadership of Pandit Motilal Nehru, but not strong enough to challenge the overriding powers of the Viceroy through constitutional means. At the same time, they were able to make life difficult for the governing authorities and campaigned vociferously for the release of an ailing Gandhi from jail, where he had been held since 10 March 1922. After medical treatment he was released on 5 February 1924.

The death of C. R. Das on 15 June 1925, at the height of his political powers and stature in the Swaraj movement, and as a truly charismatic figure on the national stage, came as a terrible shock not just to the people of his beloved Bengal but to all of India. It was overall a huge setback to the independence movement. Amiya, who at the time was just short of 10 years old, recalled later:

> I remember that about a week before he passed away, C. R. Das accompanied by his wife Basanti Devi, came down from Darjeeling to our house on Giddhapahar in Kurseong and spent a few pleasant hours with us. Though he had been ill and had come to his house 'Step Aside' in Darjeeling for some urgent rest and recuperation, no one had expected his sudden demise.

> On that sad, sorrowful day, I stood on the verandah of Deshabandhu's residence in Calcutta (on Russa Road now called Ashutosh Mukherjee Road), waiting with the others for the massive funeral procession to arrive. Gandhi stood watching

from the verandah. When finally the huge wave of people carrying the body approached the house, Gandhi went down and joined the pall bearers.

Of this tragic and untimely death of C. R. Das, Subhas as one of his most ardent admirers was to write later in *The Indian Struggle*[4]:

> June 1925 proved to be a turning point in the history of India. The disappearance of the towering personality of the Deshabandhu from the political arena was for India a colossal misfortune. The Swaraj Party, which owed so much to him, was paralysed after his death and dissensions gradually arose within the Party. Nevertheless, the Party at the time of his death was an institution of which anyone would be proud. The *Capital* of Calcutta, the organ of British commercial interests, writing after his death, compared the Swaraj Party with the Sinn Fein Party of Ireland and remarked that during forty years of its existence, it had seen nothing like it before. This discipline of the Party, according to the paper, was German in character. The weakening of the Swaraj Party served to strengthen the the forces of reaction in India and in England, while it let loose a flood of communal strife in India which had, up till then, been held back by the superior forces of Nationalism. Today (sic 1934) as we look back on the year 1925, we cannot help feeling that if Providence had spared the Deshabandhu for a few years more, the history of India would probably have taken a different turn.

After the Gaya Congress of December 1922, Gandhi himself retreated for several years from any active role on the political stage, a period which included almost two years in detention from March 1922 to February 1924 where he was not physically well. He was not to re-emerge fully on the scene and back into Congress councils in particular, until several years after the death of C. R. Das. In a letter to Sarat on 9 April 1926 from his seclusion in Sabarmati Ashram, Gandhi wrote:

Dear Sarat Babu,

Monilal Kothari has given me your message. I wish I could send you something stirring, something decisive and rapid in reply,

---

[4] Bose, *The Indian Struggle*, 145–146.

but I have no such thing in the present state of country. Meetings and resolutions, protests in the councils have been over-done. We must do something tangible so that we can feel our power. I can think of nothing else therefore but boycott of foreign cloth which in its turn is impossible without Khaddar and therefore for the ills including this wretched imprisonment, I have nothing but the Charkha. But how can I convince the people that it is a sovereign remedy? My faith in it however remains undiminished—day by day it increases. And therefore during this National Week we have some spinning wheels going on the whole of the week, night and day. We are doing it with the implicit faith that some day through it will rise a power that will enable us to realise our cherished desire.

I know that there is an alternative to the Charkha and that is rowdyism, but I am useless at it and what is more, I have no faith in it. And as a practical man, I know that our rowdyism is nothing compared to the rowdyism of the Government. I have therefore burnt my boats and staked my all on the Charkha. I invite you and all who are troubled by the knowledge of the many woes of the Nation to join me in the effort. Believe me it requires all the skill, all the discipline, all the organising power that we can summon to its aid...

Yours sincerely
M. K. Gandhi

Gandhi was seeking in his own way, but clearly enough, to continue to promote non-violence as the central creed in the national struggle, and the '*Charkha*' or spinning wheel as the centre-piece of his preferred approach. His antipathy to 'rowdyism' strongly suggests that he would have no truck with any revolutionary alternatives proposed by radical elements within the Bengal leadership including the Bose Brothers. Nor was Gandhi moved in his convictions by other prominent voices, including that of Rabindranath Tagore who in an essay entitled *Satyar Ahwaan* (Call of the Truth) written earlier in October 1921, had challenged Gandhi on the latter's belief in *Charkha* as the way forward, strongly implying that this was far too restrictive. Tagore said that God has endowed Gandhi with the power to summon men to action but Gandhiji summoned in a single narrow field. He said, 'spin and weave'. Is this a call to all-round creative activity to bring into being a new age?

In writing and commenting at length upon this turbulent decade of the 1920s, Amiya often reflected upon and contributed to the long-running historical discussion about the revolutionary credentials of the Bose Brothers. In doing so he drew particular attention to what he discerned as the strong inclination of both Sarat and Subhas towards a more revolutionary perspective, while not completely eschewing the Congress mainstream approach of Gandhian non-violent, non-cooperation. Amiya wrote in his (unpublished) memoirs:

> The years 1921–23 may be regarded as the years of preparation of Sarat and Subhas for the stellar political careers that were to follow. During these three years their ideas on the question of India's national independence began to take concrete shape. In 1921 Subhas had already joined Chitta Ranjan Das, who had given up his princely practice at the Calcutta Bar to take up the leadership of the Non-Cooperation Movement in Bengal.

> For both Subhas and Sarat the revolutionary alternative was as valid as the non-violent approach developed by Gandhi. Non-violence for them was never nor could be an end in itself. Both Sarat and Subhas were to develop and maintain close links and contacts with the revolutionaries, a primary reason given by the British for subsequent incarcerations of the brothers.

From his intimate knowledge of his father and uncle and from his own archival examinations of British intelligence files which in time became publicly accessible, Amiya considered that some of the more measured British assessments of the connections of the brothers with the revolutionaries, were by no means shy of the mark. Some 'official' information and assessments, based as they were on a spy network of often dubious local malcontents, could be wildly speculative, lurid and fearful; but it would appear that the colonial authorities were broadly correct in drawing the link between the brothers and the revolutionaries, most but not all of the latter being young men and women from Bengal.

Some of the revolutionaries such as those who were responsible for the killing of British public officials paid the ultimate price of death by execution for their activities, which in turn evoked public expressions of sympathy from Sarat, Subhas and other senior Congressmen. Such expressions were carried as a matter of course in the Swaraj Party daily newspaper *Forward* and later its successor publication *Liberty*.

As already mentioned, both Sarat and Subhas were intimately involved from the beginning with both newspapers, together with C. R. Das initially as Editor, and it could be expected that all three were among the chief determinants of editorial content. Indeed as one of the most trusted lieutenants of C. R. Das, Sarat as Managing Director of *Forward* Publishing Limited oversaw the publication of a newspaper which set an example of fearless and honest journalism, and of investigative reporting which managed to achieve access to confidential documents of the State. Amiya himself concluded that this was a classic instance when those who believed in constitutional agitation and those engaged in revolutionary activities saw common purpose based on shared goals.

In their sympathies with the revolutionaries, the brothers in any case could hardly have failed to be inspired by their mentor C. R. Das himself, who had first risen to prominence in 1909 as a young barrister with his successful defence of the then revolutionary Aurobindo Ghosh in the Alipore Bomb Conspiracy Case.[5]

As noted by Amiya, C. R. Das was later to actively participate and follow the lead of Gandhi in the Non-Cooperation Movement, but never abandoned his connections with the revolutionaries of India. As tracked by the British in their intelligence reports, these connections were to reach particular prominence with the establishment of the Calcutta Corporation in 1924, and with the election of C. R. Das as the first Mayor presiding over the Corporation and Subhas as the first Chief Executive Officer.

The British were apparently concerned that a number of erstwhile revolutionaries had been employed by the Corporation, but apparently chose to interpret this as an effort by C. R. Das to bring them under the wing of the Swaraj Party and its legitimate political activities. C. R. Das was also of course by this time a very powerful political figure and national political voice in the

---

[5] Some three dozen suspects were arrested in the Alipore Bomb Conspiracy Case (May 1908–May 1909), arising from the killing of two British nationals in a bomb attack. Aurobindo Ghosh was one of the suspects but C. R. Das as his young and eloquent defence counsel, secured his acquittal.

land, and the British authorities would have exercised particular caution in their dealings with him.

Such considerations applied less to the young Subhas. In the lead-up to his arrest on 25 October 1924 on charges of revolutionary conspiracy and subsequent incarceration in India and then Mandalay Burma, the Home Department of the Office of the Viceroy in a telegram of 28 August 1924 to the Secretary of State for India sought to put the case for the 'immediate' arrest of Subhas and two others.

> Satyandra Mitra, Surendra Ghosh and Subhash [sic] Bose are all leaders of the Jugantar (revolutionary) Party and are concerned in conspiracy to smuggle arms in large quantities into India. Subhas Bose is financing this plot as well as supplying absconders with funds. Subsequent to recent decision reached by Jugantar leaders, at the request of C. R. Das, temporarily to suspend all crime, Satyandra, Surendra and Subhas were cognisant of the plot to assassinate Tegart prepared by the Anushilan Party which Satyandra and Surendra were prepared surreptitiously to assist. Immediately prior to recent bomb outrage Satyandra, Surendra and Subhash took part in a discussion of the inner circle in regard to a proposal to assassinate H.E. the Governor. At least six independent sources of information have reported subsequent to bomb outrage, immediate likelihood of further assassinations. Threatening letters have also been received both by H.E. the Governor and the complainants in the bomb case.

The so-called 'History Sheet' of 27 August 1924 prepared in support of the telegram and call for arrest, describes Subhas thus:

> He is reported to have taken part in several conferences of revolutionary leaders at the 'Cheery Press' of which the notorious Amaranda Nath Chatterjee was the proprietor. He tried to coordinate the activities of the student and young men's organisations. He was the president of the central organisation of young men in Calcutta. He is the right-hand man of C. R. Das and his brother is Mr S. C. Bose, Barrister-at-Law, who recently worked up an agitation against Mr Justice Page. His public speeches are full of **revolutionary philosophy** [author's emphasis] and a direct call to the young men of the country to stand on their own legs.

An accompanying secret report of 25 August 1924 on a 'Conspiracy to Smuggle Arms Into India', signed off on by the

Special Superintendent of Police, Intelligence Branch CID, cites 'a very reliable source' in seeking to fully implicate Subhas in revolutionary activity:

> On the 17th July the same source reported that he had learnt that Government has succeeded in capturing a consignment of arms and ammunition which Subash (sic) Bose had arranged to import into India, that this seizure had caused a loss of about Rs. 25,000/- to the Revolutionary Party. He further learnt that another consignment was en route and that the party was endeavouring to arrange secure shelters where the arms could be temporarily stored.

> A few days later the same source reported that he had learnt from Subash Bose himself that the arms seized at Colombo were a portion of the consignment which he had arranged to smuggle into India and for which he had sent Rs. 50,000/- to a foreign country. Subash added that he had received intimation of the departure of the vessel and although he had not been informed of its route, he had sent a revolutionist to Colombo to watch for its arrival. The source added that he had learnt from Subash that these arms would be delivered either in Burma or China, where the revolutionists had an [office] for the past ten years, which would arrange to smuggle the arms into India.

> Subash also reported that they had recently successfully smuggled some falsely labelled packing cases from Rangoon to Calcutta in order to see whether the customs authorities were alert. It is interesting to note that previously this source had reported that the revolutionists had destroyed some suspicious packing cases received from Rangoon, as they feared a police raid. Subash further told the source that they were considering the possibility of bringing arms in from Burma by country craft engaged in coastal trade and also in hollowed trunks of trees brought over by timber merchants, who were prepared to assist them.

Other police reports of the period maintained that Sarat Bose was a member of a 'Secret Committee' financing the revolutionaries. On 5 June 1925, it was reported that he had paid the expenses of some revolutionaries who went to Burma ostensibly to see Subhas Chandra Bose but in reality to organise a movement there.

Whatever the truth of this and other assertions beginning to be made by the British intelligence authorities against both

Subhas and Sarat, it seems certain with the benefit of historical hindsight and on the basis of contemporary evidence, that the validity of the revolutionary alternative was becoming a key factor in the political and strategic thinking of the two brothers, during this period of the mid-1920s.

With Subhas incarcerated in Mandalay and Sarat coming into close contact with erstwhile and perhaps even active revolutionaries in the Calcutta Corporation, this development in their respective thinking seemed almost to happen in parallel rather than in any coordinated, calculated manner. For both men, ardent support for the Non-Cooperation Movement gradually yielded place to a relentless search for an alternative path to India's freedom—a path that would bring both of them into close contact with the revolutionaries.

With Sarat this eventually found particular expression in his close involvement as defence counsel for leading defendants in the spectacular Chittagong Armoury Raid of 18 April 1930, led by the inspirational Bengali revolutionary and former Bengal Congressman Surya Sen,[6] whom Amiya had seen and remembered from the corridors of 1 Woodburn Park.

Another of the leaders of the raid, Ananta Lal Singh, one of the group whom Sarat was defending, was to relate many years later to Amiya, that Sarat on one of his visits to the jail where the defendants were being held, had carried a bomb in his briefcase, to provide the revolutionaries with another option for getting out!

Whether such accounts are true or not, Lal Singh would recall of Sarat in particular, that he 'was not merely a political leader in the ordinary sense; he was also the most sympathetic friend the Bengali revolutionaries had—almost their nearest relative. We found in him a guardian angel'.[7]

For Amiya, this support for the revolutionary cause on the part of Sarat was not the product of a romantic imagination reacting emotionally to the spectacle of political violence for the cause of freedom. Rather it followed logically from a deep

---

[6] Surya Sen was executed by the British in the wake of the Chittagong Armoury Raid, and his body buried at sea in the Bay of Bengal, from a British warship.

[7] Address delivered at a memorial meeting on 8 September 1963; *Sarat Chandra Bose Commemoration Volume* (Calcutta: The Sarat Bose Academy, 1982), 31.

understanding on his part of the nature and significance of revolutionary activity at a critical period of India's freedom struggle.

It is interesting to see that Sarat himself, in a long letter of 23 April 1927 to the newly arrived British Governor of Bengal Sir Stanley Jackson centred on the detention without trial of Subhas, makes no attempt to deny the revolutionary credentials of Subhas or for that matter of himself. Rather he focuses on the iniquity of detentions without trial, challenging the new Governor to introduce 'fair play' into the equation:

My Dear Sir,

I am a stranger to Your Excellency and perhaps I owe you an explanation why I am taking the liberty of addressing you. It is because I am still in hopes that your Excellency has an open mind on the subject of 'Detentions without Trial'.

I do not pretend to be a disinterested person: for my brother Mr Subhas Chandra Bose is one of the persons under detention. But I can assure you that I am addressing you only because I feel—and the Indian public share that feeling—that he has been most unjustly detained. If I had felt otherwise I would not have taken up your time. Mr Subhas Chandra Bose was arrested under Regulation III of 1818 at the address given above on the 25th October 1924 and at a time when he had hardly recovered from the effects of a bad type of malarial fever. He took charge as Chief Executive Officer of the Corporation of Calcutta in May 1924 and his activities from May–October 1924 are well known to the Calcutta public.

During the period of his confinement, on two occasions, I believe certain charges were read out to him by a C.I.D. officer. They were as vague as possible, ie the charges. When I applied to the Government of Bengal for a copy of the said charges on the 24th of April 1925, I got a reply from the then Additional Deputy Secretary, Political department, government of Bengal on the 13th May 1925 saying that no copy could be supplied. One fails to see how any person can possibly answer any charges if no copy of the same is furnished to him and if no indication is given him of the nature of the evidence in support of these charges. I am well aware of the stereotyped reply of the Government of Bengal on this point viz, that it would be dangerous to give any indication of the evidence in support of these charges. It will suffice for the present to say that that reply has failed to convince the public.

We have heard from time to time vague rumours that the Government of Bengal charge Mr Subhas Chandra Bose with having been a party to a conspiracy for smuggling arms etc. We have also heard vague rumours that the government of Bengal would charge him with having attempted in his capacity as Chief Executive Officer of the Calcutta Corporation to arrange and distribute the water supply of Calcutta in such a way that it might be possible in the future to contaminate the supply of water to the European section of this city and poison to death the European residents of Calcutta.

The former charge could easily have been proved against him in a Court of Law (if there was anything in it) without endangering the lives of any witnesses. The numerous trials which have been held both before and since Mr Subhas Chandra Boses's arrest show to demonstration that there is nothing in the plea that witnesses will be in danger of their lives if produced before a Court of Law. The latter charge is, in my submission, too ridiculous for words; and in this connection what surprises me most is that Mr Subhas Chandra Bose could have thought of endangering the lives of members of his own family, the majority of who reside in Elgin Road, which is in the European section of this city.

May I respectfully ask Your Excellency if you consider it just or fair to incarcerate a man without giving him any opportunity whatsoever of meeting the case put up against him? It may be justice of the ex-Lord Justice type but it is not justice as one ordinarily understands it. It may be fairplay according to Indian bureaucratic standards but it is not fairplay as a sportsman fresh from England understands it.

Your Excellency said in one of your speeches in England that you desired to 'play the game'. There is an excellent opportunity in Bengal of doing it, of course if you assert yourself. Who can possibly resist the Governor of Bengal if he makes up his mind to send for Mr Subhas Chandra Bose and some other detenus and have a straight talk with them? Those detenus might be—and very probably will be—able to place facts before your Excellency of a most sensational character, more sensational even than the facts contained in the State Prisoners Memorandum to Whitehall dated 25th July 1924 and in their letter to the Members of the Indian Legislative Assembly which appeared in 'FORWARD' dated the 17th of February 1925 (both of which have been printed in pages 45 to 75 of the book entitled 'Lawless Laws' published by the FORWARD Publishing Limited). It might very well be that they will be able to expose before Your Excellency this myth of a revolutionary conspiracy and also to place facts before you showing the existence of a huge conspiracy to put innocent persons into prison.

Your Excellency might well say, why cannot the detenus write to me? My reply is what is the guarantee that their letters will reach Your Excellency without being opened or that they will reach Your Excellency at all? If the detenus attempt to place the facts before you, they run the risk of drawing upon themselves the wrath of the entire officialdom. Can Your Excellency expect them to take that risk, when there is not even the guarantee that their letters will reach their destination?

I am conscious of the fact that I am requesting Your Excellency to take a bold step, a step bolder than any that has been taken by any of your predecessors in office. I am doing so, because I feel that if that step is taken, it will help in clearing the atmosphere. Everyone recognises that an atmosphere of mutual suspicion and mutual distrust is not good either for the Government or for the people: but the misfortune is that the people's point of view is very rarely, if at all, presented before Your Excellency. I feel no doubt that you will yourself find out before long that most of the Indian gentlemen who call on you—most estimable gentlemen no doubt—really represent no one except themselves and that you will have to look to other quarters for ascertaining the opinion of the public on this subject of detentions without trial.

I shall conclude this letter with my apologies for having taken so much of Your Excellency's time. I have taken this liberty only because I feel that it is not too late to inaugurate an era of better understanding between the Government and the people.

With kind regards
Yours faithfully
Sgnd Sarat Chandra Bose

Whether coincidentally or otherwise, Subhas was released from prison by direct order of Governor Jackson just one month later on 27 May 1927, and joined his brother in a concerted effort over the next five years to unite all the forces opposed to imperialist rule. In 1927, the Swaraj Party in the Bengal Legislative Council had 39 members in a house of 140. (Although the single largest party it had lost the support of its Muslim members following the breakdown of the C. R. Das—inspired Bengal

Pact of 1924.) As a member of the Council, Sarat was able to call upon his experience before the Bar and as an Alderman in the Calcutta Corporation. He intervened and spoke on a wide number of issues ranging from the role and conduct of the police forces, to the failures of the dyarchical system of government imposed by the British.

Subhas was elected President of the BPCC during this year of 1927. Over the next two decades one or other of the Bose Brothers was to lead this most important group in the Bengal Congress, a group that represented a consistent challenge to the Gandhian leadership and their chosen path. This was particularly evident during the years from 1929 to 1932.

Sarat and Subhas questioned Gandhi's role in the freedom struggle on three principal grounds. First, they were critical of Gandhian methods used in the nationalist movement, particularly, the continuous emphasis on non-violence and the constant tendency to seek accommodation with the British authorities and prevaricate over the goal of complete independence. Second, the Bengali intelligentsia whom the Boses represented experienced what Subhas called a 'rationalist revolt against the Mahatma and his philosophy'. Third, there was a growing feeling on the part of the members of the group within the BPCC led by Sarat and Subhas that Gandhi had little understanding of the problems of the urban middle and lower middle classes. In their view, his programme was village-oriented and tended to ignore the challenges and problems of urban life.

Between 1927 and 1929, Subhas in particular sought to organise Bengali youth in support of the national struggle and to heighten their consciousness on questions affecting workers and peasants. The Bose Brothers wanted to draw the workers as well as the peasants into political struggles by encouraging their participation in the national movements. Unlike the Communists, who in India were just beginning to organise themselves, they were not in favour of class warfare. For the Bose Brothers and their supporters, the British imperialists were 'the' enemy of the working class.

Sarat and Subhas also both felt strongly at this time towards the end of the 1920s that even though the Bengal Pact of 1924 was moribund, attempts to secure the cooperation of the Muslim community should continue. They thus consistently campaigned with determination for rapprochement with the Muslim leaders and peoples of Bengal.

By 1930, it would appear that both Sarat and Subhas were increasingly disenchanted with the course of the non-violent movement and, while not eschewing the movement completely, were now moving inexorably towards the notion of revolutionary struggle. Sometime in 1930, Subhas wrote a long letter to the revolutionary leader Barindra Kumar Ghosh (brother of Aurobindo), now returned from exile in French-controlled Pondicherry and living in Calcutta.

Subhas was also living in Calcutta at the time with brother Sarat and his family at 1 Woodburn Park, sharing a room with the teenage Amiya. The latter was asked one day by Subhas to deliver in person a hand-written letter to Barin Ghosh, which he did. The original of this letter seems to have been lost to posterity, but a draft in Bengali survived with Amiya, who much later arranged to have the draft translated into English.

The letter, considered by Amiya to be a key document in properly understanding what Subhas stood for and what he was seeking to achieve, is in effect a representation of the political and socio-economic thinking of Subhas at this juncture, as well as his personal account of contemporary events. These also found expression in his book *The Indian Struggle,* written a few years later in 1934 during involuntary exile in Europe. The surviving English translation of the letter, which has gone through several refinements over time including through processes of publication, is here reproduced virtually in full.

It was important for me to meet you again, but this is perhaps not to be. As today draws to a close, tomorrow morning I have to attend court to receive the verdict and it seems that it will be quite some time before I return from there. That is why I am writing this letter to express my innermost feelings on some very important matters.

It is after a long time that you have returned to the soil of Bengal. I am very happy at your arrival here for you have come just at the right moment. I do not speak for myself alone, there are many besides me in Bengal today who are happy at your arrival; perhaps you do not even know them all.

Bengal has not forgotten you; nor has Bengal forgotten the group that you and your associates had organized; you can never be forgotten. If there is any adverse criticism about you and your comrades, in Bengal at present, or if you are criticised in future, it will be only because the country still loves you and feels that it has claims upon you; and when it does get what it expects from you it claims the right to feel fulfilled.

You and your associates have done much for the Bengalis. You have taught them a lot. You have shown them the path to immortality. You have inspired them with dreams of liberty and have given them the message that opens up the pathways to freedom. You have taught them to have self-confidence and to be fearless; you have taught them that one cannot enjoy a new life, without being prepared completely to sacrifice one's life. Above all, you have proclaimed thunderously the message of the undying spirit of Bengal through your Journal *Jugantar*. Can Bengalis ever forget any of this?

But who will carry forward the message of Bengal today? How many of those whose task it is to do so know Bengal intimately enough to carry the message of Bengal to the Bengalis? How can it be possible to understand Bengali culture by reading sixpenny English novels?

Profound dedication is needed for the understanding of Bengal. Where is that dedication today? Loud speeches and theatrical gestures may attract voters but cannot educate our people. It is indeed a matter of deep regret that Deshbandhu, who symbolized the very best in Bengali nationalism and culture, is no longer amidst us; I remember that a Maharashtrian friend of mine had once said to me, 'The death of Lokmanya Tilak has left us completely helpless. We are a widowed people'. After the passing away of Deshbandhu we realized how helpless and forlorn we were. Then I had some idea of what the Maharashtrians must have felt after the death of Lokmanya Tilak. The feeling of helplessness is with us still and I do not know when we can get over it.

During the past forty years three great men have appeared in Bengal to give shape to Bengali nationalism—Vivekananda, Aurobindo and Chittaranjan. In their lives the Bengalis discovered their lost soul and their spiritual ideal. In order to understand modern Bengal, one must understand these three great men. Those who have not understood their messages can never understand the New Bengal. Those who have not been able to comprehend the nature of their work, can never understand the significance of the culture of Bengal.

Vivekananda and Deshbandhu are no longer in our midst and Aurobindo is no longer the Aurobindo of '*Bande Mataram*', the pioneer of freedom that he was. And yet I know that their message and their ideals have not been lost. There are people in Bengal today who can still carry their message. And, as long as you and your associates are with us, how can there be any dearth of persons to carry their message? You have been the inspirer of the fiery ordeal of revolutionary struggle. I appeal to you today to appear once again to dazzle our eyes with the divine lightning, with the brilliance of 'Bijoli' in the boundless fields of Bengal, once again to thunder forth to Bengalis the message of Bengal—the message of the spirit of Bengal.

Perhaps you are witnessing directly for the first time the condition of Bengal after the loss of Deshbandhu. From all appearances, you may doubt if the Bengalis in fact remember Deshbandhu—you may feel that they are beginning gradually to forget him. But one should not always judge by mere appearances. Bengalis have not forgotten Deshbandhu, they can never forget him. I believe that with the passage of time the greatest intellects of Bengal will come to understand Deshbandhu more and more.

Of course it has to be admitted that a group of leaders and workers has emerged on the political scene of Bengal who do not understand him for they do not have the dedication and the intellect required for this understanding. They want to swear by outsiders and though the sun rises in the East every day, they expect the sun of India to rise in the West. For all their pomp and pretence, and despite all the noise with which they beat their own drums, their voice will soon be lost in the wilderness of eternity. Falsehood, deceit and artifice cannot cast their spell for long.

When you and your comrades returned from the Andaman's Jail and took charge of the journal 'Narayan', the first phase of the Non-Co-operation Movement had begun. At present on your return from Pondicherry, you are witnessing that we have reached the last phase of this Movement. During these years many of you have been engaged in what Rabindranath Tagore has described as the 'inactive exercise of solitude'.

We, on our part, have come across many trials and vicissitudes. Many of us have toiled unremittingly during these years. But though our efforts have not been quite fruitless, I have to admit that we have not been able to achieve the results that we expected. In fact truth and reality demand that in the interests of truth I must say that there is no hope of attaining full success (that is, complete independence) through the present programme of action.

Of course as the result of the Lahore Congress directive and through the earnest efforts of Mahatma Gandhi, there will be a tremendous upsurge all over India this year [1930] and this movement will lead us much further along the road to our destination. Therefore, even though we do not reach the winning post by the impetus (of this movement), we have to work heart and soul for the success of the Civil Disobedience Movement that will be launched this year.

Now that you have arrived here, do give an impetus again to Bengali hearts and do stir up their thoughts. Let our people think for themselves and let them light up the lamps of understanding in their hearts. It will be useless to go about lamp in hand in the outside like Diogenes [ancient Greek philosopher who is said to have wandered the streets of Athens with a lantern in broad daylight, searching for an honest man!] It is important, of course, to know the country thoroughly, we cannot do without reality.

I still maintain that we have to discover self-confidence, inspiration and knowledge within ourselves. We cannot have these from outside. There has been a wave of cynicism in Bengal for some time now. This is a bad sign for lack of faith everywhere and always is an obstacle to creativity. It is faith alone which can create, it is through the strength of faith alone that men can accomplish great results. I believe that if you try you can eradicate this cynicism. You must share the spiritual wealth that you have acquired in solitude during all these years.

When I was released from prison in 1927, the Congress in Bengal was in disarray. All the groups were then tired and weary through internecine feuds and strife. When Deshbandhu passed away in 1925, he left a great and unprecedented legacy for us. That wonderful legacy has been dissipated in just two years. A group was set up to take over the leadership of the Congress from those who were controlling the Party after Deshbandhu's death. The energy of the Congress was exhausted in frustrating the efforts of the rebels. Nothing new could be accomplished by Congress in Bengal which then lay in a stupor clinging to the (Legislative) Council and the (Calcutta) Corporation.

As a result of this, after Deshbandhu's death there was no movement like Tarakeshwar Satyagraha in Bengal. This listlessness was overcome last year when the Bandabilla Satyagraha was launched in Jessore District. Just as there has been a massive effort to break up the Congress after the death of Deshbandhu there was a similar effort even during his life time. Mr Shyam Sunder Chakravarty was the leader of that revolt. Many will remember even today these two instances of rebellion against the Congress.

As we encountered the state of disarray in 1927, we had to carry on work in three directions. First of all, we had to resist the split that had begun to develop within Congress; secondly, we had to continue our activities according to the Congress Programme; thirdly, the foundations had to be laid for the bigger movements of the future. I shall now indicate what we have done towards laying this foundation and I shall appeal for your help in this work.

We reached the conclusion that in order to launch a powerful movement in the country, we needed on the one hand an inspiring ideal that could lift up our spirits, and on the other we had to work among those sections of our people who were naturally endowed with the qualities of idealism, the spirit of sacrifice and deep feeling and imagination.

That is why we felt that unless we placed the ideal of complete independence before the Nation, we could not inspire our people to action. For this we had fought so hard at the Calcutta Congress; what a lot of abuse and vituperation has been showered upon us for this and immediately Mr. (J. M.) Sengupta became dead set against us. Fortunately Bengal did not forget her heritage. 'We want complete autonomy free from British control'. Bengalis did not lower the pitch of the resounding note that Aurobindo Babu had struck with these words in his journal 'Bande Mataram'. But in spite of this, through the pressure of the majority of votes from other provinces the resolution for complete independence was rejected in the Calcutta Congress [1928]. But though we lost the vote we were not really defeated; and that is why the mistake of the Calcutta Congress was rectified by the Lahore Congress [1929] adopting the resolution for complete independence.

The defeat of Bengal at the Calcutta Congress was completely wiped out at Lahore; but twelve months in our nation's life were allowed to be idled away. However, at last, the Indians have a soul-stirring ideal before them—an ideal for which even the sacrifice of one's life counts for nothing.

In order to inspire our countrymen with fresh vigour, we have to place before them the new and integral image of freedom. During all these years we have meant and explained by freedom—political freedom alone; but henceforth we have to declare that we do not want to liberate people merely from political bondage. We want to liberate them from all forms of bondage. The struggle for independence has as its aim the removal of the triple bondage of political, economic and social oppression. When all shackles are removed, we can proceed to build a new society on the basis of communism. The principal aim of our freedom struggle is to build a free and classless society. This ideal and this dream have inspired men in all ages and in all lands.

You may have learnt from many sources after your return to Calcutta that there is a wide rift between me and Mr. J. M. Sengupta. It is true that there is a rift. I shall be guilty of false-hood if I deny this fact. But I do not know if everybody has a clear idea of what the dispute is about. Some people are supposed to be of the view that a scramble for power is going on. Those who say this are either completely ignorant of facts or are deliberately spreading such lies. Even when my differences with Sengupta began to develop, we did not interfere with his possession of the 'Triple Crown'. In 1929, even as the strike was on, he was elected 'Mayor' and 'Leader of the Council' with our votes and through our efforts.

After this he was twice successively [in 1927 and 1928] offered the post of the President of the Provincial [Congress] Committee, but he voluntarily turned down our offer. Therefore, after our release from prison, we offered him three crowns; he accepted two of these and refused the third. I fail to see any scramble for power on our part in this. If we had really sought to diminish Sengupta's influence or importance, we would have proceeded to work differently after our release from prison and would not have voluntarily offered him the three crowns. There is a real difference between Sengupta and myself—between Sengupta and Young Bengal in fact. I have not yet been able to understand him or follow his ways.

I do not find any consistent harmony between his words and his deeds. I even find him contradictory in his utterances on differ-ent occasions and in different places. The reason behind this lies apparently in the lack of any dedicated work in his career. I do not know if any fixed principles guide his life at all; and above all, he does not understand Bengal. I do not think that he has any knowledge of the culture of Bengal, of the Bengali spirit or the distinctiveness of Bengal.

It is not therefore possible for him to act as the representative of Bengal. This was evident at the Calcutta Congress. On one side there was the Bengali demand for the acceptance of the Independence Resolution, on the other, there was Mahatmaji's directive for supporting Dominion Status. He went against Bengal and pleased the Mahatma by supporting him and yet he wanted to retain complete and sole influence over Bengal. The same thing was repeated at the Lahore Congress. He supported the Mahatma's original resolution by opposing all amendments to it—though most of the delegates from Bengal had supported the amending resolution.

This is not all. In Bengal he makes one kind of speech to win over the Bengalis; but when he goes outside Bengal, he talks and acts differently. In the District of Tripura he spoke in support of a parallel Government. Immediately after this in order to please the Mahatma, he signed the Leaders' Delhi Manifesto; and when I moved an amendment for the parallel Government at the Lahore Congress, instead of supporting me, he openly supported Mahatmaji's original resolution.

I admit that the exalted seat of Deshbandhu will dwarf any person who occupies it. But with dedicated effort, one can correct many of one's shortcomings and can be forgiven by others. But if this dedicated effort is lacking, how long can one continue just by being clever and by just making empty speeches? And you must be quite aware that in order to be able to lead Bengal one must be specially equipped intellectually, culturally and spiritually. The Bengali intellect does not bow down to just anybody. The Bengalis will never accept his leadership, because no peoples in India are as hyper-critical as the Bengalis. Nevertheless in spite of his mediocrity, Sengupta might have yet worked for Bengal, if he had been able to appeal to all sections of opinion. But this he could not do. He came to be dominated by an impossible conceit and arrogance.

By this time as the decade of the 1930s began to unfold, the British were convinced that not only Subhas but older brother Sarat was now working enthusiastically on the promotion of revolutionary activity both inside and outside of India. Amiya spoke of Sarat having taken 'bold strides' towards establishing links with the revolutionaries, and there is a wealth of both factual and circumstantial evidence to support this. A police report of 8 December 1931 declared:

Mr Sarat Bose is unquestionably a most dangerous opponent of government and a man who in intellectual attainments is far superior to the majority of Congress leaders in the Province. He has been for several years in direct touch with persons abroad who are likely by means of propaganda to assist the type of nationalism for which Congress stands. He did his utmost in 1930 to assist the movement sponsored by Congress, the principal object of which was defiance of the law and harassment of the Government.

There is no question that during 1930 his was one of the small cliques which virtually conducted the Civil Disobedience Movement in Calcutta, and there is every prospect of his following a similar line as soon as that movement is revived. There are good grounds too for believing that Mr Bose has supplied funds and given assistance to persons who have absconded in political cases, and that he has also interested himself in giving relief to released detenus.

He is a man with considerable influence and great powers of organisation, and in view of the fact that he will inevitably direct powers in an attempt to overthrow the government at the earliest opportunity, it is essential that he should be restrained by the operation of Regulation III of 1818.

Eight days later, on 16 December 1931, the Home Political Department chimed in with its assessment of Sarat's revolutionary credentials.

What we have here is the fact that Sarat Bose possesses a mentality which is likely to lead him to support the cult of terrorism. Not only is there source information to the effect that he assists arrested terrorists, but there are eulogies of terrorists which have continually been published in the 'LIBERTY', the policy of which he controls. There is also the employment of terrorists in large numbers in the Calcutta Corporation by the controlling group of which he is a leading member. With such mentality it is but a short step to the actual support of terrorism, and it is easy to believe the information that he does so. This information comes from eight independent sources who definitely accuse Sarat Bose during the last two years. He is particularly connected with the attempt on the life of Sir Charles Tegart and with the maintenance of terrorist absconders.

Not to be outdone and no doubt reflecting the fear which Sarat engendered in the panapoly of colonial police and governmental authorities, the Government of Bengal offered its own view.

> The Bengal Government are satisfied that Sarat Bose has for years past been cognisant of and a direct supporter of the terrorist revolutionary movement, and that, though he has not himself taken part in outrages, he has assisted them by advice and monetary support both previous to and subsequent to the commission of such outrages. In the last two years he has given support and encouragement to the Chittagong revolutionaries and absconders.

In a now much-published British intelligence report dated 5 January 1932, as the net was closing in on Sarat and following the arrest the day before on 4 January 1932 of Subhas, and on the eve of the mass incarceration of tens of thousands of followers connected in one way or another to the nationalist movement, Charles Tegart as Commissioner of Police was to conclude:

> Sarat Bose has assisted the revolutionary movement for years by means of his Purse, his Press and his Prestige. He is not the man to throw bombs himself but he is ready to provide money for their manufacture. He will probably never shoot a European official as long as he lives, but he is eager to incite young men to commit murder. Few men in this Presidency have provided so much money for revolutionary enterprises. No man is more responsible for the present cult of the revolver. No man has done as much as Sarat Bose to instill into the mind of the youth of Bengal that poisonous creed which justifies political assassination and canonises political murderers. This very dangerous individual should be dealt with under Regulation III.

Thus, it was that on 5 February 1932, Sarat was arrested and soon after joined his younger brother Subhas in Seoni Jail in central India, two among the tens of thousands of other Indians arrested and detained in a massive crackdown by the British colonial authorities against Gandhi and the independence movement. A little over one year later on 23 February 1933, an ailing Subhas left for medical treatment and enforced exile in Europe, while Sarat was eventually released from 'house arrest' at his Kurseong bungalow in the Himalayan foothills on 26 July 1935.

Subhas had left Vienna in late November 1934 to return to India without clearance from the authorities, to see his ailing father Janakinath. He managed to arrive in Calcutta on 4 December, but sadly his father had passed away on 2 December. Remaining under house arrest and close surveillance by the authorities, Subhas spent a little over a month in mourning with his brothers and then embarked for Europe again in early January 1935. That same month, his book *The Indian Struggle,* written the previous year whilst in European exile, was published by the London-based company Lawrence and Wishart, but predictably banned in India. The book seems to have been well-received in continental Europe, and perhaps somewhat ironically in Britain as well.

That same year in April, Subhas underwent a successful gall bladder operation in Vienna, and after a period of some months recuperation resumed his array of pro-independence activities in Europe. The British for their part had concluded that Subhas in Europe was the lesser of two evils, and took every opportunity to discourage his return to India.

Subhas was not to be denied and March 1936 found him aboard an Italian passenger ship the *Conte Verde,* bound for the Far East. As he expected and as the British had explicitly warned, he was detained on arrival at Bombay on 8 April 1936 and taken to prison. In the face of a public outcry over the ensuing weeks, Subhas from late May 1936, like his brother Sarat before him, was allowed to continue his detention at Sarat's Kurseong bungalow. In December of that year he was transferred to Calcutta for medical treatment and, still not in the best of health, released in March 1937.

After five years of physical separation, extended periods of detention for both, and a period in India where the freedom struggle seemed to lose much of its previous momentum of the late 1920s and early 1930s, the Bose Brothers were reunited in the long fight for 'Complete Independence', and ready to enter the next phase.

Photographs

1. Brothers-in-Arms: Sarat and Subhas

[All photos and letters are from author's personal collection, unless specified.]

2. First Meeting of the Interim Government on 2 September 1946 (Left to Right): Mr Syed Ali Zaheer, Mr Jagjivan Ram, Mr Sarat Chandra Bose, Mr Asaf Ali, Dr Rajendra Prasad, Sardar Vallabhbhai Patel, Pandit Jawaharlal Nehru, H.E. Lord Wavell

3. Amiya Nath Bose and INA Veteran Shah Nawaz Khan with INA Relief Committee in 1946

4. Netaji Subhas in the Andamans, 7 January 1944

5. Sarat Chandra Bose with Bivabati: Campaigning for Election

6. Sarat Chandra Bose: Civic Reception for Him by the People of Calcutta, 13 January 1946 (Courtesy: D. Ratan & Co., Calcutta)

7. Sarat Chandra Bose Speaking in London, July 1948

4. Netaji Subhas in the Andamans, 7 January 1944

5. Sarat Chandra Bose with Bivabati: Campaigning for Election

8. Prime Minister Jawaharlal Nehru with Madhuri Bose during His Visit to Netaji Bhawan, 2 December 1961

9. Sarat and Bivabati Welcome the Newlyweds Amiya and Jyotsna, 9 March 1948

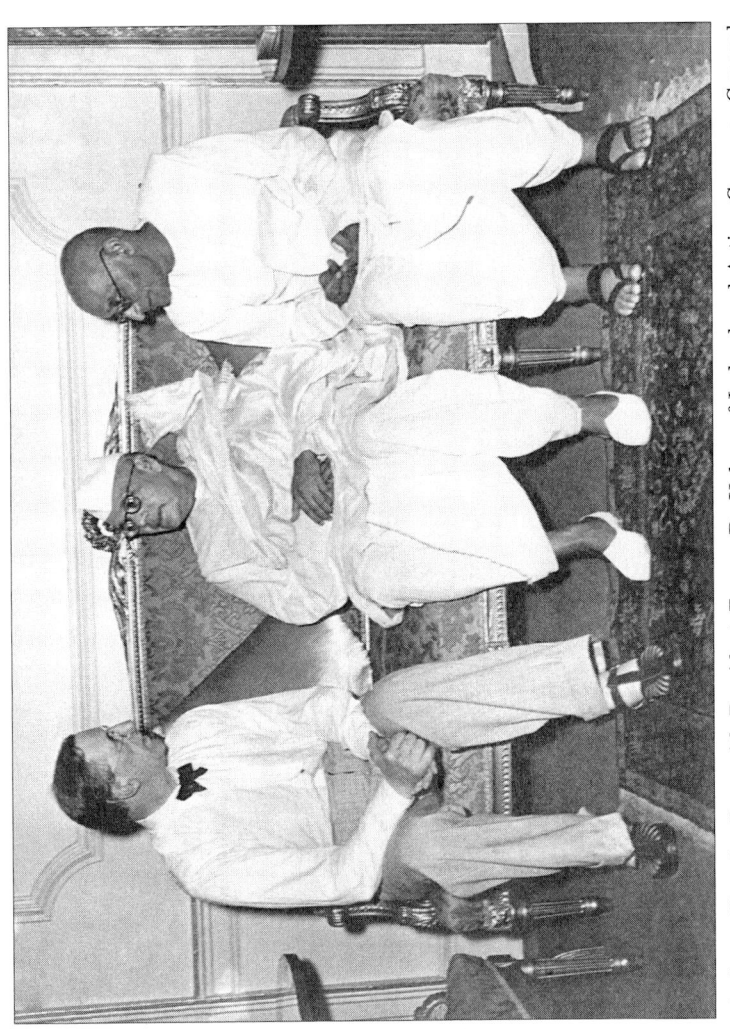

10. Sarat Chandra Bose with President Eamon De Valera of Ireland and Acting Governor-General Rajagopalachari in 1947, Calcutta

11. Subhas Chandra Bose and His then Secretary Emilie Schenkl with Amiya in Badgastein, 26 December 1937

12. Subhas Chandra Bose: Arriving at Victoria Station, London on 9 January 1938

13. Subhas Chandra Bose: Signed Portrait (Courtesy: Surya Kumar Bose)

14. Sarat Chandra Bose (Courtesy: Subrata Bose)

15. Subhas Chandra Bose

16. Sarat and Bivabati with Amiya and Their Grandchildren at Giddapahar, Kurseong

17. Amiya Nath Bose: College Days

18. Subhas in Berlin 1942

Letters

1. A Note to Bivabati from Gandhi, 29 July 1942 (pages 1 and 2)

FORWARD BLOC
(OF THE INDIAN NATIONAL CONGRESS)

PRESIDENT :
SUBHAS CHANDRA BOSE

GENERAL SECRETARY :
LALA SHANKER LAL

ORGANISING SECRETARY :
H. V. KAMATH

HEAD OFFICE :
62, BOWBAZAR STREET
CALCUTTA

Dated 14.1. 1940
38/2 Elgin Road, Calcutta.

My dear Amiya,

I cannot tell you how glad I am that you write to me regularly though I do not reply. I have got all your letters and the cutting from the London paper &c. myself. Your short article has been passed on to the staff and it will be made use of in the next issue.

I am writing this just to tell you that there is an acute and widespread demand for my book "The Indian Struggle." Reason for made the publishers to bring out an Indian edition of the book — somewhat cheaper than the original. Even without any additional chapters, it will sell in India like hot cakes. My life has been made intolerable everywhere by people asking for copies of the book. After the ban was lifted, whenever copies reached the Indian market, they were sold out in a day.

Please let me know from the publishers what I shall do about the translation. I do not know what rights I have. In several Indian languages, local publishers want to bring out translations. The Bengali translation is ready and awaits printing. If I know the terms, I shall fix up with the publishers here. This is very urgent.

If it is not possible to bring out an English edition for India owing to war conditions, I can arrange for that in India as well. Will you please let me know about this also?

I am writing this in the train on my way to Calcutta from Bombay. Once in Calcutta, I shall not have time to write. Hence these hasty, written lines.

Yours affly
Subhas

2. About *The Indian Struggle*: From Subhas to Ami,
14 January 1940 (pages 1 and 2)

Mahableshwar
30. 4. '45

Dear Amiyo,

Have you worked out the problem of electricity for every home? What is the cost? My remark quoted by you is a poser for the time being. It will cease to be one, if it is a possibility. It has not penetrated every home in the villages even in Mysore. Since you believe in it I want you to work it out & demonstrate the physical & economic possibility of electrifying every home of the seven hundred thousand villages of India.

It is a torture to suffer from fever for years. Has the medical profession declared bankruptcy?

Love to all

Bapu

3. Letter from Gandhi to Amiya Nath Bose,
30 April 1945 (pages 1 and 2)

Mandalay Jail
3. 4. 25.
Friday.

My dear Brother.

Dilip writes to say that you may be coming here during the Easter Holidays. Mandalay is exceedingly hot now and you will find the journey from Rangoon to this place very trying indeed. Personally I hardly think it worth while coming all the way from Calcutta. However, if you are keen on coming, please try to get permission from the D.I.G, C.I.D to see me as often as you like, during your stay here.

Please tell Ramiah that I have just received a parcel of books from the Corporation Library. Dilip will be able to send some books for me also. I like his books very much indeed — he has a very good choice indeed.

If you come at all, please bring some Darjeeling Tea and ত্রবু ঘৃত with you and some fine সাধখানি (সরু-মোটা) rice as well. The local rice does not seem to agree with me.

It is becoming hotter and hotter

2.

797

every day but we are told that real summer has not arrived yet. Hope this will find you all quite well.

Yours v. affly
Subhas
(S. C. Bose)

4. Message from Mandalay Jail: Letter from Subhas to Sarat, 3 April 1925 (pages 1 and 2)

My dear Subhas,

I wonder if you will get this letter before you leave. I am taking my chance. In another week or more the presidential election will be over. Apart from your name, the nominations were of Abul Kalam Azad, Abdul Ghaffar Khan & me. Abdul Ghaffar & I have formally withdrawn. Abul Kalam has also said so, but so far we have not received his formal letter of withdrawal. So there is likely to be no election but still we shall probably have to go through the formality.

Ever since the Calcutta AICC I have been greatly worried over the turn events have been taking. Gandhiji's emotional outburst at the W.C. meeting and his subsequent article in the Harijan upset me. This has been followed by other events which are disturbing. I shall not go into all these matters but I shall just point out to you that I find it extraordinarily difficult to accept pursuing the new orientation of Congress policy which involves a suppression of left elements and mass movements.

Nehru Complains: Letter from Nehru to Subhas, 9 January 1938 (page 1)

I have remained quiet in public because I dislike criticising Gandhiji or my W.C. colleagues publicly. We have to observe a certain decorum and discipline. But this quiet acceptance of this oppression has been hard on me. Matters are likely to come to a head at Haripura or even earlier. We are having a W.C. meeting at Wardha from Feb 3rd onwards, at which you will have to be present. At this meeting we shall draw up the resolutions for Haripura. We have set aside five days for this — from Feb 3rd to 8th.

The last two years have been difficult ones but the coming year is going to be far more difficult. Your job will be a terrible one. Of course I want to help you in every way I can and I shall do so. But I do not see how I can continue to associate myself with the present W.C. or something like it.

Gandhiji, Abul Kalam and others want me to function as General Secretary next year. I am quite certain that I should not do so.

3

ANAND BHAWAN
ALLAHABAD

Apart from other reasons, I do not want to tie myself down
to the enormous amount of routine activity that this
involves and which prevents all this more vital
work. But I am worried by another matter.
I would much rather not be in the W.C. although
I should like to give it all possible cooperation
from outside. I think that I can be of greater use
outside than inside. This is my present view.
Remaining outside I can retain a measure of
freedom to criticize in a friendly way and to
keep in touch with other elements. Otherwise I
disable myself and cannot prevent the crisis
which I see developing rapidly.

I have mentioned this to Gandhiji so as that
they might think about it. We shall discuss it
fully when you return —

In a few days' time I am going to the frontier
province — I shall return just in time for the W.C.
I am afraid I cannot go to Bengal before
Haripura, nor could I attend the Bengal
Provincial Conference at Haripura. You must

4

forgive me —

When you fly back I am afraid I shall not
be in Allahabad. I shall be in the frontier Prov.
If I had been here I would have asked you to
stay here for a day before proceeding to Calcutta.

You must be having a busy time in London —

Love
yours affly
Jawahar

5. Nehru Complains: Letter from Nehru to Subhas, 9 January 1938 (page 4)

4th October

My dear Ami,

Your letter of the 20th September last reached me on the 30th (along with your mother's letters of the 16th and 19th Sept.) and I was happy to learn you were all keeping well. You will have all information about me from your Jethababa, so it is unnecessary to write in detail.

I was glad to learn that your 'Nani' was proposing to take you all to the holy city of Kashi. I hope the proposal will materialize and that you will have the opportunity of seeing the 'arati' of Kasi Viswanath, the magnificent ghats of Kashi, the Manikarnika and other places of interest as also the remains of Buddhistic glory at Sarnath. Kashi is a place of special interest and attraction to Hindus and I hope you will profit both intellectually and spiritually by your stay there.

You and your brothers & sisters must

not feel depressed on account of my indefinite detention. You should always call to mind the burning words of the late Bal Gangadhar Tilak when he was sentenced to a long term of imprisonment by the Bombay High Court — "There are higher powers that rule the destinies of men and nations and it is perhaps the will of Providence that the cause which I represent will prosper more by my suffering than by my remaining free." You should also remember that you have your own duties to perform — devotion to superiors (both ... and near relations and friends of the family), love for those who are younger than you and kindness and sympathy for all who are less fortunately placed than yourself. It is by cultivating the qualities mentioned above that you can develop your intellect and elevate your soul. Try to realize every moment of your waking life that "Man does not live by bread alone".

I shall probably be late in sending you my Pujija ... having ... to my ... I am therefore sending you in anticipation my warmest love & blessings for the Pujija day. yours very affly ...Baba

6. Smuggled Letter from Prison: From Sarat to Ami,
4 October (pages 1 and 2)

4

Bose Brothers and Gandhi: Parting of the Ways

*If we come to a parting of the ways, a bitter civil war will com-
mence and whatever be the upshot of it—the Congress will be
weakened for some time to come and the benefit will be reaped by
the British Government*

—Letter from Subhas to Gandhi, 31 March 1939

Subhas Chandra Bose was elected President of the Haripura
Congress held in February 1938 in Gujarat, with the prior
blessings of Gandhi. In his path-breaking Presidential Address,
Subhas seized the strategic opportunity of a national audience
of Congress representatives from throughout British India to
articulate his vision and present a blueprint of an independent,
progressive India run on federal and socialist lines. Central
to that vision was the establishment of a 'National Planning
Commission' that would oversee the 'eradication of poverty, illit-
eracy and disease' through a comprehensive plan of reconstruction guided by government at both central and provincial levels.

By the year end, Subhas, the father of Indian planning, was
able to arrange the convening of a National Planning Committee
under the umbrella of the Congress, and had persuaded
Jawaharlal Nehru to chair the first meeting of the Committee
on 17 December 1938. This was to be the forerunner of the
Advisory Planning Board set up under the Interim Government
of 1946 and the Planning Commission of 1952 established by
the Government of independent India.

While the Haripura Congress had proceeded smoothly
enough under the leadership of Subhas, the seeds of open
ideological and political dissent were precariously close to the
surface. Fissures within Congress began to open up from the
time of the Presidential Address itself, when those on the right
of Congress of a more capitalist inclination failed to be reassured by the arguments for a distinctly Indian, non-exploitive
form of socialism.

These fault lines soon began to widen with the country-wide campaign led by Subhas for immediate resumption of the national struggle, and his insistence that under no circumstances should there be any compromise with Britain. In his capacity as serving Congress President, Subhas began what he himself termed 'an open propaganda throughout India in order to prepare the Indian people for a national struggle which should synchronise with the coming war in Europe'.[1]

Even in early 1938, Subhas was convinced that a European war was imminent. His views were not shared by Gandhi and Nehru and serious differences between the Bose Brothers on the one hand and Gandhi and Nehru on the other, can be traced to that time. As reflected in *The Indian Struggle*, Subhas had of course had any number of disagreements over the years with the analyses, methods and tactics of Gandhi, and had often been joined by Nehru; but this period saw the beginnings of a closer political nexus between Gandhi and Nehru, with the latter now clearly anointed by Gandhi as his 'heir'.

Subhas also had a strong suspicion that a section of the Congress leadership was wanting to compromise with Britain on the issue of Indian independence, and he gave expression to his suspicion in numerous public statements. On 9 July 1938, for example, Subhas as the President of the Congress issued a statement to the press to the effect that some influential leaders of the right (i.e., Gandhian) wing of the Congress had been negotiating with the British Government over the Federal Scheme as envisaged in the Government of India Act of 1935. In *The Indian Struggle*, Subhas had described this passing of a new constitution for India by the British Parliament as 'the most important political event during 1935'.[2]

The provisions of the Act were divided into two parts, the Federal and Provincial, with the proposed 'Federation' representing a new departure in that it provided for an All-India Central Government, uniting both the 11 provinces of British India and the many hundreds of semi-autonomous Indian Princely States. The federal chamber was to comprise an upper and a lower house, each with limited powers. Significantly, defence and foreign

---

[1] Subhas Chandra Bose, *The Indian Struggle* (Natyachinta Foundation Kolkata, 2005), 417.

[2] Ibid., 407–408.

policies were reserved for the British Viceroy. At the same time, financial policy and control of the administration, including the police, were also excluded from the competence of the two houses. The Viceroy also retained wide discretionary powers including the right to veto legislation, dismiss ministers, pass legislation rejected by the legislatures, dissolve the legislatures and suspend the constitution.

The provincial component of the new constitution, applicable only to the 11 provinces of British India, was in general less controversial, and in any case of less significance to those such as the Bose Brothers fighting for Complete Independence.

It was the so-called 'Federal Scheme' that attracted the rising ire and implacable opposition of the Bose Brothers, broadly supported by the left (i.e., Socialist) wing of the Congress. In his 9 July 1938 statement, Subhas declared:

> There have been from time to time statements or insinuations in the British Press to the effect that some influential leaders of the Congress have been negotiating with the British Government over the Federal Scheme as envisaged in the Government of India Act. I believe that the last statement which I noticed was that of the Manchester Guardian to which I gave an immediate and emphatic denial. In the absence of any proof, I cannot and do not believe that any influential Congress leader has been negotiating with the British Government with a view to arriving at a compromise behind the back of the Congress.
>
> I may add that there is no analogy between Provincial Autonomy and the Federal Scheme and the acceptance of office in the Provinces by the Congress should not be construed as a stepping-stone towards the acceptance of the Federal Scheme at the Centre. I have no doubt in my mind that any effort to foist the Federal Scheme on the Congress will inevitably fail. If unfortunately it succeeds, it will break the Congress, because I do not see how those who are conscientiously opposed to the Federal Scheme can take it lying down.
>
> Personally I think that any weakness shown by the Congress or any section thereof during this fateful hour in India's history will amount to treachery of the first magnitude to the cause of India's freedom. We are in such a sound strategic position today that if only we could unite and speak with one voice, we should be able to induce the British Government to concede the whole of our national demand. The slightest weakness in our attitude

towards the Federal Scheme is bound to weaken our hands and strengthen those of the British Government.

So far as I am concerned, should the unthinkable contingency arise of the Federal Scheme being adopted by a majority within the Congress, it would probably be my duty to relieve myself of the trammels of office so that I would be free to work for what I consider to be the best interests of the country namely, open, unmitigated and unrelenting opposition to the monstrous Federal Scheme.

On 15 July 1938, Subhas in a further press statement announced that reports had reached him of efforts being made by the British Government to enlist the sympathy and support of the right wing of the Congress in favour of the Federal Scheme. The conflict between the right wing on the one hand, and the left wing led by Subhas on the other, began in right earnest.

Subhas around this time began to think in terms of re-election for the Presidency of the Congress for the following year 1939. He felt that acceptance of the Federal Scheme would be a disastrous move for India and he needed to be in the best position to fight any such eventuality. This was in the face of clear opposition from Gandhi, a previously unheard-of challenge to the latter's authority and tight hold over Congress affairs.

In late 1938, Rabindranath Tagore wrote privately to Gandhi urging that Subhas be given the chance to be re-elected for a second term as Congress President. Tagore also sought Nehru's support in this matter. Subhas at the time was apparently unaware of Tagore's intervention on his behalf. Gandhi remained unmoved by Tagore's plea and continued to make it very clear to all that he was not willing to bless the re-election of Subhas as President of the Congress.

Subhas then took matters into his own hands and decided to contest the election with the support of the left wing of the Congress. For his part Gandhi determined that Pattabhi Sitaramaiyya should be his candidate for President, after Maulana Azad stepped aside and Nehru reportedly declined to run once again.

As the new year of 1939 dawned and as war clouds gathered over Europe, the machinery of Congress moved into the final stages of preparation for the identification of its President for 1939. Commenting on a meeting of the Congress Working

Committee (CWC) on 11 January 1939, the United Press of India reported that utterances of individual Congressmen favouring acceptance of Federation formed one of the subjects discussed. This almost certainly helped shape the immediate background to the now looming Congress Presidential election, and the inevitable showdown between Subhas and Sarat on the one hand, and Congress luminary and Gandhi's chief of staff Vallabhbhai Patel on the other.

An exchange of telegrams (held in the Private Collection of Amiya Nath and Jyotsna Bose) between Patel and Sarat Bose on 24 January 1939 provides an indication of the widening chasm between the two arms of Congress and between the Bose Brothers and Gandhi.

From Patel to Sarat Bose:

FEEL SUBHAS BABU'S STATEMENT PRESIDENTIAL ELECTION NEEDS COUNTER STATEMENT FROM MEMBERS WORKING COMMITTEE WHO FEEL RE-ELECTION THIS YEAR UNNECESSARY. BRIEF STATEMENT READY. IT SAYS RE-ELECTION ONLY EXCEPTIONAL CIRCUMSTANCES. NO SUCH PRECEDENT FOR RE-ELECTING SUBHAS BABU. IT REBUTS SUBHAS BABU'S CONTENTION ABOUT FEDERATION ETC AND SAYS PROGRAMMES AND POLICIES FIXED NOT BY PRESIDENT BUT CONGRESS OR WORKING COMMITTEE. COUNTER STATEMENT COMMENDS DR PATTABHI FOR ELECTION AND APPEALS SUBHAS BABU NOT DIVIDE CONGRESSMEN ON PRESIDENTIAL ELECTION.

From Sarat Bose to Patel:

RECEIVED TELEGRAMME THIS MORNING. READ MAULANA'S AND SUBHAS' STATEMENT DURING JOURNEY FROM SYLHET. IN MY VIEW SETTING UP DR PATTABHI AFTER MAULANA'S WITHDRAWAL UNDESIRABLE. COMING YEAR MORE CRITICAL AND EXCEPTIONAL FROM EVERY VIEWPOINT THAN 1937. STRONGLY FEEL NO MEMBER WORKING COMMITTEE SHOULD TAKE SIDES IN CONTEST BETWEEN COLLEAGUES. YOUR PROPOSED STATEMENT WOULD ACCENTUATE DISSENSIONS BETWEEN RIGHT AND LEFT-WINGS WHICH SHOULD BE AVOIDED. DR PATTABHI WILL NOT INSPIRE COUNTRY'S

CONFIDENCE IN COMING FIGHT. PLEASE DO NOT DIVIDE CONGRESS.

From Patel to Sarat Bose:

APPRECIATE YOUR TELEGRAMME. NOTHING BUT SENSE OF DUTY COMPELS STATEMENT. DIFFERENCE IS NOT BETWEEN PERSONS BUT PRINCIPLES. IF CONTEST INEVITABLE HOPE IT WILL TAKE PLACE WITHOUT BITTERNESS AND IMPUTATION OF MOTIVES. RE-ELECTION IS HELD TO BE HARMFUL TO COUNTRY'S CAUSE.

The response from the CWC was immediate. On the very same day 24 January 1939, Vallabhbhai Patel and other members of the Working Committee issued a statement opposing the candidature of Subhas. On 26 January 1939 Jawaharlal Nehru issued a statement from Almora in which he stated that 'Subhas Babu should not stand.' The die was cast.

It is now a matter of history that on 29 January 1939, with the full support then of the left wing of Congress, Subhas was elected Congress President, decisively defeating Pattabhi Sitaramaiyya. An allergic response from Gandhi was not long in coming. On 31 January 1939, Gandhi issued a statement from Bardoli in Gujarat on the result of the Presidential election, in which he said:

Mr Subhas Bose has achieved a decisive victory over his opponent Dr Pattabhi Sitaramaiyya. I must confess that from the very beginning I was decidedly against his re-election for reasons into which I need not go. I do not subscribe to his facts or the arguments in his manifestos. I think that his references to his colleagues were unjustified and unworthy. Nevertheless, I am glad of his victory; and since I was instrumental in inducing Dr Pattabhi not to withdraw his name as a candidate when Maulana Sahib withdrew, the defeat is more mine than his. And I am nothing if I do not represent definite principles and policy. Therefore it is plain to me that the delegates do not approve of the principles and policy for which I stand. I rejoice in this defeat ...after all, Subhas Babu is not an enemy of his country.

Meanwhile, at a meeting of the BPCC early in 1939, Sarat had been elected President of the Bengal Provincial Conference, which was held subsequently at Jalpaiguri in Bengal on 4 February 1939. In the course of his Presidential Address, Sarat returned to the attack on the so-called Federal Scheme embodied in the Government of India Act, 1935, and its overall failure to pave the way for *Purna Swaraj*[3]:

> It has however to be recognised that the ideal of *Purna Swaraj* cannot be kept in the foreground without a suitable practical issue. No such issues were, indeed, forthcoming during the last two or three years. But now we have such an issue—the issue of Federation. There is no doubt that some attempt to impose the unwanted Federal Scheme is imminent. The pronouncements of the Viceroy and other high officials are pointers in that direc- tion. This attempt must be resisted with all our strength. It is a mistake to assume that so far as the Congress is concerned, Federation is a dead issue. The Congress has certainly openly and unequivocally condemned it as totally unacceptable. But there are reasons to believe that not all individuals connected with the Congress have been able to make up their minds finally on this question. It is for this reason that the Federal Scheme deserves their special vigilance.
>
> One thing has to be emphasised in this connection. The Federal Scheme embodied in the Government of India Act of 1935 is not a true Federal Constitution at all, inasmuch as its proposed con- stituents are artificial as federal units. These latter have no firm basis in language, geographical situation and political develop- ment. The provinces of British India are partly democratic, the Indian States are almost wholly autocratic. There can be no real federation of units opposed in political principles.
>
> The second objection against the Federal Scheme is that it has totally failed to recognise the principle of self-government for the people of India. It is the old dyarchical system under a new guise, and it proposes to take foreign relations and defence out of the hands of the Indian people for all time. No self-respecting Indian can acquiesce in such a proposition.
>
> The second occasion for reviving the ideal of *Purna Swaraj* is the nearness of a world war. The conflict between the totalitarian and the so-called democratic powers is inevitable. The real oppo- sition in this possible conflict is not between totalitarianism and

[3] *Sarat Chandra Bose Commemoration Volume* (Calcutta: The Sarat Bose Academy, 1982), 356–357.

democracy but between the old and established imperial powers and the new aspirants to empires. It is certain that an attempt will be made to utilise the human and material resources of India on the side of the old Imperialists. This attempt has to be resisted. India does not wish to get entangled in this quarrel of Imperialists of different shades. This conflict is not worth a single Indian life or a single rupee of the Indian exchequer.

At the same time, Sarat was already turning his attention to support his brother Subhas in the latter's capacity as the newly re-elected President of a Congress which had been seriously divided by the election itself. Sarat clearly remained committed to the Congress, wanted to do everything possible to avoid a split, but remained openly hostile to the so-called Federal Scheme and its adverse implications for *Purna Swaraj*. After a two-day meeting on 7–8 February 1939 at the Calcutta residence of Sarat at 1 Woodburn Park and presided over by him, Congressmen and supporters from all over India who had supported the re-election of Subhas met to 'consider the situation arising out of the recent Presidential election' and issued the following statement:

> Congressmen from different parts of India who supported the re-election of Sj. Subhas Chandra Bose met again in the morning of 8 instant at 1 Woodburn Park. Sj Sarat Chandra Bose presided. They discussed the situation arising out of the presidential election in all its aspects and considered the lines that the Congress should now take.

> Out of all these discussions certain tentative conclusions emerged. It was clear that all those present were determined to do everything possible to avoid anything like a split in the Congress.

> It was also the unanimous opinion that in view of the situation in India and abroad, the Congress must stiffen its attitude of hostility towards the Federal Scheme and must utilise the present opportunity for pushing on towards *Purna Swaraj*.

> It was agreed that the programme of work and the lines of action discussed in the Conference should be embodied in draft resolutions, which will soon be issued to the press for eliciting the opinion of Congressmen all over the country. In the light of suggestions from these Congressmen, the tentative resolutions would be given final shape and sent to the All India Congress Committee on the eve of the Tripuri Congress.

The discussion related to all aspects of the Congress programme, special emphasis being laid upon the independence issue, the States' problem, the problems of Congress organisation, release of political prisoners and of continuity of parliamentary work. All those present were exceedingly optimistic that the Tripuri Congress would give a bold lead to the country with a view to winning *Purna Swaraj* at an early date.

Around mid-February 1939, Subhas became seriously ill. He requested of Vallabhbhai Patel that the meeting of the CWC scheduled for 22 February 1939 at Wardha be postponed until the Tripuri Congress which was to begin on 8 March 1939. Instead, and in an obvious bid to fatally undermine Subhas's tenure from the outset and reassert the authority of Gandhi and his supporters, Patel and other right wing members resigned from the Committee, as did Nehru.

Amiya was to observe that this was the same Jawaharlal who had written just a year earlier on 9 January 1938 to Subhas from his home at Anand Bhawan, Allahabad, which Subhas had received in London just prior to his return to India to take up his first tenure as President of the Congress.[4]

Ever since the Calcutta AICC I have been greatly worried over the turn events have been taking. Gandhiji's emotional outburst at the WC (Working Committee) meeting and his subsequent article in the Harijan upset me. This has been followed by other events that are disturbing. I shall not go into all these matters but I shall just point out to you that I find it extraordinarily difficult to accept passively the new orientation of Congress policy which involves a suppression of left elements and mass movements. I have remained quiet in public because I dislike criticising Gandhiji or my WC colleagues publicly. We have to observe a certain decorum and discipline. But this quiet acceptance of others aggression has been hard on me. Matters are likely to come to a head at Haripura or even earlier. We are having a WC meeting at Wardha from 3 February onwards at which you will have to be present. At this meeting we shall draw up the resolutions for Haripura. We have set aside five days for this from 3–8 February.

---

[4] For full text of original letter, see Private Collection of Amiya Nath and Jyotsna Bose.

The last two years have been difficult years but the coming year is going to be far more difficult. Your job will be a terrible one. Of course I want to help you in every way I can and I shall do so. But I do not see how I can continue to associate myself with the present WC or something like it.

Amiya observed with more than a touch of irony, when a real conflict arose between the right wing and left wing of the Congress, Nehru, the so-called leftist, did not seem to find any difficulty or inconvenience in joining the right wing!

The Congress Session at Tripuri in the Central Provinces of India opened on 8 March 1939. Subhas was still seriously ill, and his doctors had recommended that he should not risk the long train journey from Calcutta. Subhas, contrary to this advice, decided to attend the Session. With a dangerously high temperature, Subhas was taken by ambulance from his home to Howrah Station on the west bank of the Hooghly River in Calcutta, accompanied by his mother Prabhavati and his brother Dr Sunil Bose for the long train journey to Tripuri in central India.

Gandhi for his part decided not to go to Tripuri to attend the Congress, on the pretext that his activities in the Princely State of Rajkot were more pressing than his attendance at the annual Congress Session. He seemed content to leave to his lieutenants the messy business of reining in the recalcitrant and rebellious Subhas.

Subhas was, in the event, too ill to deliver his 1939 Presidential Address at Tripuri, and it was read out for him by brother Sarat. Subhas lay in his tent within earshot, straining to hear Sarat and the response of the audience to key messages that he had wanted placed before the people of India:

Coming to home politics, in view of my ill-health, I shall content myself with referring to only a few important problems. In the first place, I must give clear and unequivocal expression to what I have been feeling for some time past, namely, that the time has come for us to raise the issue of Swaraj and submit our national demand to the British Government in the form of an ultimatum. The time is long past when we could have adopted a passive attitude and waited for the Federal Scheme to be imposed on us.

The problem no longer is as to when the Federal Scheme will be forced down our throats. The problem is as to what we should do if the Federal Scheme is conveniently shelved for a few years till peace is stabilized in Europe. There is no doubt that once there is stable peace in Europe, whether through a Four-Power Pact or through some other means, Great Britain will adopt a strong Empire policy. The fact that she is now showing some signs of trying to conciliate the Arabs as against the Jews in Palestine is because she is feeling herself weak in the international sphere.

In my opinion, therefore, we should submit our national demand to the British Government in the form of an ultimatum and give a certain time limit within which a reply is to be expected. If no reply is received within this period or if an unsatisfactory reply is received, we should resort to such sanctions as we possess in order to enforce our national demand. The sanctions that we possess today are mass civil disobedience or Satyagraha. And the British Government today are not in a position to face a major conflict like an All-India Satyagraha for a long period.

It grieves me to find that there are people in the Congress who are so pessimistic as to think that the time is not ripe for a major assault on British Imperialism. But looking at the situation in a thoroughly realistic manner, I do not see the slightest ground for pessimism. With Congress in power in eight provinces, the strength and prestige of our national organisation have gone up. The mass movement has made considerable headway throughout British India. And last but not the least, there is an unprecedented awakening in the Indian States. What more opportune moment could we find in our national history for a final advance in the direction of Swaraj particularly when the international situation is favourable to us?

Speaking as a cold-blooded realist, I may say that all the facts of the present-day situation are so much to our advantage that one should entertain the highest degree of optimism. If only we sink our differences, pool all our resources and pull our full weight in the national struggle, we can make our attack on British Imperialism irresistible. Shall we have the political foresight to make the most of our present favourable position or shall we miss this opportunity, which is a rare opportunity in the life-time of a nation?

...Next, we shall have to work in close co-operation with all anti-imperialist organisations in the country particularly the kisan (peasant) movement and the trade union movement. All the radical elements in the country must work in close harmony and co-operation and the efforts of all anti-imperialist organisations must converge in the direction of a final assault on British Imperialism.

On all earlier occasions it had been left to the newly elected Congress President to nominate his Working Committee for the year ahead. The Gandhian right wing of Congress had lost the 1939 Presidential Election, but they were determined to defeat the Bose Brothers at the Tripuri Congress Session. Sarat himself had not joined others in resigning from the existing Working Committee, but given that all other members including Nehru had done so, there was in effect no Working Committee when the Congress Session convened at Tripuri.

At Tripuri, the Congress right wing thus decided to curb the powers of the President to nominate the other 14 members of the CWC, in addition to himself. A resolution to that effect moved by Govind Bhallav Pant and referred to as the Pant Resolution, stated:

> In view of various misunderstandings that have arisen in the Congress and the country on account of the controversies in connection with the Presidential Election and after, it is desirable that the Congress should clarify the position and declare its general policy.

> This Congress declares its firm adherence to the fundamental policies which have governed its programme in the past years under the guidance of Mahatma Gandhi and is definitely of opinion that there should be no break in these policies and they should continue to govern the Congress programme in future. This Congress expresses its confidence in the work of the Working Committee which functioned during the last year and regrets any aspersions should have been cast against any of its members.

> In view of the critical situation that may develop... Gandhi alone can lead the Congress and the country to victory during such a crisis, the Congress regards it as imperative that the Congress executive should command his implicit confidence and requests the President to nominate the Working Committee in accordance with the wishes of Gandhiji.

Supporters of the Bose Brothers moved several proposed amendments to the Pant Resolution, but they were not accepted by the majority of the delegates, principally because the left wing of the Congress was now seriously divided. In what was seen by many as a betrayal of the Bose Brothers, the Congress Socialist

Party led by Jayprakash Narayan as the largest left-wing Party, did not vote against the Pant Resolution. Thus, while Subhas won the Presidential Election, he was ultimately defeated by the Gandhian right wing at Tripuri, which through the medium of the Pant Resolution, restored and reinforced the overriding authority of Gandhi in Congress politics.

On 21 March 1939, while Subhas was still confined to his sickbed, Sarat wrote a letter to Gandhi from his home at 1 Woodburn Park Calcutta, narrating his experiences at the Tripuri Congress:

My dear Mahatmaji

I went to Jamadoba (near Dhanbad) on Saturday last (the 18th instant) to see for myself what progress (if any) Subhas was making towards recovery. On my return to Calcutta last Sunday night (the 19th instant) I found your telegramme of the 18th instant waiting for me.

First, about Subhas. I am happy to say that his fever is being steadily brought under control. During the last two days, it has not gone beyond 101.2 or 101.4. The mischief in the lungs still remains. But there is also a noticeable improvement in the condition of the right lung. The congestion in the left lung remains as before. At Jamadoba he has been strictly following the treatment, rest, and diet prescribed for him. If there is no setback, we may expect him to be free from fever in a week or so and the mischief in the lungs to disappear in a fortnight or so.

When I wired to you on the 17th saying, 'Have decided not to come Delhi now', etc., I felt that it would be better to give you in detail on a future occasion my reasons for coming to that decision. But as you found my telegram 'perplexing' and have suggested my writing, I shall indicate as shortly as possible my reason for coming to that decision.

What I saw and heard at Tripuri during the seven days I was there was an eye opener to me. The exhibition of truth and non-violence that I saw in persons whom the public look upon as your chosen disciples and representatives has (to use your own words) 'stunk in my nostrils'! The propaganda that was carried on by them there against the Rashtrapati [President] and those who happen to share his political views was thoroughly mean, malicious and vindictive, and utterly devoid of even the semblance of truth and non-violence.

I had heard from Subhas on his return from Wardha about the middle of last month that you had told him (among other things) that no obstruction would be thrown in his way. At Tripuri those who swear by you in public offered him nothing but obstruction, and, for gaining their end, took the fullest and meanest advantage of his illness. Some ex-members of the Working Committee even went the length of carrying on an insidious and incessant propaganda that the Rashtrapati's illness was 'fake', was only a political illness.

What I have stated above were facts of common knowledge at Tripuri and I feel sure that thousands of people who were there could testify to them. Shri Bhulabhai Desai went even further and sitting on the dais in the Subjects Committee pandal went on describing the Rashtrapati and his barrister brother (meaning myself) as 'Scoundrels'. In the camps, in the kitchens, almost everywhere the same propaganda was going on. The whole atmosphere was nauseating. It was because of that atmosphere that all attempts to change the wording of Shri Govind Bhallav Pant's resolution failed. The declared attitude of some ex-members of the Working Committee and some of the Congress Ministers was that 'not a word, not a comma was to be changed'.

The proceedings of the open session of the Congress were not conducted fairly or in a proper spirit. A motion by Shri K. F. Nariman (of which due notice had been given) that the consideration of Shri G. B. Pant's resolution should be postponed in view of the alarming state of the Rashtrapati's health was not allowed by Maulana Sahib to be moved on the second day of the session, for reasons which were known only to himself and the groups surrounding him. Shri K. F. Nariman having been thus choked off, Shri M. S. Aney's motion for referring Shri Govind Ballabh Pant's resolution to the AICC was taken up and was declared carried by Maulana Sahib.

Those two incidents led to demonstration on the part of a large number of delegates from Bengal, the U.P., the Punjab and some other provinces for a considerable time, which I eventually succeeded in controlling. When I was trying to pacify the demonstrators and requesting them to give Pandit Jawaharlal a hearing and had almost succeeded, the latter altogether lost control over himself and taking his stand near the microphone began describing the demonstrators as 'hooligans, guilty of fascism, goondaism and so on'. Nevertheless, I succeeded in restoring order and after a long speech by Pandit Jawaharlal Nehru, Shri M. S. Aney was allowed to ask leave of the House to withdraw his motion, which was granted. Immediately thereafter Shri Jayprakash Narain was called upon to move the resolution on 'Federation and the National Demand'. I suggested to Maulana Sahib that as it was already late the resolution may be taken up the next day but that suggestion did not find favour with him. An amendment to it sought to be moved by me was shut out by Maulana Sahib on the ground of want of notice, though I pointed out to him that the amendment was the same as moved by Pandit Lakshmi Kanta Moitra, M.L.A., in the Subjects Committee explained to him the reasons as to why I could not send in the notice that afternoon, told him that I was prepared to give notice immediately and requested him to take up the amendment next day.

This slight concession was refused, even though it was well-known to Maulana Sahib that Pandit Jawaharlal had not given notice of his resolution on 'Federation and the National Demand' and that it could be taken up in the Subjects Committee and the Congress only because the Rashtrapati had waived the rule requiring notice. In fact, the Rashtrapati had allowed Pandit Jawaharlal to move as many as six resolutions in the Subjects Committee though no notice had been given by him of any of them. I may also note in passing that no notice had been given of Shri G. B. Pant's resolution either and it could only be taken up in the Subjects Committee because the Rashtrapati had waived the rule requiring notice and had also waived the objection that its last paragraph was against the constitution of the Congress. I may add in this connection that Shri Rajendra Prasad's amendment to the resolution regarding next year's venue of the Congress was allowed to be moved by the Maulana Sahib, though no notice had been given. I can give more instances of unfairness and impropriety in the conduct of the proceedings of the Congress but I shall desist from doing so now.

All these have convinced me that two alternatives are open to men who are not lost to all sense of honour and decency, viz, allow the group which uses and shelters behind your name to rule the Congress without any opposition or put up a strong and determined and at the same time an honourable fight against them and remove them from a position they have abused. My mind has been oscillating between these two alternatives but at the moment of writing I feel we should adopt the latter alternative. This is not merely my personal opinion, it is shared by a very large body of delegates. Even if 'your representatives' are allowed to run the Congress with the support of your name, influence and prestige, this will and can continue only during your lifetime. In your absence, it will not take long for the public to sweep them aside. In a public statement after the Presidential election you described the result as a defeat of yourself. Permit me please to say that the description was totally wrong since the public had not been called upon to declare for or against yourself. There is of course some justification for describing it as a defeat for 'the High Command', i.e., of the ruling coterie of which Sardar Patel is the shining light.

We may find ourselves in the near future almost at the parting of the ways. Nevertheless, I feel that you are the only person who can pull the Congress out of the rut into which it has descended on account of the action and conduct of those who constantly take your name. It is up to you now to ascertain the truth for yourself and act accordingly. I realise that the state of your health may stand in the way of making an independent investigation into the truth of what I have said. But the time has come for you to refuse to be guided or influenced in any way by exparte reports that may be given to you. In this connection, I cannot help giving expression to a view that is held by a large number of people in the country, viz, that it is the country's misfortune that since your health began to fail, you have been cut off to a large extent from first hand knowledge and information and have become unconsciously and increasingly dependent on the group that always surrounds you and has your ear. There are honest decent people in the Congress and country who do not like the idea of running to you all the time worrying you in spite of your ill health and carrying tales to you. Their attitude has possibly put them at disadvantage so far as you are concerned. But they are still prepared to maintain their attitude if they can feel assured that you will put your foot down on all that is mean, ignoble, malicious and vindictive in the 'High Command', of which we had such a painful exhibition in Tripuri. That is the real 'corruption' which the Congress has to be purged of. The corruption we have been talking of since December last is far less serious in comparison.

My letter would be incomplete without a reference to the attitude of our Congress Ministers present at Tripuri. Those who were put in office with the avowed object of combating and wrecking the Government of India Act did their level best to wreck the Congress by converting it into a machine to register their will and make secure their own position which they thought had been threatened by the Presidential election.

At Tripuri the Congress Ministers quite openly used their influence—moral and material—in favour of one side and it is to this factor that the final outcome must above everything else be attributed. If this domination of the Congress by the Ministers continues, the Congress will end by becoming the mouthpiece of a new vested interest, and there will no longer be any free and democratic formulation of policies and programmes by it.

I desire to repeat once more that what I have said represents not merely my personal view but a large body of opinion in the country. I have purposely refrained from writing about the Congress programme laid down in the resolutions at Tripuri or, to be more accurate, the absence of any programme in those resolutions. I reserve it for a future occasion. In addition to what I have said, I ought to tell you that my own health is a very serious impediment in the way of my coming to you now. The physical and mental strain I had to undergo at Tripuri has wrecked it seriously and I feel I need respite from active political work for a few weeks. I shall try to meet you after the Easter holidays.

In the meantime, I am anxious to learn about your health and hope that we shall continue to hear about a steady improvement. I should also like to know what your tour programme for the next few weeks is, so that I may keep in touch with you at least through letters and telegrams whenever necessary.

With pronams,
Yours affly
Sarat Chandra Bose

Gandhi chose to respond to Sarat through Nehru, who wrote on 24 March 1939:

My dear Sarat,

Gandhiji arrived here this morning to see Maulana Azad and he showed me your letter to him dated the 21st March. I have read this with sorrow and surprise. There are, as we all know, differences of opinion amongst leading Congressmen on matters of policy and programme and we have often given expression to our respective view-points, although we have succeeded in pulling together. Generally speaking, Gandhiji's programme has been followed by the Congress and his leadership accepted.... It is not for me to say anything about the acting President's rulings or conduct. But I am sure you will agree with me on reconsideration that he occupied a very difficult position and conducted the proceedings with dignity and fairness. He might have stretched a point in allowing you to move your amendment to the resolution on the 'National Demand', but as it happens, you had full scope to place your point of view before the Congress. In the voting you were the one and only person who opposed the resolution. May I say how astonished I was at this for I could not conceive any Congressman who considered himself a Leftist opposing it.

...Take the question of a coalition ministry in Bengal. This may be conceivable under certain circumstances, but it is definitely a Rightist move now. I do not understand why you should desire a coalition ministry in Bengal, under dubious auspices, and yet object to the Congress ministries elsewhere which function, whatever their failings, under better circumstances.

In an acerbic and combative reply to Nehru on 4 April 1939, Sarat wrote:

The chapter of misunderstandings opened at Bardoli, where a particular group met to decide the question of the Presidentship of the Congress for the next year and arrived at certain decisions and arrangements without the knowledge and behind the back of the President and some other members of the Working Committee. Those strange and clandestine proceedings were and are wholly beyond my understanding. I wonder if you find in them that faith and understanding between colleagues to which you say you attach so much importance. I wonder if you can find any justification for the unwillingness to take the President into confidence over a matter which vitally concerned both the Congress and himself and in which he was entitled to have his say, unless that justification be sheer personal hostility towards him or reluctance to be straightforward with him.

...I am not surprised that you should find it difficult to accept certain things I said about certain individuals. A person does not like to believe such things of other men, far less of his colleagues. And you, with your temperament and training, must find it more difficult still to think ill of the set with which you have cast yourself. Do we not find evidence of this incapacity to believe that there are systems of values and standards of conduct in this world different from those followed at Eton and Harrow, among the members of the present British Government? They believe the best about Hitler and Mussolini and are profoundly shocked when they find the dictators unappreciative of cricket, the old school tie etc.

...You write that you were astonished to find me opposing the National Demand sponsored by you. No occasion for formally opposing the resolution would have arisen if I had been allowed to move my amendment. But since this opportunity was not given me, I felt that I had to record my formal protest against the resolution and I gave reasons for that attitude in my speech. In my opinion it was an ineffective, colourless demand which was not likely to lead us anywhere. Similar resolutions had been adopted year after year and they neither convinced our enemies nor heartened our people in the absence of a definite intention and plan to act if they were not accepted. In opposing the suggestion for a time limit you spoke as if a time limit was a new thing in the history of the Congress.

...As regards the desirability or otherwise of a Coalition Ministry in Bengal, I have tried in the past at meetings of the Working Committee to explain my views. Office acceptance is definitely a Rightist move. But once the Congress decides in favour of it, no distinction can or should, in my opinion, be drawn between so-called Congress provinces and so-called non-Congress provinces, provided the Congress programme is also accepted in the latter. After all, it is only an accident that the Congress Party is in a majority in some provinces—an accident which in turn depends upon the accident that Hindus find themselves in a majority in these provinces.

...Before I finish this letter, I should like to correct one more mistake. It is assumed, often as a matter of course, that what I write represents the views of Subhas also. This is not invariably the case for I do not and cannot consult Subhas about everything, nor does he do so. In this particular case, I have forwarded a copy of my letter to Gandhiji to him and it is for him to say in what matters he agrees with me and in what matters he does not. I do not hold any power of attorney for him.

Meanwhile Subhas himself wrote to Gandhi from Jealgora on 29 and 31 March 1939 to express his own disquiet about what had transpired at Tripuri:

My dear Mahatmaji,

I received your letter of the 24th instant from the train along with the enclosures.

Firstly, my brother Sarat wrote to you on his own. You will see from his letter that he got your telegram on his return to Calcutta from here and then he wrote to you. If he had not got your telegram, I doubt if he would have written.

There are, of course, certain things in his letter which echo my feelings. But that is a different matter. The main problem appears to me as to whether both parties can forget the past and work together. That depends entirely on you. If you can command the confidence of both parties by taking up a truly non-partisan attitude, then you can save the Congress and restore national unity.

I am, temperamentally, not a vindictive person and I do not nurse grievances. In a way, I have the mentality of a boxer—that is, to shake hands smilingly when the boxing-bout is over and take the result in a sporting spirit.

Secondly, in spite of all the representations that I have been receiving, I take the Pant resolution as it has been passed by the Congress. We must give effect to it. I myself allowed the resolution to be moved and discussed, despite the ultra vires clause in it. How can I go back on it?

Thirdly, there are two alternatives before you (i) either to accommodate our views with regard to the composition of the new Working Committee, or (ii) to insist on your views in their entirety. In the case of the latter, we may come to the parting of the ways.

Fourthly, I am prepared to do all that is humanly possible for me to expedite the formation of the new Working Committee and the summoning of the Working Committee and AICC. But I am so sorry that it is not possible for me to come to Delhi now (Dr Sunil has wired to you this morning on this point). I got your telegram only yesterday.

Fifthly, I was surprised to learn from your letter that the AICC Office had not sent you a copy of Pant's resolution. (This has since been done.) I was still more surprised that the resolution had not been brought to your notice till you came to Allahabad. At Tripuri, the air was thick with the rumour that the resolution had your fullest support. A statement to that effect also appeared in the Delhi press while we were at Tripuri.

Sixthly, I have not the slightest desire to stick to office. But I do not see reason for resigning because I am ill. No President resigned when he was in prison, for instance. I may tell you that great pressure is being brought to bear on me to resign.

I am resisting because my resignation will mean a new phase in Congress politics which I want to avoid till the last.

I have been attending to urgent A.I.C.C. work during the last few days.

I shall write to you again tomorrow or the day after. I am progressing. I hope your blood pressure will soon go down again.

With pronams.
Yours affectionately
Subhas

P.S. This letter is not exactly a reply to yours. I have just jotted down the points which were in my mind. I wanted to convey them to you.

In a subsequent letter soon after on 31 March 1939, Subhas appealed to Gandhi:

If we come to a parting of the ways, a bitter civil war will commence and whatever be the upshot of it—the Congress will be weakened for some time to come and the benefit will be reaped by the British Government. It is in your hands to save the Congress and the country from this calamity.... There is no doubt that there is today a wide gulf between the two main parties or blocs in the Congress. But the gulf can yet be bridged—that by you.

And further in the letter:

The letter of my brother Sarat to you shows that he is feeling very bitter. This, I presume, is due to largely to his experiences at Tripuri, because he had no such feeling when he left Calcutta for Tripuri. Naturally, he knows more about the happenings at Tripuri than I do—because he could move about freely, meet people and obtain information. But though I was confined to bed I got enough information from several independent sources regarding the attitude of responsible circles politically opposed to us—to make me thoroughly sick of the whole affair. I may say further that, when I left Tripuri, I felt such a loathing and disgust for Congress politics as I have not done for the last nineteen years. Thank God, I have got over that feeling now and have recovered my composure.

Jawahar, in one of his letters (and possibly press statements) remarked that the AICC Office had deteriorated under my Presidentship...

Subhas's angst over the happenings at the Tripuri Congress and subsequent developments but also his unshakeable optimism in the ultimate victory of the progressive forces in the country were clearly expressed in a letter of 17 April 1939 to nephew Amiya in Cambridge. Subhas was at the time in Jamadoba in Bihar where he was convalescing after his serious illness:

My dear Ami,

It is just 2 months since I took to bed. It is the worst attack I have had for a long time. I had broncho-pneumonia with some complications (liver and intestinal infection). This illness coincided with a period of political crisis causing mental anxiety. I had no rest, physical or mental—and had to work in bed, even with high fever. At times it looked as if I would never get well. But the worst is over and I am on the road to recovery. I am going down to Calcutta on the 21st inst. for the annual meeting of the B.P.C.C., A.I.C.C. meeting etc. Though temperature is nearing normal now, weakness will persist for a long time. I should go in for a change in summer, if I could afford it. Let us see.

You get the papers—so you must have seen the statements and counter-statements before the Presidential election and after. You must have also seen the accounts of the Tripuri Congress. The Old Guard had estimated that I would get 25 or 30 per cent votes at the contest—consequently the result came like a bolt from the blue. There was consternation in their ranks. They thought that not only was power (seven Provincial Governments) slipping out of their hands, but the Gandhiites as a body began to feel that their work of 20 years was undone in the course of a day. All their wrath fell on me. Since Deshbandhu's time nobody had given them such a defeat. Then came Gandhiji's statement—he came to the rescue of the Old Guard and called their defeat his own defeat. Opinion among "centrists" began to veer round. They were inclined to support us—but were not prepared to kick out Gandhiji—as they said.

My illness was the most tragic thing that occurred. Tripuri was frankly a defeat for us. But as a Bombay friend told me—it was a case of one sick man lying in bed fighting (1) 12 stalwarts of the Old Guard, (2) Jawaharlal Nehru, (3) seven provincial ministries (who were canvassing for the Old Guard), and (4) the name, influence and prestige of Mahatma Gandhi. He ended by calling our defeat a moral victory.

Our defeat was due further to the betrayal of the CSP leadership and some bungling in tactics on our side. The CSP is now being shaken to its foundations owing to revolt among the rank and file against the Tripuri policy of the leaders. The Communist Party was also sailing with the CSP but at the last moment, the revolt of the rank and file brought about a reversal of the policy decided by the CP leaders (in secret conclave with the CSP leaders).

Nobody has done more harm to me personally and to our cause in this crisis than Pandit Nehru. If he had been with us—we would have had a majority. Even his neutrality would have probably given us a majority. But he was with the Old Guard at Tripuri. His open propaganda against me has done me more harm than the activities of the 12 stalwarts. What a pity!

The immediate future is very uncertain. Negotiations are going on between Gandhiji and myself. Whether they will lead to a settlement or not—it is too early to say. It is even possible that ultimately I may have to resign.

The CSP has gone down in the public estimation, but that does not mean that M. N. Roy has gained. He is touring Bengal and is getting a good reception everywhere. Bengal naturally has a soft corner for him—but whether he will really get a position depends on his allies—whom he aligns himself with. He is too individualist and cannot go in for teamwork. That is a great drawback for him.

The Presidential election and its sequel, however unfortunate, has led to a sharpening of political consciousness. In the long run it will prove to be a great incentive to progress. Whatever the immediate future may have in store for us, we have a bright future. I say this as a realist The progressive and radical forces are 90% with us. I am sorry that Jawahar's position even among his erstwhile admirers has been badly shaken as a result of his stand before and after the presidential election and particularly at Tripuri. The delegates refused to hear him for 1½ hours and they became quiet only when Mejdada [Sarat] appealed to them to be quiet. An unheard-of thing. So long.

Love
Ever yours,
Subhas

Negotiations between Gandhi and Subhas about the formation of the CWC went on for a while but ultimately ended in failure. The AICC met in Calcutta on 29 April 1939, where Subhas tendered his resignation as President of the Congress for 1939 and this was accepted. The AICC then elected Rajendra Prasad as the President in his place.

On 2 May 1939, the new Congress President announced the members of the Working Committee before the commencement of the day's proceedings. Subhas Chandra Bose, Sarat Chandra Bose and Jawaharlal Nehru were not included in the Working Committee. The place of Nehru was not filled but in the places of Sarat and Subhas, Dr Bidhan Chandra Roy and Dr Prafulla Chandra Ghosh were taken onto the Committee.

On hearing of his resignation from the Congress Presidency, Rabindranath Tagore on 3 May 1939 sent a telegram to Subhas[5]:

> The dignity and forebearance which you have shown in the midst of a most aggravating situation has won my admiration and confidence in your leadership. The same perfect decorum has still to be maintained by Bengal for the sake of her own self-respect and thereby to help to turn your apparent defeat into a permanent victory.

It was not for naught that Gandhi at one point described Subhas as 'irrepressible'. Only days after being forced in effect to resign the Presidency of the Congress, Subhas immediately proceeded to form on 3 May 1939 a radical and socialist party within the Congress called the Forward Bloc, with the aim of rallying the entire leftist forces under one banner. To begin with, Forward Bloc functioned within Congress, but in August 1939 when Subhas along with some supporters was effectively suspended from the Congress, the All India Forward Bloc functioned thereafter in effect as a separate and independent political party.

Immediately after the formation of the Forward Bloc and in a further effort to bring the leftist forces together under one banner within Congress, and thus act as a counter weight to the better-organised Congress right wing, Subhas took the initiative to constitute a Left Consolidation Committee. This included

[5] Prasanta Kumar Pal, ed., *Rabindranath and Subhas Chandra* (Visva-Bharati, Shantiniketan, 2001), 42–43.

representatives of the Congress Socialist Party, the Communist Party of India, All India Kisan Sabha (Peasants' Organisation) as well as a group known as Royists formed under the leadership of the erstwhile Comintern leader M. N. Roy. Subhas became the Chairman of this Left Consolidation Committee, but it was never able to gain traction and gradually faded from view.

Subhas was beginning to realise that with his effective ouster from the Congress and the inability of the Left to achieve strength through unity, he was left with very limited options to continue his struggle for independence from inside India. Thus, while continuing to pursue the opportunities which arose, he began to contemplate possible avenues of external assistance to relaunch the fight against British rule in India.

* * *

Quite unexpectedly sometime in late May 1939, Amiya received a message from Uncle Subhas asking him to return to India from Cambridge during his University vacation:

> Uncle Subhas told me that on the way to India I should spend a few days in Vienna and meet with Frau Heddy Fullop-Miller (whom I had met earlier in Badgastein in December 1937). I travelled to Vienna as soon as the long vacation of Cambridge University began.
>
> After I arrived in Vienna, Frau Heddy took me to meet Prof. Dr Stiegler who was one of the founder members of the Nazi Party. By then the Anschluss had taken place and Austria was under German occupation. Prof. Stiegler through his contacts with the German Government in Berlin arranged for a meeting between me and one Mr Zellner.
>
> I met Mr Zellner in Vienna a few days later. We had dinner at the Imperial Hotel in Vienna on two occasions. He introduced himself as a senior member of the German Export Council. I came to know later that he was an important member of the Nazi Party but I am not sure that Zellner was his real name. In the course of our conversations Mr Zellner hinted that a European war that same year was very likely.
>
> I arrived in India sometime towards the end of June 1939. I reported to Uncle Subhas all that I had been told by Mr Zellner

in Vienna and that war was imminent. In the course of my conversations with Uncle it became obvious to me that I had been able to confirm some key information about the unfolding situation in Europe.

Amiya further recounted the events of summer 1939.

Soon after my return home to Calcutta, Satya Ranjan Bakshi (a colleague and a close friend of the brothers) succeeded at considerable risk to himself in arranging for several volumes of the police dossier on Uncle Subhas to be brought over to him at night to his then residence at 38/2 Elgin Road. By 1939 Uncle Subhas and his supporters had been able to make close contacts with the Indian police and administrative services all over India. Despite several efforts on the part of Uncle Subhas and his co-workers they had been unable to infiltrate the British Indian Army, the backbone of the British Raj.

Over a period of about a week, the police files concerning Uncle Subhas were smuggled out of the intelligence headquarters on Elysium Row (now Lord Sinha Road), brought to him after midnight, and then taken back at dawn. Uncle Subhas and I went through the entire dossier in the course of seven nights. Among other matters, the information contained in these files gave Uncle Subhas quite a detailed picture of the clandestine activities of various persons including that of his political co-workers, so-called friends, and even some of his own relatives. He was rather surprised to learn about the dubious role of some of the co-workers. He was also forewarned about the surveillance of his movements by one of his cousins. The information gained from the police dossier proved to be of incalculable help to Uncle Subhas in making his plan of escape from India in January 1941, and in steering clear of actual and potential enemies.

When Amiya was preparing to return to Britain to resume his studies in October 1939, his uncle Subhas told him that he had another important assignment for him. Amiya was to be entrusted with the task of delivering a hand-written letter from Subhas to the Soviet Government. In that letter Subhas sought Soviet armed assistance for the liberation of India.

Subhas held meetings with the Communist Party of India (CPI) to enlist their support in approaching the Government of Soviet Russia. According to the CPI representative at those meetings, Soli Batlivala, the CPI agreed and 'acted accordingly'. It was finally decided by Subhas to send a direct communication to Moscow through Amiya. Mr Batlivala recalled what had transpired at those meetings[6]:

> I represented the Communist Party of India in the meetings with Subhas Chandra Bose in October 1939 after the Second World War had just commenced.
>
> I took notes of what he said, because I had to report back to the party.
>
> He said—'I trust Soviet Russia as one State which will not be interested in colonising India. So I would be ready to welcome military help from Soviet Russia to secure our (India's) freedom from the claws of the British Imperialists. I do not see any possibility of securing our freedom without the help of a modern equipped army. The strategy I suggest is: We in India launch a full-scale national movement for freedom; at the same time Soviet Russia marches in from the North, declaring they are coming in allies of nationalist India, which is struggling to free itself from imperialism. He was positive that our country would rise like one man and welcome them. Between the pincers of the Soviet Army and the nationalist upsurge in every village and town of India, the British would be squeezed out in no time'.
>
> He was emphatic that Soviet Russia could be trusted not to take advantage of that situation and occupy the country. Their theory and practice of Revolution, to which they are openly wedded, would not permit them to do so. They would not double-cross us. He, therefore, sought our help to communicate his offer to the Moscow powers. I conveyed this to the CPI Polit Bureau and returned our reply to Netaji. The CPI did not look upon the scheme with favour. They termed it 'opportunism'. But if a message was written and given to them, they would see that it reached Moscow.
>
> He (Subhas) informed us that Amiya was going and could be trusted to contact intelligently. He could have the ropes in Rome, London and further. After some exchanges, the CPI accepted the suggestion and acted accordingly.

---

[6] Soli Batlivala was a prominent, Kolkata-based member of the Communist Party of India, who responded to a request for information from Amiya with this hand-written, self-explanatory message dated 6 March 1972.

Thus, Amiya started on his journey back to England with two letters to deliver—one from the CPI to the British Communist Party and the other from Subhas Chandra Bose to the Soviet Government. Amiya recalled:

> Uncle Subhas told my father about my 'Russian' mission, but he requested him not to disclose it to my mother. He assured him that if anything were to go wrong, he would himself disclose the whole matter to my mother. Such was the level of trust between the brothers. Sarat not only agreed to Subhas taking such an enormous risk with his own life but also with his son's life.
>
> I was thus ready to embark on my mission. Uncle Subhas advised me to carry the two messages in the pocket of my overcoat. As I were to find out later, he clearly had a good understanding of the minds of intelligence officers. I said to Uncle—'If I get caught with your message, you would certainly be hanged'. He replied that he would gladly take that risk.
>
> Thus in October 1939, I proceeded to Bombay, accompanied by my parents, Sarat and Bivabati, and Uncle Subhas. Uncle Subhas had asked me to book a passage to Europe on an Italian steamer. But when we arrived in Bombay, I was told by the Superintendent of Police of Bombay that I would not be permitted to return to Europe by an Italian boat (though in October 1939 Italy still had not entered the war). So arrangements had to be made for me to travel by the Imperial Airways. So we proceeded to Poona from where I took the Tata Airways flight from Poona to Karachi.
>
> From Karachi I took a seaplane to Basra where we stopped for the night. From there to Corfu, Greece for another overnight halt, and finally to Bordeaux in France. I spent the night in Bordeaux and next morning left for Poole seaport in England.
>
> On landing at Poole seaport as I came down from the seaplane I was met by an officer of the New Scotland Yard. In perfect Bengali, he asked me to follow him. I wondered what he knew. It was October and quite cold but I could feel my shirt becoming wet with perspiration. I was interrogated for nearly three hours. Several of my books in the suitcase were taken away. The interrogating officer also confiscated my shaving stick and my spare shoes. But my overcoat pockets were not searched. I took my suitcase and overcoat and hurried along to board the train to London.
>
> As planned, I contacted Rajani Palme Dutt and handed him the message from CPI for the CPGB. He told me that I should go to a

hotel in Bristol from where a Soviet agent would collect Subhas' message to the Soviet Government. I proceeded accordingly and the message was collected from me by the designated agent at the Bristol hotel.

We know that there was no response from the Soviet Government to the proposal from Subhas Chandra Bose. Somewhere in the Soviet archives can be found that letter from Uncle Subhas for armed assistance to India in her struggle for independence.

* * *

Meanwhile on 3 September 1939 Subhas, while addressing a huge public meeting of around 200,000 people on the sea beach in Madras, had been informed by a member of the audience about the declaration of war by Britain on Germany. He declared at that public meeting that this was India's 'golden opportunity' to strike for her freedom, and soon after initiated efforts to mobilise the Indian people for immediate resumption of the national struggle. That same day, the Viceroy Lord Linlithgow declared India as a belligerent on the side of Britain and issued an ordinance containing the most stringent powers for the suppression of internal disorder.

In *The Indian Struggle,* Subhas wrote[7]:

On September 6th [1939], Mahatma Gandhi, after meeting the Viceroy Lord Linlithgow, issued a press statement saying that in spite of the differences between India and Britain on the question of Indian independence, India should cooperate with Britain in her hour of danger. This statement came as a bombshell to the Indian people, who since 1927, had been taught by the Congress leaders to regard the next war as a unique opportunity for winning freedom. Following the above statement of Gandhi, many leaders belonging to the Gandhi Wing began to make public declarations to the effect that though they demanded freedom for India, they wanted Britain to win the war. As this sort of propaganda was likely to have a very unfortunate effect on Indian public opinion, the Forward Bloc, which was by now an all-India organization, commenced counter-propaganda on a large scale. As against the Gandhi Wing, the Forward Bloc took the line that the Congress had since 1927 repeatedly declared that India should not cooperate in

[7] Bose, *The Indian Struggle,* 426–428.

Britain's war and that the Congress should now put that policy into practice. The members of the Forward Bloc also declared openly that they did not want Britain to win the war because only after the defeat and break-up of the British Empire could India hope to be free.

Apart from the general propaganda carried on by the Forward Bloc, the writer made a lecture tour throughout the country, in the course of which he must have addressed about a thousand meetings in the course of ten months.

[Author: These meetings included a well-attended Anti-Imperialist Conference of October 1939 in Nagpur Central Provinces, and an All India Students' Conference held at Delhi in January 1940 over which Subhas presided. His Presidential address at the Students' Conference provides a firm directive to the political line that he wanted his country to follow: '...*we now have a supreme opportunity for winning liberty for India. Such a rare opportunity we can miss only at our own peril. Posterity will never forgive us if we do not rise to the occasion'.*]

That the British Government should permit such anti-British and anti-war propaganda came as a surprise to many, including the writer. The fact, however, was that the British Government was afraid that if drastic measures were taken against the Forward Bloc, it would provoke the Congress and the public in general to launch a campaign of passive resistance against the British Government. Because of sheer nervousness on the part of the British Government, the Forward Bloc was able to continue its anti-British and anti-war propaganda, though in the course of this propaganda many members were thrown into prison.

The propaganda of the Forward Bloc found an enthusiastic echo all over India. Mahatma Gandhi and his followers thereupon realized that the policy of cooperation with Britain would not find any support among the public and would surely lead to the loss of their influence and popularity. Consequently, they began to alter their attitude gradually.

More strange even than Gandhi's attitude was the attitude of Nehru. From 1927 to 1938, he had figured prominently in all the anti-war resolutions of the Congress. Consequently, when the war broke out, people naturally expected him to take the lead in an anti-war policy.... Not only did Nehru not adopt this policy, but he used all his influence in order to prevent the Congress from embarrassing the British Government while the war was on.

In March 1940, the annual session of the Congress was held at Ramgarh in Bihar, which was indecisive on the question of an anti-war policy. At the same time an All India Anti-Compromise Conference was also held at Ramgarh convened by the Forward Bloc and Kisan Sabha. Maulana Azad presided over the Ramgarh Session of Congress while Subhas chaired the Anti-Compromise Conference.

Amiya observed that it became known throughout the country and outside that the latter meeting was attended by a larger number of persons and aroused greater enthusiasm among the people than the Ramgarh Session of Congress. Amiya also recorded that Aung San who later took a leading role in the freedom struggle in Burma, went to Ramgarh at that time and had long discussions with Subhas. Aung San also met with Sarat in Calcutta. In his book on Burma's Constitution, the Burmese political leader Dr Maung Maung wrote[8]:

> Thakin Aung San visited India in March that year (1940) to attend the Ramgarh Session of the Indian National Congress. With him were Thakin Than Tun who was destined to become the top Communist in Burma and his bitter political enemy. The delegation visited places and met several leaders, and Aung San came back more impressed with Subhas Chandra Bose than with Mahatma Gandhi.

In June 1940, Subhas had what would prove to be his last meeting with Gandhi. In what he describes in *The Indian Struggle* as a 'long hearty talk', Subhas sought once again to convince the Mahatma of the need for him to 'come forward and launch his campaign of passive resistance' but Gandhi remained non-committal. Gandhi insisted that the country was not prepared for a fight and any attempt to precipitate it would do more harm than good to India, but added that 'if his (the writer's) efforts to win freedom for India succeeded, then his (Gandhi's) telegram of congratulations would be the first that the writer would receive.'[9]

Thus by this time there remained a clear division in the ranks of the Indian freedom fighters, the one led by Gandhi which still emphasised a negotiated, non-violent solution, and

---

[8] Maung Maung, *Burma's Constitution* (Martinus Nijhoff, 1959), 43–44.
[9] Bose, *The Indian Struggle*, 431–432.

the other led by Subhas which posited that independence would only materialise through armed struggle.

Subhas was arrested soon after on 3 July 1940 and detained without trial, but the Forward Bloc national civil disobedience campaign for immediate independence continued apace. In October 1940, Gandhi, now sensing the revolutionary stirrings both among the public-at-large and within and across the ranks of the Congress, decided finally to commence resistance to India's involvement in the British war effort, but this time not on a mass scale as before in the early 1920s and 1930s. Thus by October 1940, both Congress and Forward Bloc were committed to an anti-British and anti-war policy albeit adopting different methods of struggle and with varying intensity.

The campaign began the following month in November 1940 and retribution from the British authorities was swift. Within a short time, all the Congress Ministers in the eight Congress-controlled Provinces were arrested and imprisoned along with hundreds of other influential persons, and thousands of others. Along with the earlier suspension by the Viceroy on 11 September 1939 for the duration of the war, of the federal provisions of the Government of India Act of 1935, this crackdown spelt the end of Congress participation in government until after the end of the war in 1945.

Subhas for his part decided to start a hunger strike in jail and was determined to get out of prison either dead or alive. He began a fast unto death on 29 November 1940. The British Government became nervous and apprehensive of the possible repercussions in the country in the case of Subhas's death in prison. He was thus released unconditionally on 5 December 1940 and brought to his residence at 38/2 Elgin Road, Calcutta. Though Subhas was a free man, a host of plain clothes policemen and police agents kept a close watch on the house around the clock.

Subhas began making plans to escape from India. He had detailed private discussions about this matter with Sarat at 1 Woodburn Park. Preparations for the escape and knowledge of the arrangements were kept to a very intimate circle, without any single person with the exception of Sarat, knowing the full plan. Extreme caution had to be exercised, not least as Subhas already knew from his earlier secret perusal of police dossiers together with Amiya that there were informers around the house with links to the police authorities.

In the early hours of 17 January 1941, Subhas in disguise as a Pathan slipped out of the house on Elgin Road and after a perilous journey arrived in Peshawar. Subhas crossed the Indo-Afghan border and arrived in Kabul, where he was delayed for about two months. Continuing overland, he eventually reached Berlin by air from Moscow sometime in April 1941.

* * *

The year 1939 had marked a turning-point for both Subhas and Sarat. While Subhas was fully preoccupied in promoting the Forward Bloc agenda of 'an uncompromising struggle with British Imperialism for winning Indian independence', Sarat pursued the same policy both inside and outside the Bengal Legislative Assembly. At the historic Bengal Political Congress in Jalpaiguri (north Bengal) in late 1939 over which he presided, Sarat endorsed an ultimatum to the British Government for immediate transfer of power.

Soon after on 13 December 1939, Sarat moved a resolution in the Bengal Legislative Assembly demanding self-government. The Congress High Command responded by suspending Sarat from the Congress in January 1940. The same month the Bengal Provincial Congress hitherto led by the Bose Brothers was also de-recognised by the Congress High Command and an Ad Hoc Congress was formed both inside and outside the Legislative Assembly. Kiran Sankar Roy became the leader of the Ad Hoc Congress Parliamentary Party in the Bengal Legislative Assembly.

While Gandhi and his followers were coming round to the realisation that Britain was not going to concede an unequivo-cal undertaking on independence for India either now or later, Subhas left India unable to convince them that the war was India's opportunity to strike for her freedom through a mass uprising.

At the same time, Gandhi and Nehru were faced with a conun-drum. The events of 1939 surrounding the election of Subhas at the Tripuri Congress and his obvious widespread popularity had come as 'a bolt from the blue' to both Gandhi and Nehru, and it now seemed in 1941 that that had not abated. They perceived that leadership was slipping out of their hands and out of their control, and as Gandhi became more isolated, signs of friction began to emerge between him and his chosen heir.

The profound and ill-disguised disappointment of the Bose Brothers in the reluctance of both Gandhi and Nehru to take full advantage of the predicament in which Britain found herself at this time, and to confront them head-on, would only have added to the pressure.

Meanwhile in the midst of rising communal tensions in Calcutta and Bengal, Sarat from this time turned his attention to bringing down the communal Muslim League Ministry in Bengal led by well-known Muslim leader Khwaja Nazimuddin. By the latter part of the following year 1941, Sarat as a leader (and still suspended from Congress) of the rebellious Bose Group of the Congress Party in the Bengal Legislative Assembly had together with his old sparring partner Fazlul Haque of the Krishak Praja Party successfully negotiated the formation of the Progressive Coalition Party. This new coalition had the numbers and was thus able to defeat the Muslim League government of the day.

Thereafter, the Progressive Coalition Party being the majority party in the Bengal Legislative Assembly was called upon by the British Governor of Bengal to form a new Ministry under the leadership of Fazlul Haque. It had been intended that Sarat would join the Cabinet as Home Minister, but sadly this was not to be. On 11 December 1941, just a day before the Coalition Ministry was to take office and just a few days after the British and United States Declarations of War on Japan, Sarat was arrested and detained by the British authorities as a 'danger to the security of India'.

At the same time Congress representatives from Bengal belonging to the Gandhi Wing, arrested and detained a little over one year before in October 1940, were suddenly set free. Sarat was taken immediately to Presidency Jail in Calcutta, then via Trichinopolly and Mercara jails to Coonoor in south India, where he was held until September 1945.

With Subhas now out of India and pursuing his vision of internal armed struggle triggered and inspired by outside forces, and Sarat languishing under detention with his own frustrated vision of a free, united and secular India to take its place in a community of resurgent Asian nations, the parting of the ways between Gandhi and the Bose Brothers had come. But there was never to be a complete estrangement between them.

For Subhas and his Provisional Government and Indian National Army (INA) fighting against British forces in Burma and even for a brief time on the soil of Mother India herself, Gandhi remained for them the 'Father of the Nation'. Subhas addressed him as such in appeals broadcast from the battlefields. In one particular instance, Subhas implored Gandhi to maintain his resolve for a united India, in the face of the rising star of Jinnah and increasing strength of his Muslim League and the machinations of the British.

Where Gandhi's attitude to Subhas was concerned, Maulana Azad was to write later in his autobiography *India Wins Freedom*[10]:

> I also saw that Subhas Bose's escape to Germany had made a great impression on Gandhiji. He had not formerly approved many of his actions, but now I found a change in his outlook. Many of his remarks convinced me that he admired the courage and resourcefulness Subhas Bose had displayed in making his escape from India. His admiration for Subhas Bose unconsciously coloured his view about the whole war situation.

Incarcerated as he was far from Calcutta in an isolated corner of south India, Sarat was to all intents and purposes cut off from the mainstream of political developments during the war years. News of the exploits of his younger brother and of politics within India, including the rise of the Muslim League, did reach him, but there was little he could do to offer public comment or otherwise influence the course of events for the four years that he was locked away.

That he did follow unfolding events as best as he could and had strong opinions on certain aspects is known from his surviving jail diaries. He held particularly strong views on the looming threat of partition, and hoped that Gandhi would find the will and the support to stand fast before Jinnah, the British, and for

---

[10] Maulana Abul Kalam Azad, *India Wins Freedom* (Orient Black Swan, 2009), 40.

that matter the growing voices within Congress itself beginning to talk freely of partition.

Gandhi for his part always held Sarat in high esteem. It was then no real surprise that after September 1945 when Sarat was released, an increasingly embattled Gandhi sought the intervention of Amiya to persuade his father to rejoin Gandhi and the Congress. Amiya was to regret later that he had so will-ingly—and successfully—complied with Gandhi's plea for him to persuade his father Sarat to rejoin the Congress and its chosen constitutional path to independence. With hindsight, Amiya felt that a more successful role for Sarat might have been outside the Congress, helping to harness the spirit of revolution which was clearly evident in the country for a time during the course of late 1945 and early 1946.

British intelligence reports from around that time appear to substantiate Amiya's conviction that revolution was in the air, and that the resumption on 21 November 1945 of the trials by the British of INA senior officers now in captivity would provide the spark. Calcutta itself was for several days from this time, in the estimation of British Intelligence Officers, on a knife-edge.

The demonstrations were reportedly initiated by the student community, soon supported by workers organisations including Communist-controlled trade unions. The demonstrations, as noted by the British and other commentators, were markedly non-communal with participation by Muslims, Hindus and Sikhs in significant numbers, and thus in the image of the INA itself. The British also noted that the demonstrations, though widespread and with a semblance of spontaneity, were still well-organised and well-managed, with relatively few casualties.

The British further observed that the demonstrations that had begun in support of the INA were of a political nature, and were markedly 'anti-Police, anti-European and anti-Government'. From one of their reports at the time entitled *Report on the Calcutta Disturbances*:

There is no doubt at all that there is a feeling of great perturbation among the European community. There is a growing feeling that authority in India as represented by the existing government is steadily losing its grip and that if steps are not taken now to reas-sert that authority, a situation will arise by which government will

cease to be able to exercise any authority at all, and the country
will be plunged into an orgy of lawlessness and bloodshed.

And from the conclusion of a related report of the same period
entitled *Calcutta Disturbances in Retrospect*:

Seen in retrospect the results of these three days of agitation,
especially as it was not sponsored by Congress, bodes ill for the
future. The ordinary forces of law and order were very nearly over-
whelmed by the magnitude of their task. There are indications
that many Indians, who ordinarily do not engage in politics, and
many of those who have relations in the (British) Indian Army,
have been captivated by the glamour and ideals of the I.N.A.
I.N.A slogans such as 'Jai Hind' and 'Azad Hind' are now being
introduced for greetings between individuals both in letters and
in speech.

It is an almost universal opinion, even among Indian members
of the public, that the whole handling of the I.N.A Trials, and
indeed the very decision to hold public trials in India, is a mistake on the part of the Government. Since propaganda concerning them has been unbridled and allowed to go unchecked by
Government, the effect has been seriously to influence persons
who otherwise might have kept out of politics and political
trouble, and the Indian Independence Movement as a whole,
and feeling against Government, have received considerable
impetus as a result.

There is a general feeling of pessimism in European circles as to
the future and this feeling is not confined to non-officials. Doubts
have been expressed that the loyalty of the Indian Army, if called
upon to quell disturbances as they may have to be, may have been
affected by this insidious I.N.A propaganda.

This feeling of pessimism is engendered to a large extent by
the opinion—shared alike by many loyal Indians and most
Europeans—that H.M.'s Government and the Government of
India do not know their own minds as to how they will deal with
the immediate future of the Indian political problem. They feel
matters are just drifting for the worse.

There is a general desire that an unequivocal statement should
be given by H.M.'s Government as to what their real intentions
are. It is felt, naturally very strongly amongst the European
Community, that Government should either be determined to
maintain Law and Order in a firm manner until such time as they

are prepared to hand the country over to Indians, or that they should decide to name a date in the near future for the handing over and clear out of the country altogether.

This indecision on the part of H.M.'s Government affects the manner in which Indian Government servants, however loyal they may be, carry out their duties. Strong action and firm decision by Government gives confidence to its servants. If once Government loses the support and loyalty of its Indian servants, it is finished.

This is realised by Congress and other agitators who have already been exhorting the Police in public speeches to turn on their masters at their right moment. Students think it "gratifying" that Indian police officers and men were not prominent in quelling the disturbances, and "Amrita Bazar Patrika" (newspaper) has asked why Indian police officers and men were conspicuous by their absence.

For Sarat, recently released from his long detention in Coonoor and now very much present in Calcutta together with Amiya, the INA-inspired demonstrations could not have failed to persuade them that India was at last awaking from its long slumber. They would have seen clearly that the prophecy of Subhas concerning the catalytic role of the INA was becoming a reality.

Certainly, the British saw fit to place Sarat at the vortex of these events in their argument that 'the whole episode was an organised disturbance,' citing one of the main reasons for this conclusion as 'the choice of locality in which rioting first started and its proximity to Sarat Chandra Bose's house'; and while the British had also acknowledged that the events had not been sponsored by Congress, they still saw the hand of Congress elements in the troubles, and Sarat was by now back in the Congress fold and a prime suspect.

Thus, it is no surprise to find Sarat's name being given prominence in the intelligence reports among the national leaders with whom the British had to reckon, and to whom the British had to turn to bring the situation under control. At least one such report places Sarat in conference with the Governor of Bengal Richard Casey, together with other leaders, on the third day of the demonstrations, that is 23 November 1945.

The British further reported that on the early afternoon of the same day, Congress vehicles carrying loudspeakers went around the worst affected areas in Bhowanipur, south Calcutta (the immediate area of Sarat's 1 Woodburn Park residence) broadcasting a message 'to the effect that Jawaharlal Nehru had sent a wire requesting all students and other elements to cease creating further mischief and that further hooliganism would prejudice Congress interests in the future and be a slur on Congress as a whole'. The demonstrations continued.

So it happened that Sarat did indeed re-enter the Congress mainstream, and in particular did all that he could to bolster Gandhi in the latter's final efforts to prevent partition, first of India itself and then of Bengal. Gandhi also joined Sarat, Muslim leader Suhrawardy and others in Bengal in 1947 in a courageous and ultimately successful campaign to prevent any repeat of the 1946 mass communal killings in Calcutta and Bengal.

Sadly by this time, the star of Gandhi was waning and that of his chosen heir Nehru was in the ascendant. As will be seen in the following chapter, neither the Bose Brothers nor Gandhi was able to stem and overcome the gathering momentum towards the monstrosity of partition. Historians are left to ponder on what might have been had the brothers and Gandhi been able to form from the beginning, a united front in the long struggle for the independence of India.

5

Partition: A Bitter Pill

...the tragic history of the partition of this country and how jaundiced and weak-kneed statesmanship, supped full of an irrational despair, found in that pernicious partition the panacea for the ills of the country. March 1947 to August 1947 was the period of gigantic national suicide...

—Sarat Chandra Bose, inaugural address to All-Bengal
Subhasist Students' Conference, Calcutta, 26 December 1949

As the struggle for independence laboured on, the question of the unity of the many different peoples and communities of what was then imperial India was never far from the minds and considerations of the various protagonists. Among the many different shades of ethnicity, caste, language, region and religion, that of the religious divide between Hindus and Muslims posed probably the greatest preoccupation and challenge. Throughout the pre-independence period of the twentieth century, tensions between the two communities had simmered and periodically surfaced and re-surfaced in different parts of India and had led to bouts of inter-communal riots and strife.

In the early part of the 1920s, Gandhi, as the undisputed leader and dominant figure in the Congress movement, sought to draw the Muslims of India into the burgeoning nationalist movement and into the Congress sphere of influence, though not necessarily into the Congress itself. Gandhi reached out to Indian Muslims in their time of unhappiness and disaffection with the treatment of Turkey in the wake of the Great War, and with a perceived lack of recognition on the part of the victors including Britain, of Turkey's then leadership of the Muslim world via the Caliphate or Khalifate.

Gandhi encouraged the formation of Khilafat Committees throughout the country to give expression to their grievances and for the continuation of the Caliphate. Various commentators have noted better cooperation and relations between Hindus and Muslims at the time of the Khilafat Movement, as it came to be known; but the campaign and the architecture of Khilafat Committees came to an abrupt end with the constitutional abolition of the Caliphate on 3 March 1924 by the new President of the Turkish Republic, Mustafa Kemal Attaturk.

The Khilafat movement swiftly collapsed, and the All-India Muslim League began to re-emerge as the predominant voice of Muslim India, gradually more strident and communal as the years slipped by.

Reflecting the views of Sarat and Subhas, Amiya questioned the political judgement of Gandhi in seeking to ally the Khilafat campaign with the Non-Cooperation Movement.

> The sponsoring of the Khilafat movement by Gandhi was a momentous event in the history of India. He launched his Non-Cooperation Movement in 1920 after entering into an alliance with the Khilafat leaders, brothers Mohammed Ali and Shaukat Ali. It is also in connection with the Khilafat movement that Gandhi came in contact with Maulana Azad for the first time. By taking a leading part in the Khilafat movement, Gandhi introduced religion into Indian politics. Hindu–Muslim participation in the Khilafat Movement was a very undesirable move and it had tragic consequences. It was an opportunism for which there could be no political justification. The Khilafat Movement died when Kemal Pasha exiled the Khalifa Abdul Majid and abolished the Caliphate.

> The Muslim masses were drawn into the Non-Cooperation Movement by Gandhi not on the basis of any socio-economic programme, nor for the attainment of freedom of India, but with the slogan of 'Islam in danger' raised by the Ali brothers. By associating the Indian National Congress with the Karachi Resolution of the Khilafat Conference of 1921, Gandhi exploited religious sentiments of the Muslim masses for political purposes. Such exploitation no doubt gave Gandhi an immediate political gain, but it had unfortunate long-term political consequences.

In September 1924, following the collapse of the Caliphate earlier in the year in March, Gandhi initiated the convening of a Unity Conference in Delhi, which was judged at the time to have been a success. As related by Subhas in *The Indian Struggle*,[1] 'Gandhi

---

[1] Subhas Chandra Bose, *The Indian Struggle* (Natyachinta Foundation Kolkata, 2005), 135.

at the time of the Conference "embarked on a three weeks" fast as a self-imposed penance for the wrongs committed by members of different communities, who by their actions disturbed inter-communal peace in India.' Subhas also noted that a formula was devised at the Conference for promoting unity among the different communities, and a Conciliation Board of fifteen members was set up to intervene whenever and wherever any communal trouble arose; but that in spite of the success of the Conference, practical results did not follow.

Further efforts at this time towards Hindu/Muslim reconciliation were initiated by Swaraj Party leader and founder C. R. Das, through the so-called Bengal Pact brokered by him on behalf of the Party with Bengal's Muslim political leaders. Briefly that agreement, reached during the first half of December 1923, allowed for fairer representation of Muslims in Bengal's political life, consonant with their position as the majority community in Bengal, including in the legislative bodies. Predictably, the agreement raised great passions, with C. R. Das receiving strong support from the Muslim community but mixed reactions from Hindus. Tellingly, the annual session of the Indian National Congress held later in December 1923 in Coconanda in southern India, rejected the Pact.

C. R. Das himself, even in the face of concerted personal attacks on him from some quarters, always insisted that Swaraj could not be won without Hindu/Muslim unity. With the untimely death of Das on 16 June 1925 at the peak of his stature, influence and political power, the Pact disintegrated, leaving a legacy of separatist feeling and bitterness towards the Congress among the Muslim body politic.

At this time, Subhas still languished in jail in far-away Mandalay, with opportunities to influence events in India limited by distance and the British censor. Back home in India, Sarat was a direct witness as communal strife again raised its ugly head in his own city of Calcutta in 1926, with bloody riots and attacks on temples, mosques and gurdwaras. In July of that year in the midst of the troubles, Sarat undertook a tour of several districts of Bengal in an effort to organise a firm response against the riots, but by now he had come to the painful realisation that the Bengal Pact could not be enforced, and that a strategic opportunity had once again been lost by the Congress.

Even with the realisation that the Bengal Pact had not been able to survive the double blow of Congress rejection and the death of its chief architect and source of inspiration C. R. Das, Sarat persisted with his efforts to promote Hindu/Muslim reconciliation and unity. In a letter of 31 July 1926 written to Subhas in Mandalay in the wake of his aforementioned tour of Bengal districts, Sarat wrote from home in Calcutta.

[A]fter staying at Rajshahi for a couple of days, we went to Puttia Natore and Naogaon. In spite of the communal conflict in the adjoining district of Pabna, Rajshahi has kept her head cool. We succeeded in forming a volunteer organisation in the Rajshahi District to combat communal troubles and to do relief work in the villages etc. If all the districts of Bengal work on these lines, I think we shall steadily (though perhaps slowly) solve the communal question. Of course, preachers (specially reliable Mahomedan preachers) and trained instructors are needed to make the volunteer organisation a success. I very much wish I were able to devote more time to this work, but unfortunately that is not to be...

I believe you have read in the papers that the Working Committee of the Congress at their last meeting held in Calcutta have resolved that both communities should accept the resolutions passed at the Unity Conference of 1924 and proceed on those lines. I think it was a right decision. The Pact has become so thoroughly odious to both Hindus and Moslems that it would be wise to drop it and wait for a more suitable opportunity for entering into some other (and if possible, a better) agreement between the two communities. Of one thing I feel certain and that is, separate electorates must go; otherwise the question cannot be solved.

This letter and other evidence belie the politically motivated accusations of that time against the Bose Brothers, to the effect that their support for the Indian revolutionaries who were largely from Bengali Hindu communities, somehow meant that they were not sympathetic to genuine Muslim grievances. Both Sarat and Subhas very clearly understood and believed that the leadership of Bengal could not be properly exercised by anyone who championed only Hindu aspirations.

The constitutional evolution charted by the imperial authorities from the Government of India Act of 1919 to the successor Government of India Act of 1935, via the Simon Commission of

1927 and the three Round Table Conferences in London in the early 1930s, if anything only added fuel to the fires of division and tension between and within Indian communities—particularly between Hindus and Muslims.

Of particular note in this constitutional process was the issuance on 17 August 1932 by the British Government of Labour Party Prime Minister Ramsay MacDonald, of the so-called Communal Award which among other things sought to readjust the electoral balance of communities in provincial legislatures, particularly where representation of Hindus and Muslims was concerned.

Under the earlier Lucknow Pact of 1916 negotiated by the imperial authorities, fairer representation for Muslims had been called for, but a bias towards non-Muslims remained. In Bengal, for example, the ratio of representation was determined as 60 per cent for non-Muslims and 40 per cent for Muslims, which was an improvement at the time for Muslims but still not consistent on religious lines, with Muslims being in the majority in the province.

The Communal Award of separate electorates had the effect of moving representation forward in favour of the Muslim community, and also catered for lesser minorities including Sikhs, Christians, Anglo-Indians and Europeans. A distinct category for the Scheduled or Depressed Classes was withdrawn on the objections of Gandhi under the terms of the so-called Poona Pact of 24 September 1932 between Gandhi and the acknowledged leader of the Depressed Classes Dr B. R. Ambedkar. Gandhi did not object to a larger number of reserved seats for the Depressed Classes instead of having them as a completely separate category.

Sarat and Subhas watched from detention as the Communal Award began to ignite disagreement and tension within their home province of Bengal, not only between the two major Hindu and Muslim communities, but also within the Congress machinery itself. For their part Hindu leaders and representatives were enraged by what they saw as the down-grading of their political status. At the same time, some Muslim leaders slowly but surely began to become incensed by the more intemperate claims of Hindu representatives concerning general qualification and eligibility to participate in the legislatures.

By 1936, during the tenure of Jawaharlal Nehru as Congress President, schisms had begun to emerge between the Congress national leadership and the Congress provincial leadership in Bengal. The BPCC moved to agitate against the Award both as an anti-national and divisive measure between Muslims and Hindus, and more strategically as an inherent component of a new Constitution under the Government of India Act of 1935. Congress at the national level had formally condemned the Act in its entirety, including in its election manifesto. However, while reaffirming policy opposition to the Constitution and specifically the Award, Congress objected to the proposed direct agitation methods of the BPCC.

In one particularly forthright exchange of letters with Nehru, Sarat, now out of detention and Acting President of the BPCC, and clearly perceiving the Communal Award as a formidable barrier to Indian unity, progress and independence, in the course of the exchange wrote (from Simla) on 19 September 1936.[2]

> The Congress election manifesto makes it clear that the rejection in its entirety of the new Act by the Congress inevitably involves the rejection of the communal decision. Even apart from the Act as a whole, the communal decision is wholly unacceptable as being inconsistent with independence and the principles of democracy; it encourages fissiparous and destructive tendencies, hinders the normal growth and consideration of economic and social questions, is a barrier to national progress, and strikes at the root of Indian unity.... The attitude of the Congress is, therefore, not one of indifference or neutrality. It disapproves strongly of the communal decision and would like to end it.
>
> The Congress election manifesto also makes it clear that the Congress will carry on agitation for the rejection of the new Constitution; and, as the rejection of the new Constitution inevitably involves the rejection of the communal decision, it follows that agitation against the new Constitution inevitably involves agitation against the communal decision. Congressmen and Congress-minded men in Bengal feel that agitation for the rejection of the new Constitution and non-agitation for the rejection of the communal decision cannot logically and consistently go together...

[2] *Sarat Chandra Bose Commemoration Volume* (Calcutta: The Sarat Bose Academy, 1982), 230–232.

We regret we cannot agree with the view that the said resolution of the Executive Council of the BPCC is in any way opposed either to the spirit or the letter of the Congress election manifesto. We are of the opinion that agitation by Congress organisations against the communal decision cannot and ought not to be characterised as an 'attempt by one community to get some communal favour from the British Government at the expense of another; nor can it be condemned as "the effort of one community only to change the decision in the face of the opposition of another community." ...We maintain further that a country-wide agitation by the Congress and by organisations subordinate to it against the communal decision is extremely necessary for the purpose of paving the way for an agreed solution of the communal problem.

For his part, Nehru had sought to challenge the wisdom or otherwise of agitation against the Award in Bengal, and at the same time to reassert Congress national authority over the recalcitrant Bengalis. In an earlier letter of 3 September 1936 to Sarat, he had written[3]:

Any big scale organised agitation against the communal decision at this stage will inevitably divert attention from the vast political and economic questions that face India and the World today. It is obvious that the British Government will only yield to considerable pressure. Our job is to organise that pressure. That pressure can come only effectively on the political plane. So far as the communal decision is concerned the Congress has used the strongest language in condemning it. Whenever occasion arises it will repeat this condemnation, as a group and individually. Ordinarily if this matter comes up in the legislature or otherwise it will be the duty of the Congress to express that condemnation by vote. Obviously one cannot bind down any political party to vote in a particular way unless one knows how the matter comes up. But if an organisation has a clear opinion on a subject, voting follows that opinion. It may be necessary to move amendments or to face the situation in some other way. But the general background of the Congress attitude is quite clear.

I must confess to you that my mind is full of the vast upheavals that are taking place in the world today, of the tragic conflict in Spain and the inevitable effect of all this on India...

[3] Ibid., 227–228.

The Bose Brothers, for whom the entire concept of separate electorates was anathema and had drawn trenchant and sustained criticism from them over their political lifetimes, now found themselves treading a fine line between support for fair electoral representation of all communities, and the defence of the legitimate interests of the Hindu community as the largest minority in Bengal. If they could have had their way, they would clearly have done away with the Communal Award altogether. Subhas was to write in *The Indian Struggle*[4]:

> The whole object of the Communal Award embodied in the White Paper seems to be to divide India still further, so that the effect of the meagre constitutional reforms may be sufficiently neutralised. Attempt has been made to provide representation in such a manner that the points of difference among the Indian people, if any, will be given exaggerated expression in the Legislatures and not their points of agreement. The entire scheme is based on the pernicious principle of 'Divide and Rule'. In trying to divide the people, attempt has naturally been made to placate those elements—the Moslems for instance—who according to the official estimate, are likely to be more pro-British than the others...
>
> In 1906, therefore, at the instance of the Viceroy, Lord Minto, and by pre-arrangement, some Moslem leaders for the first time broached the proposal of separate electorate. This demand was at once given effect to, because the constitutional advance made in the Morley-Minto Reforms of 1909 had to be neutralised. Separate electorates for Moslems were continued in the Government of India Act 1919.
>
> The experience of the last fourteen years has shown that in spite of separate electorates and in spite of an official bloc in the Legislatures, the Government could be defeated repeatedly. Therefore the British Government found it necessary to divide the Indian community still further so that the chances of a united opposition against the British Government in the future Legislatures would be considerably minimised. Hence the proposal to give separate electorates to Indian Christians, women, Depressed Classes etc. in addition to Moslems, Europeans, Anglo-Indians and Sikhs.

[4] Bose, *The Indian Struggle*, 365–366.

The principle of 'Division before concession' reminds one of a similar policy followed in Ireland, when Ulster was separated before the Constitution of the Irish Free State was conceded by the British Government. In the case of India, it is needless to say, that on a basis so sectarian and reactionary, no constitution can thrive.

For the Bose Brothers, from the beginning there was never the slightest doubt that all of the peoples and communities which constituted imperial India should become one free, independent, and united sovereign entity. As passionate sons of Bengal, one of the provinces of British India with a Muslim majority, Sarat and Subhas understood more than most the sensitivities of religious divides, and the overriding imperative of resolving these and other differences in the creation of a sovereign nation state.

Sarat and Subhas belonged to that blessed part of humanity which stands for the dignity of the human being regardless of background and differences of birth, caste and creed. The examples of their father Janakinath and of C. R. Das were strong influences, and both brothers imbibed the teachings of Ramakrishna and his disciple Swami Vivekananda.

* * *

By the early years of the 1930s, the broad concept and then mantra of 'Pakistan' had begun to emerge in academic and intellectual circles in both Britain and the subcontinent, and gradually gained political traction and currency through the rest of the decade and thereafter. The genesis of the name seems to have derived from an acronym resting on Punjab, Afghan (North West Frontier) Province, Kashmir, Sind and BaluchisTAN, thus PAKSTAN and changed to Pakistan for ease of pronunciation. This may have first been articulated by a Punjabi Indian student in England Choudry Rahmat Ali (1895–1951), in a 1933 pamphlet written while he was at Cambridge University entitled: 'Now or Never: Are we to Live or Perish Forever' also termed by him as 'The Pakistan Declaration.'

Muslim leader Mohammed Ali Jinnah paid little heed at first, and in a meeting with Rahmat Ali and his friends in 1934 where they sought Jinnah's support for the Pakistan concept, Jinnah was less than enthusiastic and is widely reported to have counselled them: 'My dear boys, don't be in a hurry: let the waters flow and they will find their own level.'

Writing in 1934, Subhas was to observe in *The Indian Struggle*[5]:

> Pakistan is, of course, a fantastic plan and an impractical proposition—for more reasons than one. India is geographically, historically, culturally, politically and economically, an indivisible unit. Secondly, in most parts of India, Hindus and Muslims are so mixed up that it is not possible to separate them. Thirdly, if Muslim states were forcibly set up, new minority problems would be created in these states which would present new difficulties. Fourthly, unless Hindus and Muslims join hands and fight the British, they cannot liberate themselves and their unity is possible only on the basis of a free and undivided India.

By the end of the decade and the beginning of the 1940s, there had clearly been a marked shift in Jinnah's thinking. At the Lahore Session of the All-India Muslim League in March 1940, Jinnah gave his full support to the so-called 'Pakistan Resolution' moved by Bengali Muslim leader Fazlul Haque and adopted by the Session. This in effect signalled for the first time League aspirations for the partition of the subcontinent, and the beginnings of the end of real efforts towards communal accommodation.

It is interesting to note that the Resolution had not in fact used the terminology 'Pakistan'; this was a sobriquet ascribed by the news media to the Resolution, and which fired the imagination of all protagonists and communities both in positive and negative ways. The Muslim world of India seemed largely supportive, with mixed reactions from Hindus and other non-Muslims.

It is no surprise that the eventual partition of the Indian subcontinent into India and Pakistan and the subsidiary division of two of the most fabled and influential provinces of British India, namely Bengal and the Punjab, should have been hotly contested by the Bose Brothers until the very end. Even after the event, on 20 February 1950 just hours before his sudden death, Sarat put the final touches to what he termed 'An Appeal to India and Pakistan,' for East Bengal—by then part of Pakistan—to

[5] Ibid., 404.

join the Indian Union as a distinct and separate state, and thus achieve at least some form of reunification with fellow Bengalis next door in the new Indian state of West Bengal. This appeared as a signed editorial the following day 21 February 1950, along with the shocking news of his death, in his own newspaper *The Nation,* which he had established on 1 September 1948.

Several years earlier on 15 March 1947 in a statement to the press in Calcutta, only months before independence for India and Pakistan, Sarat—by this time estranged from Congress and with his back increasingly to the wall—had prophetically warned[6]:

> By accepting religion as the sole basis of the distribution of provinces, the Congress has cut itself away from its moorings and has almost undone the work it has been doing for the last 60 years.... To accept that concept [i.e. of religious or theocratic states] in the year of grace 1947 and to apply it to India will mean pushing her back into the medieval ages. It is obviously a reactionary and anti-revolutionary step and shuts out progress for long years to come. It will further aggravate the communal problem and will make its solution extremely difficult if not altogether impossible. As the population of India all over the country is composite in character, this sort of communal segregation or religious quarantine is neither desirable nor feasible. We have to find out a solution that applies to the entire country. The solution of the communal problem lies ultimately in social justice, and so far as our collective life is concerned, in an emphasis on the political and economic aspects and interests of life and in the divorce of religion from politics and economics.

Amiya commented extensively through lectures and in his own writings, on the roles of his father and uncle in the increasingly desperate fight against partition and for the unity of India. In the final years leading to partition and independence, Amiya himself played an active role in the accompanying deliberations and negotiations, as his father's political aide and confidante.

With all that has been written about partition and notwithstanding a veritable mountain of available archival material, it remains difficult to identify any precise moment or action from where it could be said that partition was inevitable. Some

---

[6] *Selected Speeches and Writings of Sarat Chandra Bose 1947–1950* (The Sarat Bose Academy, 1954), 1–2.

observers would trace that inevitability to the thrust of British imperial policy itself, namely, the tactic of divide and rule that British colonial authorities adopted in other parts of their colonial empire, Ireland and Palestine being two such instances cited by Subhas. Others might point to age-old religious divides.

Still others argue that the answer is to be found in the events of the final few years leading to independence for both India and Pakistan in August 1947. The mantra of 'Pakistan' itself, as has been mentioned previously in this chapter, generated its own momentum, particularly as the revived Muslim League under the leadership of Jinnah grew in confidence, stature with the Muslim masses, and influence with the imperial authorities, particularly from the early 1940s.

For the Bose Brothers, it can safely be said that they believed that nothing was inevitable, and that resistance to any moves towards partition no matter how late in the day was more than fully justified. Presciently, the brothers were entirely correct in insisting that partition would not solve communal problems neither in the short nor longer terms.

For Amiya, the most fertile seeds of partition were to be found in the positions taken by the CWC under the direction of the Congress High Command on the conduct and outcome of the Provincial Elections held in mid-January 1937, under the auspices of the Government of India Act of 1935.

In those elections (based on communal electorates and restricted franchise) Congress contested 1,161 of the total of 1,585 seats available in the 11 provinces of British India (Assam, Bengal, Bihar, Bombay, Central Provinces, Madras, North West Frontier, Orissa, Punjab, Sind, United Provinces) and won 716 of those, with absolute majorities in six (Bihar, Bombay, Central Provinces, Madras, Orissa and United Provinces) and constituting the largest single party in three others (Assam, Bengal and North West Frontier).

Congress contested only 56 of the 482 seats set aside for Muslim voters, of which it won 28; it did not secure a single Muslim seat in the United Provinces, Bengal and in the Punjab; and, it did not even contest any Muslim seats in Sind, Bombay and Bihar. Its greatest successes with Muslim seats were achieved in Madras where it obtained four and the North West Frontier Province where it won 15 under the guidance of local

Congress Pathan Muslim leader Khan Abdul Ghaffar Khan, popularly known as the 'Frontier Gandhi'.

Congress had done well, but had made no real attempt to reach out to the Muslim electorate even in the face of a still relatively weak Muslim League, which performed poorly in the elections. There were already worrying signs of a shift in the image of Congress from one of a nationalist to a predominantly Hindu organisation.

Amiya believed that Gandhi's techniques of political propaganda did not help with the Muslim masses. He spoke to the Indian people in the language of a Hindu saint and utilised Hindu religious symbols to garner support. An inevitable consequence in Amiya's view was the alienation of Muslims from the Congress movement.

Amiya further noted that the CWC finally met at Wardha from 5 to 8 July 1937 after a five month delay, to discuss the outcome of the Provincial Elections and consequent formation of ministries in the Congress majority provinces. During this time, the Congress leadership had wrestled with the imperial authorities on the question of the overriding constitutional powers of the imperial provincial Governors.

Key items on the agenda at Wardha were the outstanding issues of office acceptance, that is of ministerial positions and coalition ministries. As Sarat had to leave Wardha early, he wrote letters to Gandhi and Nehru, the latter in his capacity as Congress President for 1937 as well as 1936. The CWC agreed on the principle of office acceptance but rejected the proposal for coalition ministries. Congress was thus directed by its leadership to form ministries in the Congress majority provinces only.

Provincial Congress Committees were forbidden to form coalitions of any description with other political parties including the Muslim League, whether Congress was in an absolute majority or, as in the case of Bengal, the single largest party. Indeed Congress demanded that any parties wishing to join them in government would in effect have to forego any separate party affiliation, and identify and merge with the Congress.

In the United Provinces, Congress reneged on a pre-election power-sharing agreement with the Muslim League when the Congress found themselves winning an absolute majority of seats in the elections. To add salt to the wound, Congress allowed that Muslim League members could join them in government in the United Provinces, but only upon renouncing the League and joining Congress! Amiya drew attention to remarks by Congress Muslim leader Maulana Azad in his autobiographical book, *India Wins Freedom,* on the readiness of the Muslim League to join ministries in the Hindu majority provinces and Azad's visit to the United Provinces.[7]

> Chaudhari Khaliquzzaman and Nawab Ismail Khan were then the leaders of the Muslim League in the UP (United Provinces). When I came to Lucknow for forming the Government, I spoke to both of them. They assured me that they would not only cooperate with the Congress, but would fully support the Congress programme. They naturally expected that the Muslim League would have some share in the new Government. The local position was such that neither of them could enter the Government alone. Either both would have to be taken or none. I had therefore held out hopes that both of them would be taken into the Government. If the Ministry consisted of seven members only, two would be Muslim Leaguers and the rest would all be Congressmen. In a Cabinet of nine, the Congress majority would be still more marked. After discussion with me, a note was prepared to the effect that the Muslim League Party would work in cooperation with the Congress and accept the Congress programme. Both Nawab Ismail Khan and Chaudhari Khaliquzzaman signed this document.

Azad further noted that Nehru did not honour this agreement entered into by him (i.e., Azad), and the negotiations with the Muslim League failed.

> [T]his was a most unfortunate development. If the League's offer of cooperation had been accepted, the Muslim League Party would for all practical purposes have merged with the Congress. Jawaharlal's action gave the Muslim League in the UP a new lease of life. All students of Indian politics know that it was from the UP that the League was reorganised. Mr Jinnah took full advantage of the situation and started an offensive which ultimately led to Pakistan.

[7] Maulana Abul Kalam Azad, *India Wins Freedom* (Orient Black Swan, 2009), 170–171.

Amiya concluded, and this was a central theme in his many lectures about this period, that by its actions centred on the 1937 elections and aftermath, the Congress made it clear to the Muslims of India that in a united India, Muslims could never expect to share political power in an equitable manner. They were therefore led to believe that they could only achieve such power if India was divided into Hindu and Muslim majority areas.

This hegemonic position of the Congress High Command flew in the face of the ongoing endeavours of the Bose Brothers for acceptance of the principle of coalition throughout the 11 provinces of British India. Amiya recounted that in December 1936, Subhas had been brought from house detention in Kurseong in the Himalayan foothills to the Calcutta Medical College for urgent medical treatment.

> I had a number of interviews with him then. He asked me to tell Sarat Bose to work for coalition ministries all over the country, if necessary with the assistance of the Muslim League, so that relations between Hindu and Muslim communities could be improved and in consequence the unity of India preserved and strengthened. Both the Bose Brothers firmly believed in and tried to put into practice the principles behind the Bengal Pact of C. R. Das, which sought broadly to give Muslims fairer representation in national and provincial legislative bodies.

Amiya observed that the immediate background to Subhas's concerns at that time, centred on the preparations by the Congress, Muslim League and various political parties for the Provincial Elections. These were in fact held shortly after in the following month of January 1937. Neither Congress nor the Muslim League was in any way satisfied with the new Constitution under the 1935 Government of India Act, but both decided to participate. By this time, all the important Congress leaders except Subhas were out of prison.

In respect of Congress, the decision to participate was taken in the course of the annual session of the All India Congress Committee (AICC), presided over by Nehru as the Congress President for 1936 and held in Calcutta late October 1936. Meetings of the 15-member CWC were held at the 1 Woodburn Park residence of Sarat. Different Congress leaders were placed in charge of electoral preparations in the various provinces, with Sarat accepting responsibility for both Bengal and the Punjab.

Soon after this AICC session, an Anti-Office Acceptance Committee had been formed with Sarat Chandra Bose, Rafi Ahmed Kidwai, Sardar Sardul Singh Caveesher and Srimati Vijaylaxmi Pandit as its leading members. Jawaharlal Nehru supported this Committee but did not become a member as he was then still Congress President. The primary purpose of the Committee was to campaign for Congress participation in the elections, but non-acceptance of ministerial positions so as to paralyse and wreck the Constitution from within the legislatures.

Subhas felt that Sarat was pursuing the wrong tactics. He felt sure that the right wing of Congress would in the end decide to accept office in the different provinces where the results of the elections would enable them to do so, and successfully eliminate representation of the left wing of Congress on the grounds that the latter were against office acceptance. Subhas was just as sure that Nehru would accept office at the bidding of Gandhi and effectively isolate the left wing, including Sarat.

In Bengal itself, Sarat wanted the political space to be able to forge Hindu/Muslim alliances involving Congress, in this case specifically with the Muslim-based Krishak (peasant) Praja Party (KPP) led by long-time Bengali Muslim leader Fazlul Haque, in preference to a rejuvenated Muslim League led by fellow Bengali Muslim Khwaja Nazimuddin.

Sarat, who was then the leader of the Bengal Congress, had little confidence in the nationalist predelictions of Nazimuddin, and thus worked in close cooperation with the KPP to defeat the Muslim League. However in the wake of the elections where the three dominant parties, that is, Congress, KPP and Muslim League, each won almost the same number of seats (52, 50 and 50 respectively, according to the tabulation of Amiya), the eventual refusal of the Congress High Command to sanction coalitions involving Congress, saw Sarat's vision denied. A disappointed Fazlul Haque was thus thrown into the arms of the Muslim League.

A coalition Ministry dominated by the Muslim League in alliance with the KPP and generally more sympathetic to Muslim interests was thus formed on 1 April 1937 in Bengal with Fazlul Haque as Premier and Nazimuddin as Home Minister. Nalini

Ranjan Sarkar, a confidante of Gandhi, defected from Congress and joined the cabinet as Finance Minister. The President and CWC expelled Sarkar from the Congress Party for 20 years.

The Bengal Congress which had won 52 seats in the elections, and was thus the largest single party in the Bengal Assembly, was consigned to opposition in the Assembly. A further attempt by Sarat some months later in August 1937 to ally Congress with the KPP in a coalition ministry was again refused by the CWC under Nehru as Congress President.

Sarat was not to be denied. In August 1937, political prisoners in the Andaman Islands had begun a hunger strike demanding repatriation to India. This matter developed quickly into a major political issue, and Sarat initiated a campaign throughout the country in support of the Andaman prisoners and political 'detenus' in general. Sarat's ceaseless agitation for the release of these prisoners reflected badly on the less active Muslim League Ministry in Bengal, and Sarat emerged for a time as the most powerful figure in Bengal politics.

Also during this period, Sarat began to advocate publicly for a socio-economic programme of a socialist nature. In October 1938, in the course of his presidential address to the Mysore State Students Conference, Sarat openly declared his faith in socialism, though not fully agreeing with Marxian thought. He advocated a form of socialism which would be particularly Indian in nature. By November 1938, a large number of Scheduled Caste members and a major section of the KPP were again ready to support Sarat Bose in the formation of a coalition ministry with the Congress Party. Thus by December 1938, Sarat was tempted to again seek to break the Muslim League-dominated Ministry in Bengal. As related by Amiya:

> On 15 December 1938, Sarat again went to Wardha to attend a meeting of the Congress Working Committee and also to again seek the support of Gandhi and other Congress leaders, for a coalition ministry in Bengal including the Congress. Soon after Sarat's arrival in Wardha, prominent Calcutta businessman G. D. Birla accompanied by Nalini Ranjan Sarkar, arrived in Wardha to discuss the situation in Bengal with Gandhi.
>
> The emergence of a Congress coalition ministry in Bengal under the leadership of a confirmed socialist such as Sarat Bose, was

anathema to the Marwari capitalists of Calcutta. G. D. Birla suggested to Gandhi that Sarat Bose should be removed from the leadership of the Congress Party in the Bengal Assembly and that Nalini should be entrusted with the responsibility of forming a coalition ministry in Bengal.

It was widely reported in the press that Gandhi gave a patient hearing to Birla and Sarkar and asked them to take their proposal to the Congress President and other Congress leaders. As Subhas was then the Congress President, Birla and Sarkar did not pursue the matter. But under the diktats of Birla, Gandhi successfully sabotaged Sarat Bose's further attempt as a member of Congress to break the Muslim League-led ministry in Bengal. Sarat's efforts were foiled in a subtle manner by Gandhi because he did not want to weaken the economic predominance of the Marwari capitalists in Bengal.

On the wider canvas of relations between Muslims and Hindus throughout British India, the damage arising from the conduct and aftermath of the 1937 elections had been done. By 1940 Jinnah was openly pushing the vision of an independent Pakistan, an idea towards which he had been openly dismissive only a few years earlier. How did it happen that a man who had once been regarded as the 'Ambassador of Hindu–Muslim unity,'[8] becomes the most powerful protagonist of the partition of India and the creation of an independent state of Pakistan?

Contrary to popular contentions and contemporary folklore, Jinnah's personal ambitions had less to do with his dramatic change of heart than his sense of 'Muslim injury under Congress rule'. It was his very negative perception of Congress-ruled provinces post-1937 elections that prompted him to call upon Muslims in India to celebrate their 'deliverance from tyranny, oppression and injustice' when the Congress provincial governments resigned en masse in November 1939.

It was thus abundantly clear to Amiya that

> The turning point in Jinnah's career came after the 1937 elections when Congress refused to share with him the spoils of office in those Indian provinces where there was a substantial

---

[8] A sobriquet conferred upon Jinnah by Indian independence activist and the 'Nightingale of India' Sarojini Naidu, lauding his role in the Lucknow Pact of December 1916 promoting Hindu–Muslim unity.

Muslim minority. Jinnah was a man of towering vanity and he took Congress's action as a personal rebuke. It convinced him that he and the Muslim League would never get a fair deal from a Congress-run India. The former apostle of Hindu/Muslim unity became the unyielding advocate of Pakistan, the project he had labelled an 'impossible dream' barely four years earlier.

It had not helped in the immediate aftermath of the 1937 elections, Jinnah had tried to initiate discussions with Gandhi for some sort of rapprochement between Hindu and Muslim political leaders. In May 1937, he sent a message to Gandhi, but received a letter from the latter dated 22 May 1937 declining a discussion. Jinnah made a further attempt, but this time Gandhi asked him to talk to Azad, seen by many as a Congress puppet. Jinnah thus abandoned his overtures.

In his capacity as Congress President for 1938, Subhas also sought to reach out to Jinnah in a further effort to settle the increasingly vexed communal imbroglio. While the exchanges, both written and face-to-face (in May 1938), between Subhas and Jinnah were from all accounts civil and mutually respectful, and generally absent the animosity between Jinnah and Nehru in particular, the situation by then had become much more complex. Jinnah held his ground in insisting that the Muslim League was to be considered as the authoritative and representative voice of Muslims in India and that the League should be considered as being on an equal footing with the Congress.

By this time Jinnah clearly saw Congress as the voice of the Hindu community and not of Muslims. Jinnah reminded Subhas that it had not helped that during his tenure as Congress President in 1937, Nehru in one of his statements had asserted that there were only 'two parties in the country, namely the British Government and the Congress'.

With Congress through Subhas and its Working Committee unable to concede that it did not and could not represent Muslims, the efforts of Subhas in his role as Congress President to reach an accommodation with Jinnah came to nought. Subsequently with the withdrawal of Congress in 1939 from all forms of provincial and national governance, mass imprisonment of Congress leaders from the early 1940s (including Subhas in July 1940, Sarat in December 1941 and Gandhi himself in August 1942), and the clash from August 1942 with the British Government and imperial authorities over the Quit India movement, the Muslim League and Jinnah were given room to consolidate and build on the separatist momentum generated from 1937. Thus by 1944, with the momentum of the Second World War now leaning clearly towards Britain and its allies, Jinnah was now fully recognised by the imperial authorities as a factor to be reckoned with. He was now in direct contact with the Viceroy and the British Government about the shape of things to come in what was still imperial India. By the time of the release of Gandhi from imprisonment on 6 May 1944, partition was now very much a part of the political discourse in both the Muslim League and the Congress, with some Congress luminaries actively supporting the concept as inevitable in one form or the other.

Foremost among these was Congress stalwart and Gandhi confidante Chakravarti Rajagopalachari, who from 1942 had sought to devise a settlement between the Congress and the League, and to come to a common understanding on the way forward. Even prior to Gandhi's release, what became known as the C. R. Formula for the partition of India between Hindu and Muslim majority areas had been discussed between Rajagopalachari and Jinnah with the tacit blessing of Gandhi. The latter was thus left with little choice but to deal with the matter as it gathered momentum, and directly with Jinnah whose position had hardened into a demand for an independent Pakistan.

In what he called 'Stray Thoughts of my Own' written during his detention at Coonoor Camp in southern India, Sarat wrote on 31 July 1944 with a sharp tone of regret.[9]

> Gandhiji's acceptance of Rajaji's formula is nothing short of a tragedy in India's political life. He, who not long ago declared vivisection of India to be a sin, has now blessed it! And yet, he says he has not changed! Very probably his coming discussions with Jinnah will end in smoke [Gandhi was to say somewhat ruefully and laconically on his return after the meeting with Jinnah in September 1944, in response to what he had brought back from Jinnah, 'Only flowers']. But there can be no doubt that they will consolidate Jinnah's position further in his own community and encourage him to make even more extravagant demands.

[9] *Sarat Chandra Bose Commemoration Volume*, 181–182.

I cannot help feeling that Gandhiji has been making blunder after blunder since 1937, acting on the advice of Jawaharlal and Maulana Azad. If he (Gandhi) had agreed to the formation of coalition ministries in 1937, Jinnah and his followers would have been satisfied and Hindu–Muslim differences would have been narrowed down. But that was not to be, as Gandhiji preferred to tag along with Jawaharlal and Maulana—the former a muddle-headed theorist, the latter Jawaharlal's ditto man.

When I asked Gandhiji at a meeting of the Working Committee in Delhi (I think it was in 1937) as to whether there was in his opinion any difference between a pure Congress ministry and a Congress Coalition ministry provided the programme was the same, he said there was none. But he was not prepared to throw his weight in favour of a Congress coalition ministry. He asked me to discuss the matter with Rajendrababu and Sardar. I discussed it with them, but nothing came out of it.

They had all made up their minds in favour of pure Congress ministries. Jawaharlal was thinking all the time that I was supporting a Congress coalition ministry, because of Bengal's peculiar position. He never appreciated that it would have the effect of liquidating Muslim suspicion of and opposition to the Congress. The great 'leftist' was prepared to support acceptance of offices at Gandhiji's bidding but he had not the foresight to take the step I advocated.

Acceptance of offices in 1937 was a blunder. I pressed again and again my viewpoint that the seven provinces in which the Congress had absolute majority should combine to create a deadlock and make the working of the 1935 Constitution impossible. If the Constitution had been wrecked in seven provinces, the British Government would have been in great difficulty. Alternatively, I pressed for Coalition Ministries, at least in the (Congress) minority provinces! But neither the one nor the other was accepted. There was a dead wall between me and my colleagues.

In a broadcast from somewhere in Burma on 12 September 1944, where he was now the Head of the Provisional Government of Azad Hind and Supreme Commander of the multi-religious, multi-ethnic INA comprising both male and female personnel, Subhas issued a clarion call to his countrymen and women.

You are all aware that Gandhiji and Mr Jinnah are discussing the Hindu/Muslim question in Bombay and that Gandhiji is prepared to come to an agreement with the League even if it means conceding the League demand of Pakistan. I know that you are all very anxious to know what we Indians abroad think about Gandhiji's attempt to pacify the League. It is clear that Gandhiji and other Congress leaders wish to compromise with Britain after settling with the League.... The very idea of a compromise with the British is repugnant to us; it will, we very strongly feel, mean the perpetuation of our slavery.

Friends, we have resolved to create a united and free India; therefore, we shall oppose all attempts to divide her and cut her up into bits.... Personally, I have great respect for Mr Jinnah, President of the Muslim League. I, and my party, have been in close contact with him and have cooperated with the League in the past and I am opposed neither to the League nor to its illustrious leader. But, I vehemently oppose the Pakistan scheme for the vivisection of our motherland.

Even by this time, Sarat and Subhas were increasingly becoming voices in the wilderness on the question of partition. Indeed from the time of his disappearance in August 1945, that of Subhas was to be heard no more, and Sarat was left with an ever-diminishing band of cohorts to carry the burden of doing all that they could to save the territorial integrity of India. When that cause was irretrievably lost, Sarat switched his efforts to a last-ditch attempt to prevent the partition of Bengal. As will be discussed in the following chapter, it was all too late and his efforts were in vain.

On 6 January 1947, Sarat finally resigned from the CWC and sent the following message to the Congress President[10]:

I have served on the Working Committee in spite of serious differences with my colleagues since May last over the acceptance of the Cabinet Mission statement and scheme but I regret I cannot do so any longer. The resolution drafted by the Working Committee stultifies the Congress, makes the Constituent Assembly a subservient body, irreparably destroys the integrity of India and actually compels provinces to accept grouping against their will and to surrender provincial autonomy while giving them misleading assurances that no compulsion or interference is involved and that provincial autonomy will remain intact.

[10] Private Collection of Amiya Nath and Jyotsna Bose.

A Constituent Assembly acting in accordance with the British Government's interpretation and mandate cannot possibly frame a constitution for a sovereign republic of India. I tender my resignation from the Working Committee membership.

Sarat Bose

On 1 August 1947, Sarat relinquished for good his membership of the Congress movement which he had actively served for three decades, and announced the formation of his Socialist Republican Party. In a press release of the same day to mark the occasion, Sarat regretted the failures of the Congress.[11]

The Indian struggle has entered a new phase. The sufferings and sacrifices of the people during the last twenty years raised hopes in their minds that independence of India free from British influence and control was within their grasp. The acceptance of the June 3 Plan by the two major political organisations in the country has, for the time being, dashed those hopes to the ground. We have today a dismembered India and, instead of independence, Dominion Status under British influence and patronage.

The Flag of Independence was unfurled at the session of the Indian National Congress which was held in Lahore in the year 1929. The people rallied under that flag and were prepared at all times for the utmost sacrifices in order to make independence a reality. Why then have we failed? We have failed because of weakness and vacillation on the part of our leaders, we have failed because of anxiety on their part to accept compromises even on matters fundamental, we have failed because of their failure at all critical moments to give a bold and correct lead to the country.

As Sarat somewhat ruefully reflected in a speech entitled 'I Warned My Countrymen', at the launch in New Delhi on 13 April 1948 of the Hindi Daily 'Netaji'[12]:

[Y]ou all remember that the Congress has since the year 1929 been fighting for an independent and united India. The election manifesto which was issued by the Congress Working Committee in the year 1945—I was then a member of the Congress Working Committee—made it absolutely clear that the Congress would

[11] *Selected Speeches and Writings of Sarat Chandra Bose 1947–1950*, 9–13.
[12] Ibid., 37–42.

resist partition and Pakistan. Signs of weakness appeared in the Congress leaders from the year 1946 when the British Cabinet Mission came to this country. Weakness increased from month to month until I felt compelled, in the beginning of the year 1947, to resign my membership of the Congress Working Committee. Shortly thereafter—to be exact in March 1947—the Congress Working Committee passed a resolution recommending the division of the Punjab into two provinces - one predominantly Muslim and the other predominantly Non-Muslim.

On the 15th of March, 1947, I raised my voice of protest and sounded a note of warning against the resolution passed by the Congress Working Committee with reference to the Punjab.... My warnings went unheeded and members of the then Congress Working Committee suggested one compromise after another and eventually accepted Pakistan and the division of the country. In the month of April or the beginning of May, 1947, Mahatma Gandhi came to Calcutta and I met him at Sodepur and discussed with him the situation in the country. As most of you are aware, Gandhiji was against partition. I requested him again and again to assert himself and resist partition.

I told him in the course of discussion that I clearly visualised that two things would happen immediately partition was effected. One was that the North-Western Frontier province would pass into the hands of the League. The next was that Kashmir would be swallowed up by Pakistan. Gandhiji was against partition but he did not agree with me that the two results I had mentioned to him would flow from it and he gave me his reasons for disagreeing with me.

Towards the end of May 1947 I came to Delhi and had discussions with Gandhiji and also with Mr Jinnah. I have not the slightest doubt myself that if the Congress leaders had displayed a certain amount of statesmanship the partition of Bengal could have been prevented. Whether the partition of the Punjab could have been prevented is more than I can say. It is for the leaders of the Punjab to express themselves.

Then came the June 3 Plan, popularly known as the Mountbatten Plan. Two days after the announcement of the Plan I said at New Delhi that HMG's India had dealt a staggering blow to the cause of Indian unity and independence, a blow from which we might not be able to recover for many years....

On my return to Calcutta from Delhi I issued a statement on 8th June 1947 saying among other things that British Imperialists

had won.... I said further that what had been said by the partition-
ists to the Hindus of Eastern Bengal and the Hindus and Sikhs
of Western Punjab namely, that Western Bengal and Eastern
Punjab would come to them respectively was a mere sop...

Two weeks after that I said in a message to the *Free Press Journal*
of Bombay that the June 3 Plan marked the triumph of British
diplomacy and that Congress would rue the day when it accepted
Dominion Status, conceded Pakistan, and demanded the partition of the provinces.

The time has now come for the Indian people to judge whether I
was right or the Congress leaders were right. After what happened
immediately after 15 August 1947, all over the country, I believe
I can claim that every word of what I said has come out true.

On 24 June 1947, I said that acceptance of the June 3 Plan marked
the triumph of British diplomacy. To those words I shall add that
it also marked the bankruptcy of Indian statesmanship and the
betrayal of the nation by eminent Congress leaders.

Sarat was to express on many occasions his deep and bitter disappointment at the course of events, not only around partition
but also against what he saw as the failure of the new India and
its leaders. At the All-Bengal Subhasist Students' Conference
in Calcutta on 26 December 1949, he reminded his 'Young
Comrades' of the dreams of Subhas for complete independence
unsullied by Dominion Status and a form of socialism adapted
to Indian conditions.[13]

I must recall in this connection the tragic history of the partition
of this country and how jaundiced and weak-kneed statesmanship, supped full of an irrational despair, found in that pernicious partition the panacea for the ills of the country. March
1947 to August 1947 was the period of gigantic national suicide,
in the course of which all reactionary elements of and in the
Congress and the Hindu Mahasabha, casting to the winds the
advice of Mahatma Gandhi, clamoured for a self-inflicted death.
Warnings given to them went unheeded, drunk as they were
with the heady wine of despair. Their propaganda machine
worked and they kept the whole country etherised upon the
surgeon's table for the knife to be applied. What followed is

[13] Ibid., 118–119.

recent memory—blood-bath, and caravans of homeless refugees pouring in from the east and west of India. But partition is now a fait accompli and we have to accept it and decide upon our course of action in the present set-up.

Do you realise what havoc two years of Congress rule have caused in our country? On 15 August 1947 India started as one of the most solvent countries in the world. Now she has been reduced to one of the poorest by the reckless actions and thoughtless inactions of her Prodigal Sons, the eminent Congress leaders! Her Sterling balance is depleted, her development projects all but stopped, India is going about in the west with a beggar's bowl in her hand. Inside the country, the picture is no better. Corruption, favouritism and nepotism are running rampant, and black-marketeers, profiteers and corrupters of public morals are at large with the Government looking on helplessly, almost pathetically.

In his own interpretations of the seeds of partition, Amiya laid heavy stress on the events of 1937 and the behaviour of key protagonists both then and later. He was to argue forcefully in various lectures and seminars that if Gandhi, Nehru and Patel had in 1937 agreed with Sarat and Maulana Azad on the principle and formation of coalition ministries, Jinnah and the Muslim League would not have seen the need to pass the so-called Pakistan Resolution in Lahore in 1940. Pakistan might thus not have come into existence at all. Rajmohan Gandhi was to reflect in his epic biography of his grandfather[14]:

Gandhi was often in agony. He felt that partition would lead to more violence, not less, but his Working Committee and ministerial allies thought the opposite. He felt that details of the division should be settled between the Congress and the League, without the mediation of the Raj; they disagreed. Having 'scotched' his Jinnah card, they seemed set also on a large army for India and on large-scale industrialisation. The charkha had been forgotten. He had been rejected on several fronts.... Aware that desire for power had influenced their acceptance of Partition, he yet refused to obstruct his 'sons' while they collected crowns or medals for their faithful toil of three decades, and he knew that the trophies were thorny.

---

[14] Rajmohan Gandhi, *Mohandas: True Story of a Man, His People and an Empire* (UK: Penguin, 2006), 613 and 617.

Nehru for his part sought to move a major share of the responsibility for partition towards Gandhi, telling British author Leonard Mosley more than a decade later[15]:

> The truth is that we were tired men, and we were getting on in years too. Few of us could stand the prospect of going to prison again—and if we had stood out for a united India as we wished it, prison obviously awaited us. We saw the fires burning in the Punjab and heard every day of the killings. The plan for partition offered a way out and we took it...if Gandhi had told us not to, we would have gone on fighting, and waiting. But we accepted. We expected that partition would be temporary, that Pakistan was bound to come back to us.

Sarat and Gandhi remained in close personal touch, and in what may have been their last face-to-face meeting sometime in September 1947 at which Amiya was present, the latter noted Gandhi's poignant reflections:

> My writ no longer runs and I could not have prevented partition even if I wanted to. Sardar, who has always been my yes-man, has become the no-man. Whatever I say, he says no. Rajendra Babu has kicked the ladder by which he rose. Jawaharlal simply delights in contradicting me.

On Gandhi's sudden death at the hands of a Hindu fundamentalist assassin on 30 January 1948, Sarat issued the following statement from his Woodburn Park residence, prior to leaving Calcutta the same day for the funeral in Delhi:

> The sad and tragic news of the death of the Father of the Nation at the hands of a foul assassin has staggered me. No language is strong enough to condemn such an outrage. The country is orphaned and God alone knows what is in store for it. Mahatmaji is dead. When comes such another?

One month later on 28 February 1948, in his Presidential Address to the All-India Sugar Factory Workers' Conference in Meerut, Sarat mourned the loss of Gandhi[16]:

[15] Leonard Mosley, *The Last Days of the British Raj* (London: Weidenfeld and Nicolson, 1961), 248.

[16] *Selected Speeches and Writings of Sarat Chandra Bose 1947–1950*, 25–26.

We meet today under the shadow of a great calamity. The Father of the Nation is no more with us, and we who are orphaned seem to be moving in a sort of vacuum, paralysed by an over-powering sense of despair and frustration. The present appears dark, and the future blurred. But the immortal spirit of Gandhiji is there to give us light and inspiration, and we shall be guilty of betraying the trust he reposed in us if we succumb to our sense of personal loss and sorrow.

His death in the darkest hour of India's history has made our responsibilities all the more onerous, and the only way to offer true homage to the departed great is to shoulder those responsibilities with grim determination and accomplish the work left unfinished by him—the work of winning Complete Independence for India.

In the same address, Sarat went on to explain what he meant by Complete Independence:

The basic fact that forces itself on our attention is that India is yet to achieve her independence. The 15th of August 1947 was in the nature of a sad anti-climax. It did not witness the consummation of the mighty struggle India had waged against a foreign imperialistic power for several decades. It only marked the ignominious acceptance of the status of a Dominion within the British Commonwealth and the price we had to pay for it was the loss of the unity of India. It was a betrayal of the noble ideal our predecessors and we had cherished and fought for, for so long—the ideal of an undivided and independent India free from foreign influence and control.

And the pity of it is that the betrayal was on the part of some of our top-ranking Congress leaders, who had made no small contribution to the freedom movement of the country. Lured by the elusive prospect of a safe journey to the promised land of freedom, they demanded the division of India and the creation of two dominions and unfortunately failed to realise that that would not solve the communal problem but would only aggravate it.

6

A Free and United Bengal

Bengali Muslims, Hindus, Christians and Buddhists have a
common mother tongue and are bound together by racial, social,
cultural, economic and other ties, and a Free and United Bengal
where they can fully cooperate with one another is essential for
their social, economic and political progress

—Free and United Bengal,
Draft Basis of Agreement, 25 May 1947

As the prospects for a united India began to fade and the inevitability of partition of the subcontinent into India and Pakistan loomed on the horizon, Sarat Bose turned his attention to saving the territorial integrity of Bengal. It was clear by early 1947 that a united, predominantly Muslim province of Bengal remaining within the new state of India was a lost cause and simply not going to materialise. This left the option of a third independent sovereign state of Bengal, along with India and Pakistan.

Historians and other commentators differ on whether this was in any way a realistic option, with some tending to argue that Sarat was isolated on the issue and that it was all too late. Others, including Sarat himself contended that there remained a broad base of consensus and support among Bengalis themselves, majority Muslims and minority Hindus alike, for Bengalis to remain united as a political as well as a cultural and social entity, regardless of the religious divide. If this could only happen as a sovereign state, then so be it.

What is clear is that arraigned against Sarat and a small number of prominent allies including Shaheed Suhrawardy and Fazlul Haque from the Muslim League and also erstwhile colleagues from the Bengal Congress was a formidable 'cartel' of both Muslim and Hindu fundamentalists, political leaders from both camps, Congress leaders such as Nehru and Patel, and Marwari business leaders in Calcutta.

Jinnah for his part appeared to remain ambivalent, perhaps sensing that a far-away eastern territory of Pakistan was not going to work in the longer term, and that a united, sovereign Bengal was a better prospect than seeing all or part of Bengal absorbed into a new State of India living side-by-side with the new Pakistan. The prospective loss of the then predominantly Muslim city of Calcutta to new India would also have figured in his calculations. As late as June 1947, Jinnah indicated to Sarat, if not support then at least acceptance of a united, sovereign Bengal which could take its own constitutional decisions on whether to join either of the other two entities India and Pakistan, or remain independent.

As the partition timetable of the Mountbatten Plan came into play and as the clock ticked towards midnight, Sarat turned to Gandhi in a last-ditch effort to salvage a united Bengal from the ruins of the imminent partition of the Indian subcontinent.

At this time in mid-1947, Amiya had been constantly by his father Sarat's side since the latter's release from detention on 14 September 1945, fully engaged in supporting him as his political secretary, sounding-board and adviser. In connection with the dramatic but tragic events around partition which began to unfold in early 1947, Amiya recalled that even before Mountbatten arrived in India as Viceroy on 22 March 1947, the CWC had passed a resolution on 8 March 1947 with reference to the Punjab which recommended its partition into two provinces—one predominantly Muslim and the other predominantly non-Muslim. In the course of a press interview the same day, the Congress President Maulana Azad announced that the principle of division underlying the resolution also applied to Bengal. In connection with this resolution, on 15 March 1947, Sarat issued his now much-cited—and prescient—statement to the press[1]:

> I think I ought to raise my voice of protest and sound a note of warning against the resolution passed by the Congress Working Committee with reference to the Punjab. The resolution in question recommends a division of the Punjab into two provinces—one predominantly Muslim and the other pre-dominantly non-Muslim. In the course of a press interview the Congress President has announced that the principle of division underlying the resolution applies also to Bengal.

[1] *Sarat Chandra Bose Commemoration Volume* (Calcutta: The Sarat Bose Academy, 1982), 393–394.

I confess that the resolution has surprised me not a little. By accepting religion as the sole basis of the distribution of Provinces, the Congress has cut itself away from its moorings and has almost undone the work it has been doing for the last sixty years. The resolution in question is a violent departure from the traditions and principles of the Congress. And I am forced to the conclusion that it is the result of a defeatist mentality. A sort of fear complex seems to have worked havoc in the minds of many of us.

To my mind a division of Provinces on a religious basis is no solution of the communal problem. Even if the Provinces were to be so divided, Hindus and Muslims will still have to live side by side in them and the risk of communal conflicts will remain. Supposing we divide Bengal and the Punjab on the basis of religion, what about the Muslims in western Bengal and the Hindus in eastern Bengal, or about the Muslims in eastern Punjab and the Hindus and Sikhs in western Punjab? What again is going to happen to the minority religious groups in the other Provinces of India? Are we going to have Hindu, Muslim, Sikh, Buddhist, Christian, Parsee and other religious states or pockets throughout the country?

The resolution of the Congress Working Committee pushed to its logical conclusion would mean the creation of such religious states or pockets and the result would be that the risk of armed communal conflict or clashes would increase hundredfold. The concept of religious or theocratic States is not a new one, but all the advanced countries of the world have dismissed it or grown out of it. To accept that concept in the year of grace 1947 and to apply it to India will mean pushing her back into the medieval ages. It is obviously a reactionary and anti-revolutionary step and shuts out progress for long years to come. It will further aggravate the communal problem, and will make its solution extremely difficult, if not altogether impossible. As the population of India all over the country is composite in character, this sort of communal segregation or religious quarantine is neither desirable nor feasible.

We have to find a solution that applies to the entire country. The solution to the communal problem lies ultimately in social justice, and, so far as our collective life is concerned, in an emphasis on the political and economic aspects and interests of life and in the divorce of religion from politics and economics. Whether we are Hindus or Muslims, Sikhs or Christians, our political and economic problems and interests are the same for all of us. In socialism, therefore, and in all it means lies a solution of this vexed communal problem. Any division of the country or of the provinces on religious basis will not help us in bringing about amity, not to speak of unity, which the Congress has so long stood for. An overhasty surgical cure will involve us in confusion and disaster.

Amiya never ceased to point to this tragic prophecy of Sarat, and to the chequered communal history of the subcontinent since then. Partition on communal lines did not bring peace, but created enemies across borders, and Hindu/Muslim conflict and enmity inside India itself remained depressingly familiar. Until his dying day, Sarat was to insist that the answers and solutions were to be found not in religious divide, but in social justice and better lives for the people of the subcontinent.

When Sarat realised that in spite of his strong opposition, Congress leaders such as Nehru and Patel, as well as prominent business leaders were bent upon partitioning India, he concentrated his efforts on saving the unity of Bengal. He started to focus and advocate in terms of a 'Free and United Bengal' as a socialist republic, independent both of India and Pakistan.

On 10 May 1947, Sarat met Gandhi at Sodepur near Calcutta, at 2 pm, to have preliminary discussions with him on the proposal for a United Bengal. Later in the afternoon of the same day between 4 and 6.30 pm, Sarat was on hand at his 1 Woodburn Park residence in Calcutta, for discussions with Bengal Congress leaders Kiran Sankar Roy and Surendra Mohan Ghose.

Later the same evening at Woodburn Park, from 7.30 pm, a meeting was convened by Sarat where Bengal Muslim League leaders Suhrawardy and Abul Hashim joined the aforementioned Bengal Congress luminaries, along with Bengal Congress stalwart Satya Ranjan Bakshi. Here, the scheme for a United Bengal was the only item on the agenda and was thus discussed in some detail. Time was short, but Sarat was moving as quickly as he could.

Sarat met with Gandhi again at Sodepur at 7 pm on 13 May 1947, to report to him about the progress of talks he was having with the Bengal Congress and Bengal Muslim League leaders. Gandhi at this point expressed his satisfaction with the talks between the two groups, the one Hindu and the other Muslim, and indicated his support for 'a Free and United Bengal'.

Further meetings between the Bengal Congress and Bengal Muslim League leaders were held in Woodburn Park on 15 May, 17 May and 19 May 1947. On 20 May 1947, a tentative agreement was arrived at between them, which was signed by Sarat on behalf of the Bengal Congress group and by Abul Hashim. By this time, the latter held the most senior position in the hierarchy of the Bengal branch of the Muslim League as General Secretary, and signed on behalf of the League.

The terms of this draft agreement hammered out at 1 Woodburn Park were as follows[2]:

1. Bengal will be a Free State. The Free State of Bengal will decide its relations with the rest of India.
2. The constitution of the Free State of Bengal will provide for election to the Bengal Legislature on the basis of joint electorate and adult franchise; with reservation of seats proportionate to the population amongst Hindus and Muslims. The seats as between Hindus and Scheduled Caste Hindus will be distributed amongst them in proportion to their respective population, or in such manner as may be agreed among them. The constituencies will be multiple constituencies and the votes will be distributive and not cumulative. A candidate who gets the majority of the votes of his own community cast during the elections and 25 per cent of the votes of the other communities so cast will be declared elected. If no candidate satisfies these conditions, that candidate who gets the largest number of votes of his own community will be elected.
3. On the announcement by his Majesty's Government that the proposal of the Free State of Bengal has been accepted and that Bengal will not be partitioned, the present Bengal Ministry will be dissolved and a new Interim Ministry brought into being consisting of an equal number of Muslims and Hindus (including Scheduled Caste Hindus), but excluding the Chief Minister. In this Ministry the Chief Minister will be a Muslim and the Home Minister a Hindu.
4. Pending the final emergence of a Legislature and a Ministry under the new constitution, the Hindus (including Scheduled Caste Hindus), and the Muslims will have an equal share in the services including Military and Police. The services will be manned by Bengalees.

---

[2] Copies of this Agreement with original signatures are included in the Private Collection of Amiya Nath and Jyotsna Bose.

5. A Constituent Assembly composed of 30 persons, 16 Muslims
    and 14 Hindus will be elected by the Muslim and non-Muslim
    Members of the Legislature respectively, excluding the
    Europeans.

    1, Woodburn Park   Sd/- Sarat Chandra Bose
    Calcutta   Sd/- Abul Hashim
    20th May 1947

Once signed, the agreement was then dispatched by special
messenger to Gandhi, who was at the time in Patna. At a press
interview on 23 May 1947, Sarat said[3]:

> If the Free State of Bengal comes into being, it will be a Republic
> and its nature and character will be Socialist. Details of the
> Socialist Republic will have to be worked out, if and when,
> Bengal will have a Constituent Assembly of her own. There is
> no difference as far as fundamentals are concerned between me
> and those with whom I had discussions on the subject since the
> last five months.

> I want to impress upon the public of Bengal and the rest of India
> that the cure for communalism is not communalism. We have to
> approach things for an altogether different and healthier out-
> look—and that is the socialistic outlook.

> The solution I have offered is the creation of Socialist Republics—
> call them Free States, if you will, that is the expression that has
> been used in the terms of the agreement that were published this
> morning. By the word 'Free' I mean freedom not only from political
> bondage, but also freedom from social and economic servitude.

Gandhi himself was not long in responding, and on 24 May
1947 wrote to Sarat from Patna suggesting some changes in
the draft agreement of 20 May 1947, thus signaling his positive
engagement with what Sarat and his Bengali Hindu and Muslim
cohorts were trying to bring about[4]:

> My dear Sarat,

> I have your note. There is nothing in the draft stipulating that
> nothing will be done by mere majority. Every act of Government

[3] Private Collection of Amiya Nath and Jyotsna Bose.
[4] Ibid.

must carry with it the cooperation of at least two-thirds of the Hindu members in the Executive and the Legislature. There should be an admission that Bengal has a common culture and common mother tongue—Bengali. Make sure that the Central Muslim League approved of the proposal notwithstanding reports to the contrary. If your presence is necessary in Delhi, I shall telephone or telegraph. I propose to discuss the draft with the (Congress) Working Committee.

Yours
Sd/- Bapu

Upon receipt of Gandhi's letter of 24 May on the following day 25 May 1947, Sarat immediately convened a further meeting that same day at Woodburn Park. The draft agreement of 20 May was readily amended by both Congress and Muslim League representatives in line with Gandhi's suggestions. The amended draft agreement now read[5]:

Basis of Agreement:

Bengali Muslims, Hindus, Christians and Buddhists have a common mother tongue and are bound together by racial, social, cultural, economic and other ties, and a Free and United Bengal where they can fully cooperate with one another is essential for their social, economic and political progress.

Terms:

1. Bengal will be a Free State. The Free State of Bengal will decide its relations with rest of India. The question of joining any Union will be decided by the Legislature of the Free State of Bengal by a two-thirds majority.

2. The constitution of the Free State of Bengal will provide for election to the Bengal Legislature on the basis of joint electorate and adult franchise, with reservation of seats proportionate to the population amongst them in proportion to their respective population or in such manner as may be agreed among them. The constituencies will be multiple constituencies and votes will be distributive and not cumulative. A candidate who gets the largest number of votes of his own community cast during the elections and at least 25 per cent of the votes of the other communities so cast will be declared elected. If no candidate

---

[5] Ibid.

satisfies the condition laid down in the previous sentence, that candidate who gets the largest number of votes out of the total votes polled will be elected.

3. On paragraph 1 and 2 being accepted by both parties, the present Ministry will be dissolved and an interim Ministry brought into being consisting of an equal number of Muslims and Hindus (including Scheduled Caste Hindus), but excluding the Chief Minister. In this Ministry, the Chief Minister will be a Muslim and the Home Minister a Hindu. The Interim Ministry is to be treated by H.M.G. as an Independent Indian Government.

4. Decisions to be taken by the Interim Ministry are not to be taken by a bare majority but by a two-thirds majority. Similarly, decisions to be taken in the present Bengal Legislature are not to be taken by a bare majority but by a two-thirds majority of its members excluding the European Members.

5. Pending the final emergence of a Legislature and a Ministry under the new constitution, the Hindus (including Scheduled Caste Hindus) and the Muslims will have an equal share in the services including Military and Police. The services will be manned by Bengalees. Merit shall be the determining factor in the matter of recruitment to the services.

6. A Constituent Assembly composed of 30 persons, 16 Muslims and 14 non-Muslims will be elected by the Muslim and non-Muslim members of the Legislature respectively, excluding the Europeans.

7. As far as Bengal is concerned, H.M.G. is to transfer power either to the interim Ministry mentioned in paragraph 3 or to the Constituent Assembly mentioned in paragraph 6.

Thus, it was that on 26 May 1947, Sarat Bose was able to reply positively to Gandhi and forward to him an amended draft agreement which incorporated all of Gandhi's suggestions[6]:

My dear Mahatmaji,

I am very grateful for the suggestions contained in your note of the 24th instant which was handed over to me by Deben Dey yesterday. We have been discussing the terms almost every day and trying to improve upon them. Day before yesterday, I had a long discussion with Kiran and some members of the Bengal

---

[6] Ibid.

Legislative Assembly. Last night I had a discussion with Abul Hashim and Satya Babu. As a result of the discussions, I have re-drafted paragraphs 1 and 2 of the terms and forwarded them to Shaheed (Suhrawardy) this morning. I enclose copies of re-drafted paragraphs 1 and 2 herewith for your consideration.

As regards your suggestion that every act of Government must carry with it the co-operation of at least two-thirds of the Hindu members of the executive and legislature, I have not been able to discuss the matter with Shaheed. He is leaving for Delhi this afternoon by air. If I come to Delhi, I shall discuss it with him there. If, in the meantime, he sees you, you may put the matter before him and ask for his reactions.

As regards your suggestion that there should be an admission that Bengal has common culture and common mother-tongue—Bengalee—the discussions I initiated in January last and have been carrying on since then have been on the basis that Bengal has common culture and common mother-tongue—a basis agreed to by all the parties to the discussions. In one of Shaheed's statements made last month, he made that admission. There should, therefore, be no difficulty in incorporating the admission in the terms.

So long today. With Pronams,
Yours affectionately,
Sd/- Sarat Chandra Bose

MAHATMA GANDHI,
NEW DELHI.

P.S. Shaheed and Fazlur Rahman will discuss the terms with Jinnah and his Working Committee. From the conversations I have had with them, I have gathered that if the Congress and the Muslim League in Bengal could come to an agreement, Jinnah may not stand in the way.

Amiya argued strongly in his reflections and comments on this critical period, that in May 1947 the majority of Congressmen in Bengal remained in favour of a free and united Bengal. Those not in favour were, he said, influenced by pro-partition propaganda largely financed by the influential Hindu Mawari capitalists of Calcutta, with Shyama Prasad Mukherjee of the Hindu Mahasabha as the main spokesman.

A section of the Muslim League led by its Bengal Chairman Maulana Akram Khan was also against the formation of a 'Free and United Bengal', but most of the other leaders of the Bengal Muslim League including Abul Hashim were in favour. In any case where the League was concerned, the final decision would rest ultimately with Jinnah.

As could by now be expected, the British imperial authorities and the British Government at home were following developments closely. They were no longer disguising their rising impatience to be gone from the subcontinent as an imperial power, as articulated by British Prime Minister Attlee and Viceroy Mountbatten, and no doubt increasingly apprehensive as to what would be the nature and outcome of their handover of power.

On 28 May 1947, the British Governor of Bengal, Sir Frederick Burrows, wrote a long letter to Mountbatten regarding the proposal for a Free and United Bengal. This letter has been declassified and released, and merits reproducing in full:

GOVERNMENT HOUSE, CALCUTTA,
28 May 1947
S E C R E T

Dear Lord Mountbatten,

You will believe me when I say that I was both relieved and delighted to receive your telegram of the 23rd May informing me that H.M.G. had agreed to your having authority to recast the forthcoming statement, so far as Bengal is concerned, in the light of the circumstances prevailing on the 2nd June. It is primarily to bring you up to date as regards Coalition prospects in Bengal, as far as I can do so, that I am now writing. I say 'as far as I can do so' because both Suhrawardy and Kiran Shankar (sic) Roy have left for Delhi to take the matter up with their respective High Commands and the final decision 'to coalesce or not to coalesce' will now be taken there.

I can therefore only give you the position as it was this weekend when they left Calcutta for Delhi and my own estimate of the prospects. Suhrawardy proposes to seek an interview with you on your return at which to give you the final result of his efforts there. Should Kiran Shankar Roy also ask to see you and be given an interview it would help you to complete the picture.

I should perhaps recall that there have been latterly two sets of negotiations proceeding concurrently—those between Suhrawardy, with some of his followers, and Kiran Shankar Roy and Sarat Bose for the formulation of certain points of agreement as the basis of a future Coalition Government and of a separate constituent assembly formed under its aegis to draft a constitution for the sovereign independent 'Free State of Bengal'. The other set of negotiations to which, so far as I know, only Suhrawardy and Kiran Shankar Roy are parties, was inaugurated at my suggestion and directed to the formation of a Coalition government here and now without any binding commitment as to the future constitutional or 'international' set up of the Province.

The two sets of negotiations are not mutually antagonistic in any way but rather complementary. I felt that while some progress was undoubtedly being made in the long term negotiations, these had already been in progress since the New Year and finality was not likely to be attained before the critical date of June 2nd. It was common ground between the three of us that the object of those negotiations would almost certainly be defeated if it once became known for certain the H.M.G. had decided to link the possibility of partition in B E N G A L with any decision to partition India, and we therefore decided to try to secure the immediate setting up [of] a Coalition without any definite commitments but obviously on the basis of a tacit recognition of the ground already covered towards agreement in the discussions to which Sarat Bose and a wider circle on both sides have been parties. Suhrawardy and Roy were both impelled to my proposal for a short cut by their conviction that only by getting a Coalition set up in time to avert reference in the statement of June 2nd to the possibility of partitioning Bengal could we hope to escape a holocaust in Bengal.

The discussions in which Sarat Bose has figured are still proceeding and have been the subject of a good deal of discussion in the Press—not all of it unfavourable. Documents purporting to be heads of agreement actually reached between the three protagonists have been shown to me from time to time—I telegraphed a recent edition to you in my No. 125-C of the 19th May, and while I cannot say that finality has been reached even by the principals to the discussion, there is probably enough agreement to justify the formation of a Coalition on that basis now if the High Commands would agree.

It is true that the formula has not been put to or accepted by either Party's Working Committee in Bengal and that the newspapers controlled, on the one side, by the Mahasabha (which is pressing for partition) and, on the other, by the faction which is critical of Suhrawardy on personal grounds, are strongly critical both of the main idea of an independent but united Bengal and of some of the details (e.g joint electorates). But I know for a fact that some of the 'rebels' in Suhrawardy's camp have approached Kiran Shankar Roy with almost identical proposals as the basis of a future coalition if only he will deal with them rather than with Suhrawardy: and Suhrawardy claims to have talked over the hitherto hostile Chairman of the Muslim League Party in Bengal, Maulana Akram Khan. Suhrawardy has considerable support among his personal followers and I believe him when he says that, if Congress will 'play', he is confident he could bring his Party up to support his move for a united and independent Bengal, as they all want at all costs to avoid partition. He is not, however, prepared to burn his boats unless he can be assured that Kiran Shankar Roy will be able and willing to bring the Bengal Congress in, with or without the approval of his own High Command. Roy for his part has gone so far as to tell me and others that he will resign his position as leader of the Congress Assembly Party in Bengal if the High Command will not listen to him, as he is not prepared to take responsibility for the bloodshed that will ensue; but I must confess I share Suhrawardy's apprehension that, if Nehru and Patel prove adamant, Roy is not the man to move them and Bengal will be sacrificed on the altar of Nehru's All-India outlook.

The plan to form a Coalition without firm conditions and, if necessary, in the faces of the respective High Commands has not matured and I doubt if it will do so now as the Provincial parties have not been approached. Though Suhrawardy and Roy might get together in Delhi, I doubt if they would defy their respective High Commands without more definite assurance of the support of their parties here. But if the High Commands would agree to a Coalition of this kind at once—either without conditions or on the Suhrawardy-Roy-Bose formula—I am confident that both Suhrawardy and Roy could put it over down here:

Gandhi is on the side of avoiding partition and there has been some sign, this last week, of a revulsion of feeling among the Hindus (especially of East Bengal) against partition if it can be avoided. Short of the Cabinet Plan of May 1946, partition can only be avoided by maintaining, for the time being at all events, a right to stay out of either Hindustan or Pakistan.

The reason for this in a nutshell is that the Hindus of Bengal are determined not to surrender their ideal of a link with a Hindu centre (and the protection they think that would afford to a Hindu minority) unless they can be guaranteed that they will not be forced under a Pakistan centre and, lacking that guarantee, they demand partition: the Muslims, on the other hand, while not so adamant about joining a North Western Pakistan, are determined not to come under a Hindu-controlled centre. To be independent, for the time being, of either Hindustan or Pakistan is the only platform on which they can unite.

And a united Bengal ought to be a viable proposition in peace time, however defenceless it might prove in war. It is something to which we could hand over power with a clear conscience that it represented the greatest measure of agreement of the population and I believe it would offer the best chance now remaining of a peaceful hand over. The alternative of partition is politically and economically a deplorable prospect, especially for Eastern Bengal, but as I cannot be sure that Suhrawardy and Roy will bring off Coalition to avert it, I must now deal with this possibility.

All our information—and there is plenty of it—goes to show that if as a result of the discussions beginning on the 2nd June it appears that partition is being forced on Bengal or that the Hindus can have partition for the asking, the Muslims will refuse to take it lying down and will adopt every form of resistance, in the course of which much blood will be shed and much property devastated, especially in Calcutta, the loss of any interest in which will be the greatest blow, financially and in prestige, to the Muslims of Eastern India.

In the Province generally there is a feeling of pessimism and almost of resignation to the prospect of renewed communal strife on an unprecedented scale and in some parts the wildest ideas are current regarding the preparedness of the rival community to launch a planned campaign of violence the moment the signal is given. Calcutta is particularly "jittery"—I enclose a copy of a document which Kiran Shankar Roy handed to me on Saturday with the comment, merely, that it was handed to him by a Muslim. I have had this checked up by our Intelligence and have reason to believe that this particular document represents merely a collection by the Congress Party of the rumours prevalent (among Hindus and Muslims alike) in Calcutta and that most of the assertions of fact in it are palpably false: but that exaggerated rumours of this sort are being freely circulated and given ready credence by both sides is undeniable.

Other panicky reports that have recently come to notice in Calcutta are that the 2nd June (earlier dates have already been mentioned but discarded when nothing eventuated) will be marked by a planned attack by the Muslims on Hindu life and property in Calcutta and elsewhere: that the prospects of peace are so gloomy that a four-day continuous curfew covering the 2nd June is in contemplation: that the Ministry will be dismissed and rule u/s 93 inaugurated with a view to maintaining law and order for a period round about the 2nd June (curiously enough Suhrawardy when he saw me just before leaving for Delhi on Monday quite unexpectedly and inconsequentially asked me at what date I proposed to dissolve the Ministry and go into Section 93): and, finally, that simultaneously with the forthcoming announcement martial law will be enforced.

There is no doubt that both sides are preparing for trouble—though preparations are not on the scale suggested in Kiran Shankar Roy's paper—and that both sides have bombs and firearms and other weapons to an extent hitherto not experienced in communal disturbances in Bengal. But to my mind most dangerous of all is this mentality that a struggle is inevitable, that "the other side" are only waiting for a signal to begin it and that one must therefore be on one's guard night and day for the outbreak of the trouble. In such an atmosphere the smallest incident occurring round what the public regard as the critical date (June 2nd) may cause people to say 'This is it' and may start the widest conflagration.

In this superheated and explosive atmosphere I deemed it necessary to give a broadcast last night (copy enclosed) with a view to steadying public opinion. Certain leaders also have of themselves circulated a statement appealing for calm (enclosure 3): copies of this were widely dropped over Calcutta from the air yesterday. We are, of course, taking all possible precautions, unobtrusively and without provocation, to be prepared for an outburst should there be one following on publicity being given to transactions at Delhi on and after the 2nd June. But what I really have in mind in acquainting you with this aspect of the position down here is to give you material (which I believe Suhrawardy and Kiran Shankar Roy will confirm and reinforce) for impressing on the All-India leaders of both sides the danger of the position in Bengal—the danger of widespread communal strife, followed almost immediately, as it inevitably would be in present circumstances, by a complete breakdown of our feeding arrangements for Calcutta and the deficit pockets of the Province (largely in East Bengal).

A serious outbreak of communal strife at this moment might well cost us more lives by famine in the next few months than

the rioting itself. If, therefore, and this is the point I am leading up to, division of India becomes inevitable and with it
the opportunity to the Hindus to partition Bengal, it is in my
opinion of supreme importance that if that is by any means an
agreed decision or even a decision acquiesced in by the All-India
leaders, these (and from my point of view especially Jinnah)
should, if it is humanly possible, be got to the microphone at
the earliest possible moment to say that all should acquiesce
in the decisions taken at Delhi and to appeal in the strongest
possible terms for their peaceful implementation. Though the
response in Calcutta, so far, to the Gandhi–Jinnah appeal to
abjure violent means has not been conspicuously favourable in
practice, I believe that a strong indication by Jinnah (if he can
be got to give it) that the decision is accepted by him as the best
that can be got and as worthy of acceptance and working out,
for what it is worth, in peace and amity, would have a most
steadying effect on Muslims down here and, incidentally, on
Hindu apprehensions.

Yours sincerely,
F J BURROWS

Meanwhile, and also on 28 May 1947, the India–Burma
Committee of the British Cabinet met in London where the
future of Bengal was on the agenda for discussion and certain
decisions were taken. According to these records, which are now
public, those present at this meeting at 10 Downing Street, held
at 11 am, were Prime Minister Attlee (in the Chair), Sir S. Cripps,
Mr Alexander, the Earl of Listowel, Viscount Addison, Mr C. P.
Mayhew, Mr A. G. Bottomley, Mr A. Henderson, and Lord
Chorley. Also invited and present were Rear-Admiral Viscount
Mountbatten of Burma, Field Marshall Sir Claude Auchinleck,
Sir D. Monteath, Lord Ismay, Lieutenant Colonel Erskine Gum,
Sir N. Brook, Mr S. E. V. Luke, Mr G. M. Wilson and Mr F. F.
Turnbull (Secretariat).

That part of the Minutes dealing with 'The Future of Bengal'
stated:

Viscount Mountbatten drew the Committee's attention to the
report in the News Chronicle of 27th May of an interview given
by Pandit Nehru, in the course of which he had said that Congress
could agree to Bengal remaining united only if it remained in the
Union of India. This statement would no doubt receive the widest

publicity in India and was an example of the tendency of the Indian leaders to make public statements from which they could not subsequently withdraw. The Viceroy was afraid that, in view of this development, the prospect of saving the unity of Bengal and securing its establishment as a third Dominion in India had been gravely prejudiced; indeed, he thought that, if Pandit Nehru had completely committed himself, the only means by which the partition of Bengal could be avoided would be by Mr Jinnah's abandonment of his claim to the Province for Pakistan and by his acceptance of a position, similar to that of an Indian State, a quasi-independence in close relationship with one or other of the Dominion Governments. If it proved impossible to avoid the partition of the province, the future of Eastern Bengal would present very difficult problems, since it was clearly not a viable unit. This area might possibly submit a claim for recognition as a separate Dominion in order to secure the assistance and backing of His Majesty's Government. The Committee agreed that, in the event of the partition of Bengal, Dominion status could not be granted to Eastern Bengal alone; it would have to unite with one or other of the Indian Dominions.

It can, thus, be reasonably concluded that up to the end of May 1947, now less than three months away from the final departure of the British imperial authorities, partition was inevitable but the possibility of a united Bengal as a separate entity was still on the table. Mountbatten as Viceroy had noted in a Top Secret telegram of 28 April 1947 to Governor Burrows, 'Do not forget that my scheme leaves the door open to a united but independent Bengal belonging neither to Pakistan nor Hindustan. Jinnah would raise no objections to this.'

According to Mountbatten's own records, two alternative broadcast statements were recorded by him in London on the same day of the Committee Meeting, that is 28 May 1947. Broadcast 'A' was to be used if it appeared likely that Bengal would be partitioned, and broadcast 'B' if it appeared that Bengal would remain unified.

In the event neither broadcast was put to air at the time, and for the last days of May and the first week of June 1947, Sarat and his allies both Hindu and Muslim, Congress and League, accelerated their now frantic efforts to save the day. On 30 May 1947, Sarat left Calcutta for Delhi on an afternoon flight accompanied by Satya Ranjan Bakshi. Their objective was further discussions with Gandhi, this time face to face, on a 'Free and United Bengal'.

These duly began the following evening of 31 May 1947 at Bhangi Colony in Delhi, immediately after a prayer meeting conducted by Gandhi which itself had been preceded by a meeting there of the CWC. Commenting on the latter two events on the following day 1 June 1947, the Hindustan Standard of Calcutta reflected a robust position on the part of Gandhi against partition in general, and decrying the concept of Pakistan:

> New Delhi, May 31, 1947. The Congress Working Committee met at 3 pm today at the Bhangi Colony, New Delhi, where Mahatma Gandhi was staying. The Committee after three hours session adjourned the meeting to meet again at 3 pm tomorrow. It is understood that the discussions were of a general character which centered around the stand which the Congress should take in the forthcoming talks with the Viceroy especially in the light of Mahatma Gandhi's uncompromising stand in regard to the division of India.

On the same evening, Gandhi in his prayer meeting said: 'Even if the whole of India burns we shall not concede Pakistan, even if the Muslims demand it at the point of the sword.'[7]

Sarat's meeting with Gandhi in the evening of 31 May 1947 was followed by further discussions between 1 and 4 June 1947, involving Gandhi, Suhrawardy and Maulana Azad. The amended agreement was approved by Suhrawardy, who in turn met with Jinnah to elicit his support and open the way for his final approval.

On 5 June 1947, Sarat himself met with Jinnah, who agreed to Bengal remaining united and becoming independent with a Constituent Assembly of her own. Sarat met Jinnah and then Gandhi again on 6 June 1947, to convey his thanks to them for supporting the proposal for a 'Free and United Bengal'.

Sarat was later to freely acknowledge his debt to Jinnah in a statement issued on 12 September 1948 on the death of Jinnah[8]

---

[7] Michael Edwardes, *The Myth of the Mahatma: Gandhi the British and the Raj* (UK: Constable, 1986), 250.

[8] Private Collection of Amiya Nath and Jyotsna Bose.

[I]n justice to him I must disclose that in June 1947, he agreed in his conversation with me in New Delhi to Bengal remaining united and becoming independent with a Constituent Assembly of her own to decide to which Union she would accede. What he agreed to was conveyed by me to Mahatma Gandhi immediately and it will be remembered that on or about 8th of June 1947 Mahatmaji said in a prayer meeting that 'he had been taken to task for supporting my move'.

No doubt relieved by the assurances from Jinnah and also in receipt of reassurances of full support from Gandhi, Sarat left Delhi for Calcutta on a morning flight on Saturday 7 June 1947, seemingly more confident about the prospects of saving Bengal. Almost immediately after Sarat's departure for Calcutta, the carefully, albeit hastily constructed plan for a free and united Bengal began to unravel.

Sarat and Amiya were completely taken aback and thrown off balance by a report only two days later in the Hindustan Standard of 9 June 1947, of a statement from Gandhi after his prayer meeting of 8 June, which said:

Referring next to the move for United Sovereign Bengal, he said that some people had told him that the move was a sinister one. The Hindus were fed up and wanted to divide the Western from the Eastern Bengal. The Bengal Muslim League had also rejected the unity plan. But some people are still persisting with it and it was said to be due to the fact that he (Gandhiji) was behind the move. He wanted to make it clear that he could never support any questionable practice. He was told that money was being spent like water to buy votes in favour of United Bengal. He appreciated unity but not at the cost of honour and justice. He was taken to task for supporting Saratbabu. He was undoubtedly his friend. He was in correspondence with him. But he would never be guilty of supporting anything that could not be publicly and honestly defended. That was his universal practice. He did not believe in questionable means even to secure a worthy end.

That same day on 9 June 1947, Sarat fired off the following telegram to Gandhi:

Request you publicly disclose names of your informants and details of information regarding money being spent like water to buy votes for United Bengal and hold public enquiry to ascertain

truth Stop If information false punish informants if information
true punish bribegivers and bribetakers Sarat Bose

Gandhi telegrammed his reply on 10 June 1947:

New Delhi 10th June Sarat Chandra Bose Woodburn Park
Calcutta Received angry wire Anger unworthy Wrote Sunday
Must not publish names How can bribegivers and takers be
punished by private persons except Bar Public opinion Be calm
and steadfast Bapu

Sarat was not to be denied and responded to Gandhi on 11 June
1947:

Express Mahatma Gandhi Bhangi colony New Delhi No anger in
me or in my wire Made only a request Stop Did not expect you
give currency rumours before ascertaining truth Stop Awaiting
your letter shall not publish names without your consent Sarat
Bose

Worse was to come in a letter from Gandhi written by him on 8
June 1947 but not received by Sarat until 13 June 1947. Sarat
had deliberately avoided dealing with Nehru and (Sardar) Patel
whom he knew were firmly against the idea of a sovereign Bengal
in any circumstances, and Gandhi's letter confirmed for Sarat
his reservations about dealing with them:

My dear Sarat,

I have gone through your draft. I have now discussed the scheme
thoroughly with Pandit Nehru and Sardar. Both of them are
dead against the proposal and they are of the opinion that it is
merely a trick for dividing Hindus and Scheduled Caste leaders.
With them it is not merely a suspicion but almost a conviction.
They feel also that money is being lavishly expended in order
to secure Scheduled Caste votes. If such is the case, you should
give up the struggle at least at present for the unity purchased
by corrupt practices would be worse than a frank partition, it
being a recognition of established division of hearts and the
unfortunate experiences of the Hindus. I see also that there is
no prospect of transfer of power outside the two parts of India.
Therefore, whatever arrangement is come to has to be arrived at
by a previous agreement between the Congress and the League.
This as far as I can see you can't obtain. Nevertheless I would

not shake your faith unless it is founded on shifting sand consisting of corrupt practices and trickery alluded to above. If you are absolutely sure that there is no warrant whatsoever for the suspicion and unless you get the written assurance of the local Muslim League supported by the centre, you should give up the struggle for unity of Bengal and cease to disturb the atmosphere that has been created for partition of Bengal.

Love
Bapu

Sarat replied almost immediately in a letter of the following day 14 June 1947:

My Dear Mahatmaji,

Your kind letter of the 8th instant was to hand yesterday afternoon. I note that both Jawaharlal and Vallabhbhai are dead against the proposal. As regards their opinion that it is merely a trick for dividing Hindus and Scheduled Caste leaders. I cannot subscribe to it. Having had conversation with some Muslim League leaders in and from January last, and subsequently with some Congress leaders, I can say definitely and emphatically that there was nothing in the nature of trickery. I am unable to understand what Jawaharlal and Vallabhbhai mean by saying that they feel that money is being lavishly expended in order to secure Scheduled Caste votes. It is possible to deal with facts, but not with mere feeling or suspicion. I must say however that the feeling of suspicion that money is being expended to secure Scheduled Caste votes is entirely baseless.

My faith remains unshaken and I propose to work in my own humble way for the unity of Bengal. even after the raging and tearing campaign that has been carried on in favour of partition, I have not the slightest doubt that if a referendum were taken, the Hindus of Bengal by a large majority would vote against partition. The voice of Bengal has been stifled for the moment, but I have every hope that it will assert itself.

With Pronams

Yours affectionately
Sarat Chandra Bose

Mahatma Gandhi
Bhangi Colony
New Delhi

As a direct witness to this episode, Amiya often raised the question how it could have come to pass that Gandhi who supported the 'Free and United Bengal' movement until 6 June 1947 withdrew his support on 8 June 1947 only two days later, during his post-prayer meeting speech and in his letter to Sarat Bose of the same date. At his prayer meeting, Gandhi had stated that the Bengal Muslim League had also rejected the unity plan, but Amiya insists that this was not correct. Gandhi was fully aware that a majority of Bengal Muslim League leaders were in favour of a free and united Bengal. It was also well known that Maulana Akram Khan's opposition to the proposal was due more to his personal dislike of Suhrawardy than the proposal itself.

Amiya reiterated that in any event it was known to all including Gandhi that the final decision on this question from a Muslim perspective rested only with Jinnah, who wielded almost dictatorial powers within the Muslim League organisation. Gandhi knew directly from Sarat when they met on 6 June 1947 that Jinnah had agreed to Bengal remaining free and united and had also agreed to give necessary directions to the Bengal Muslim League. If he (Gandhi) had any doubts in the matter why did he not ask Sarat during their Delhi meeting to 'get the written assurance of the local Muslim League supported by the centre?'

It was ironic that on 9 June 1947, still perhaps unaware of the tectonic shift in Gandhi's position on the matter of partition, Sarat had written to Jinnah, thanking him and suggesting what might be Jinnah's tactical approach to 'Muslim members of the Bengal Legislative Assembly'[9]:

My dear Jinnah,

I have to thank you most sincerely for your courtesy and cordiality towards me and for the consideration you gave to my suggestions. Bengal is passing through the greatest crisis in her history, but she can yet be saved. She can be saved if you will kindly give the following instructions to Muslim members of the Bengal Legislative Assembly:

(i) at the meeting to be held of all members of the Legislative Assembly (other than Europeans) at which a decision will be taken

---

[9] *Sarat Chandra Bose Commemoration Volume*, 85–86.

on the issue as to which Constituent Assembly the province as a whole would join if it were subsequently decided by the two parts to remain united, to vote neither for the Hindusthan Constituent Assembly, nor for the Pakistan Constituent Assembly, and to make it clear by a statement in the Assembly or in the press or otherwise, that they are solidly in favour of Bengal having a Constituent Assembly of her own; and,

(ii) at the meetings of the members of the two parts of the Legislative Assembly sitting separately and empowered to vote whether or not the Province should be partitioned, to vote solidly against partition.

The request I am making to you is in accordance with the views you expressed to me when we met. But it seems to me that if you merely express your views to your members and not give them specific instructions as to how to vote, the situation cannot be saved. I hope you will do all in your power to enable Bengal remain united and to make her a free and independent state.

If Muslim members of the Bengal Legislative Assembly vote solidly as suggested in paragraphs (i) and (ii) above, I think Lord Mountbatten will be compelled to convene another meeting of all members of the Assembly (other than Europeans) at which a decision can be taken on the issue as to whether the province as a whole desires to have a Constituent Assembly of her own.

I shall be coming to Delhi again on the 13th or 14th and shall call on you on the 14th or 15th.

Thanking you and with kind regards,

Yours sincerely,
Sarat Chandra Bose

Quaid-e-Azam M. A. Jinnah
Barrister-at-Law
10 Aurangazeb Road
New Delhi

Amiya who had been closely associated with the negotiations regarding the United Bengal movement with a variety of different Muslim League and Congress leaders, confirmed that 'there was not an iota of truth' in Gandhi's allegation that money was being spent like water to buy votes in favour of a United Bengal.

Also according to Amiya, Gandhi knew all along that Nehru and Patel were dead against the proposal of a united sovereign Bengal, and in spite of their opposition, had supported the movement until 6 June 1947. What then caused the volte-face on 8 June 1947?

For Amiya it was difficult to accept that Gandhi could change his stand on such a crucial issue within such a short time. He doubted that it was the well-known opposition of Nehru and Patel which made Gandhi suddenly change his political stand on a 'Free and United Bengal'. Rather it seemed to Amiya that the real reason for Gandhi's change of heart was to be found in the pressure exerted on him by the Hindu, non-Bengali capitalist lobby which had its main investments at that time in and around Calcutta.

The leaders of this business community did not want to lose their influence in shaping political policies which in their view might have had adverse economic and financial consequences for them and their interests. They certainly did not want to allow the emergence of a free, united and socialist Bengal which might threaten their economic predominance. They had reached the conclusion that partition of Bengal was best for their economic interests and acted accordingly.

Of the other actors on the stage, Jinnah in Amiya's view was first and foremost a practical politician. He appreciated even in 1947 that it might not be possible for Pakistan to keep its control over the province of East Pakistan for any length of time, as had also been predicted by Mountbatten. Jinnah therefore supported the proposal for a Free and United Bengal, as Amiya believed, not out of any generosity of heart but because he was primarily a realist. In view of Jinnah's ceaseless campaign for the partition of India, it was not possible for him to concede unification of the whole of Bengal with India in 1947. Formation of a 'Free and United Bengal' gave him a way out, and he had therefore welcomed the proposal.

Where other politicians were concerned, the voices of Nehru and Patel proved decisive. They were resolutely against the creation of a third sovereign nation in addition to India and Pakistan, and carried the CWC with them on the issue, leaving Gandhi and a somewhat reluctant Mountbatten floundering in the backwash and struggling to keep up. On 14 June 1947, Gandhi addressed the AICC Meeting in New Delhi, asked the Congress to accept the partition of India, and supported the AICC resolution to that effect.

Nehru and Patel effectively won the day with their insistence that the Bengalis through the existing legislature of the Bengal National Assembly be given the choice of union with either of the two emerging nations India and Pakistan, or partition into two components the one majority Muslim to join Pakistan, the other majority Hindu to join India. There was never any real doubt by this late stage that the eastern part of Bengal would go to Pakistan, and the western part including Calcutta, to India.

In yet another spirited attempt to save the day for India and Bengal, as late as 1 July 1947 Sarat was calling for the 'mobilisation of all leftist and revolutionary forces' and for a meeting to be convened on 11/12 July 1947 to prepare a 'plan of action'. A circular letter to this effect was issued:

Tel: PK. 2248.   1 Woodburn Park
                                                   Calcutta 20

.   1st July, 1947

Dear Friend,

The acceptance of the June 3 Plan (Ed: The Mountbatten Plan) by the two major political organisations in the country has created a situation which calls for the mobilisation of all leftist and revolutionary forces. India stands divided; two of the major provinces are being partitioned. The domination and exploitation of the two Indias by British Imperialists will continue, but possibly in a more subtle and insidious form, under the name of Dominion Status.

The sufferings and sacrifices of the people in the cause of Indian unity and independence and the heroic fight that was put up outside India's borders by Indian soldiers and civilians under the leadership of Netaji Subhas Chandra Bose for the liberation of India have not yielded the desired result.

At this critical juncture we cannot afford to sit quiet. I, in common with many friends, feel that we should meet at an early date, review the situation, exchange thoughts and ideas and decide upon a definite plan of action which might lead the country to unity and freedom. For that purpose, a small conference has been arranged to take place in Calcutta at Belgachia Villa, 64 Belgachia Road (Tel. BB 1040) on 11th and 12th July, 1947.

I cordially invite you to attend the conference and shall feel thankful if you will kindly accept my invitation. I hope you will excuse short notice and make it convenient to attend.

An early reply will oblige. With kind regards,

Yours sincerely
Sgnd SARAT CHANDRA BOSE

No record has yet been found of what transpired at this meeting, or even if it actually took place. Whatever the case, the die was cast and on 14/15 August 1947, despite the herculean efforts of Sarat and others, Bengal was again divided as it had been early in the twentieth century. But there has been no reunification within a few years as there was then, and most of historic Bengal remains divided into Bangladesh as a sovereign state (since 1971) and West Bengal as a province of India.

Sarat was thus acutely distressed not only by the vivisection of British India, but also by the failure to save Bengal itself from partition. Most of all he had been deeply disillusioned by the conduct of the Congress High Command, which he saw as having reneged on its fundamental principles and its commitment to 'Complete Independence'. This, as was noted in the previous chapter, led to his resignation from the CWC on 6 January 1947, and from the Congress movement itself on 1 August 1947. Thereafter, the post-Congress political life of Sarat centred on the promotion and consolidation of Left unity.

* * *

Under the auspices of his 1 August 1947 press statement, already cited in the previous chapter as marking his final and complete break with the Congress, the indomitable Sarat on that same day launched his own Socialist Republican Party (preceded by an embryonic Azad Hind Party which had sought to cater principally for the returned servicemen of the Indian National Army, but which was superseded by subsequent developments). The Socialist Republican Party would continue the struggle for Complete Independence and a socialist form of government adapted to the particular conditions and circumstances of India:

The crisis that has overtaken India because of the June 3 Plan was not entirely unexpected, regard being had to all that has happened since the year 1939. It may also be said that such crises sometimes appear in periods of transition. We must, however, overcome the crisis that has overtaken us and for that purpose we must strengthen and consolidate all the leftist and revolutionary forces in the country. We have to distinguish real leftists and revolutionaries from pseudo ones. We have to distinguish between those who offer lip service to the ideology and programme of Netaji and those who really believe in it and are prepared to take upon themselves the completion of his unfulfilled task. We have to rally people of all communities—Hindus, Muslims, Sikhs, Christians, Buddhists and others—who do not subscribe to communalism in any shape or form and are prepared to undertake the work of reunifying the country on a socialist basis.

The communal poison that has entered into our souls has to be completely eradicated if India has to live and that can only be done if we are able to approach all the problems facing us from the nationalist and socialist points of view, and form ourselves into a cohesive, well-knit and disciplined Socialist Republican Party for the purpose of implementing the ideology and programme of Netaji.... I have decided to form such a party immediately and I announce its formation today under the name of the Socialist Republican Party.

I appeal to friends and co-workers all over the country and to the people at large—the unknown soldiers who are and will be the makers of India's destiny—to join the party in their thousands and tens of thousands and to serve the cause of Freedom, Democracy and Socialism with undying faith and devotion.

The aims and objectives together with the Manifesto of the new Party were reproduced in a booklet entitled *What We Believe,* on 21 October 1948, the fifth anniversary of the launch in Singapore of the Provisional Government of Azad Hind. In addition to standing for the 'Complete Independence' of an India free from British or any other foreign influence and control, the Socialist Republican Party called for the ending of autocratic rule in the Indian States, the setting up of Socialist Republics on the basis of linguistic groups, and the establishment in India of a Union of Socialist Republics.

Sarat had for some time given serious thought and consideration to his conception of a new, egalitarian and socialist India and had earlier articulated his thoughts while in jail in Coonoor, where his diary entry of 29 January 1944 reads:

> I conceive my country as a Union of Socialist Republics—an immense melting-pot in which the characters of all the races and nationalities comprised in it will be mixed and out of which a new 'worldism' will arise which will recognise no frontiers, no races, and no classes.

Underlying principles of the Party and its Manifesto included freedom of development, equal rights in particular those of Indian women, universal education and religious freedom, and the fundamental right to food and shelter. The Party chose to accept 'unconditionally' the ideology of Netaji Subhas Chandra Bose, and considered the completion of his unfulfilled task as the main aim of its political, social and economic activities.

From this point, Sarat moved to the next stage of his strategy, namely, to bring together all of the socialist forces in the country under the one banner. It was his firm conviction that if the socialist, leftist and progressive parties could be brought together on one platform 'welded together on some fundamental bases', the forces of reaction and the foreign and indigenous vested interests that were in alliance with them could be defeated.

By this time, Sarat together with his supporters and fellow travellers on the Left spectrum of politics in the new India were confronted with a now-governing Congress Party, which in the period immediately prior to and in the several years after the Transfer of Power on 15 August 1947 had undergone a seismic shift to the Right. This had included the state of West Bengal where a new Congress provincial government led by Chief Minister Dr Prafulla Chandra Ghosh, had sought to deal with political unrest through repressive legislation of civil rights (the Special Powers Bill).

This had in turn triggered a counter movement towards further consolidation of the Left parties, including Forward Bloc and the CPI together with Sarat's Socialist Republican Party, among others. On 6 December 1947, Sarat presided over a mass rally at Shraddhananda Park in Central Calcutta, held in protest against the 'anti-people policies' of the Congress in West Bengal. Among the other speakers were a young CPI Member of the West Bengal Legislative Assembly, Jyoti Basu, and an old friend and political ally of both Subhas and Sarat, Satya Ranjan Bakshi.

At the national level, the challenges for Sarat and his allies, if anything, seemed more formidable. In the several years following 15 August 1947, Sarat repeatedly warned about the corruption, nepotism and cronyism which had come to characterise Congress rule. He also felt that the 'Right-wing Congress leadership's blundering policy' had led the country from one form of slavery to another and was bound to result in complete political and economic ruin of the country.

In the Manifesto for his election campaign of June 1949 for a seat in the West Bengal Legislative Assembly, referred to in more detail later in this chapter, Sarat reflected upon the previous two years:

> I have been watching closely and with anxiety the work of our legislatures, central and provincial, since the attainment of Dominion Status on the 15 August 1947. I have been noticing with consternation the progressive deterioration in our administrations, central and provincial, since then and the rapid increase in them of nepotism, favouritism, and corruption. The State machinery is being run by a handful of capitalists and those who were until yesterday reactionaries and exploiters have now become our masters and benefactors: No wonder that black-marketing, profiteering and graft have increased in geometrical progression. The Press has been gagged, civil liberties of the people have been ruthlessly suppressed and the demands of the exploited, the repressed and the neglected have been met by lathis, teargas, batons, bayonets, bullets, as in British times. Inflation has not been checked, prices of the necessaries of life have been soaring higher and higher and food and clothing are beyond the reach of the poor and middle classes. Our one-party legislatures, central and provincial, are merely registering the dictates of the few high and mighty. They have not the mind to conceive, the intelligence to construct, the power to create.

It was in this context that Sarat, increasingly conscious of the imperative for what he saw as the leftist and progressive forces to be heard, on 1 September 1948 launched a new daily news-paper *The Nation.* This he saw as a vehicle for those voices in a new India dominated by the forces of capitalism and plagued by nepotism and corruption.

As the key figure in the creation of the newspaper, Sarat was invited by his colleagues to write the editorial for the first issue of *The Nation,* which also heavily reflected the Manifesto of the Socialist Republican Party:

I have been asked what is the necessity for a new paper. My answer is, that at no time in the history of contemporary India has the need for a really free and liberty-loving press been so impera-tive as it is today. The country has been and is passing through a grave crisis. Stupendous problems, bigger than anything that has ever confronted our country, are crying for solution.

The liberty that we have achieved as a result of negotiations with the British imperialist power has, during the last twelve months, proved to be an oppressive mirage to the common man. Corruption, bribery, nepotism, profiteering and black-marketing have all entered into an unholy conspiracy to crush the life out of our people. Little schemes of reconstruction, announced from time to time by our ruling authorities with a flourish of bugles, horns and trumpets, have all but foundered.

It is only an independent and fearless press that will have the courage to criticise and the intelligence, foresight and wisdom to construct, that can liberate the country from the parlous condition in which it is now. The existing newspaper press in India has on the whole failed to stand up to the test. With a few honourable exceptions, it shows from end to end of the country drab uniformity and chronicled regimented news and views. 'The Nation' will attempt to revive and restore the pristine glory of the newspaper press in India.

What does 'The Nation' stand for? It stands for the Complete Independence of India, independence undiluted and undefiled, free from British or any other foreign influence and control, beyond the reach of any power on earth. It regards Dominion Status as a snare to our feet and will ceaselessly warn the people not to suffer the country to be betrayed with a kiss.... It believes in complete equality of sexes and in the right of our women to take their due and proper place in the social, cultural, economic and public life of the country. It will demand of the State that religious freedom, secular education and civil liberties should be guaranteed to all. Lastly, it will demand that in a free and liberated India all must have the right to claim food and shelter in return for their due contribution to society.

* * *

The first major test of the strength of Left unity came with Sarat's decision to contest a South Calcutta Bye-Election on 12 June 1949, for the West Bengal Legislative Assembly. Virtually all leftist parties rallied behind him, and in an acknowledgement of their strongly supportive role, Sarat noted in his campaign election manifesto issued from Glion in Switzerland on 3 June 1949:

> I could not help feeling that the Government had somehow received information regarding my illness and the medical advice that had been given to me to proceed without delay to Switzerland for treatment and cure [from a heart attack in late April 1949] and that was what had led them at long last to declare the vacancy. But though I was due to leave Calcutta within a week of that announcement and the election would take place in my absence, it did not take me a minute to decide that I should contest the seat. I decided that the fight that I, with the help and cooperation of progressive and leftist forces, have been carrying on since the 19th August 1947 has to be carried into the legislatures as well as for the purpose of carrying us to victory.

With Sarat duly absent in Switzerland for medical treatment, but with Amiya at home as the link with key supporters and coordinating the campaign, he won with a thumping majority (19,030 for Sarat, 5,780 for his Congress opponent Suresh Das). All mainstream newspapers, except of course *The Nation*, were predictably arrayed against and attacked Sarat, vociferously supported the Congress candidate, and were thus left exposed. *The Nation* for its part celebrated the victory under banner headlines: **RESURGENT PEOPLES' REBUFF TO HIGH COMMAND; RESOUNDING VICTORY FOR SARAT BOSE;** and, **CONGRESS NOMINEE FLOORED.**

Sarat noted this overwhelming defeat of the Congress candidate with a typical witticism in a June 1949 edition of *The Nation* stating, 'Those who are left are right, and those who are right are left behind.'

Sarat returned to India on 21 January of that year 1949, 'only to spend his body and mind on the process of Left unity. It was mainly due to his sustained work that a conference was held in Bombay on 8/9 April 1949'.[10] Sarat presided over the conference, which gathered together 75 representatives of various leftist parties from across India, including his own Socialist Republican Party and the Forward Bloc.

The meeting aimed to devise ways and means to bring about co-ordination among these parties and form an effective opposition to the prevailing Congress Government. Sarat oversaw the creation of a provisional Leftist Co-ordination Council, elected by the conference participants with Sarat as chair. The immediate aims were to bring about cohesion of leftist activities all over India, and the formation of a common general programme for different existing parties on an inter-provincial and cooperative basis.

By this time, the frantic pace set by Sarat both in his professional and political life was beginning to take its toll, and wife Bivabati, Amiya and others were becoming increasingly concerned. Hardly had Sarat returned to Calcutta from the Bombay meeting, then he began to suffer from chest pains which led to a heart attack some time later in the month of April 1949. On the strong recommendation of his younger brother Sunil, a renowned heart specialist practising in Calcutta, Sarat left on 11 May 1949 from Calcutta for the Clinique Valmont in Glion Switzerland, where he arrived some days later. (As previously noted, it was from here that he had conducted his victorious South Calcutta Bye-Election campaign of June 1949.)

After several weeks of treatment and recuperation at the Clinique, Sarat on 9 July 1949 flew to London, where a heart specialist gave him an all-clear. He returned to India via Geneva, arriving just in time for a second, follow-up meeting of the putative Leftist Coordination Council in Bombay on 23 July 1949. Perhaps reassured by what appeared to be an effective treatment and recuperation in Switzerland and the positive diagnosis of the London Doctor, Sarat sought to operate as before with scant attention to his health and without paying any heed to the

---

[10] Anjan Bera, ed., *Interpreting a Nation* (Kolkata: Netaji Institute for Asian Studies, 2001), Introduction liii.

remonstrations of his immediate family. He resumed in earnest his mission of uniting the leftist parties in India, to forge an opposition force to the governing Congress, and thus save the country from what he saw as the depredations of the Congress. On 20 August 1949, at a huge public reception for him in Calcutta, to the shock and consternation of those around him including Amiya, he suffered a second major heart attack. He was consequently confined to bed, but even then would not slow down. From Geneva in July, he had announced his decision to convene at an early date, a United Socialist Conference, to be followed by the formation of a United Socialist Congress. After consultations with representatives of most of the leftist parties, the dates had been set for 25–27 September 1949 to be held at Nagpur. The meeting now had to be postponed, but not for long.

The United Socialist Conference was duly held 28–30 October 1949 at 38/2 Elgin Road, the home of Janakinath and family in Calcutta, now renamed Netaji Bhawan by Sarat in honour of his missing brother Subhas. In the event, Sarat was not able to be present and remained confined to his home due to continuing fragile health and medical treatment. His Presidential Address as the convenor of the Conference, attended by more than 300 representatives of Leftist parties from throughout India, was read out by a member of the Organising Committee Tridib Choudhury, after which delegates were invited to take the floor.

In his address, in welcoming the participants, tracing the evolution of events so far, and outlining the way ahead, Sarat turned the attention of the meeting to what became the fundamental aims and objectives for the Bharatiya Samyukta Samajbadi Sabha or United Socialist Organisation of India (USOI), with Sarat as its first President.

Not surprisingly, the programme for the USOI agreed at the Conference, very much mirrored those of his Socialist Republican Party, with an emphasis on universal principles of social justice and human rights, and with a socialist programme adapted to Indian conditions. A Union of Socialist Republics constituting greater India, where the principle 'from each according to his ability to each according to his needs' would remain central to the vision of an India free of exploitation both internally and from abroad, would be established.

Positive actions expected of the State would include: (a) socialisation of all public health services and provision of medical aid for all, (b) full employment and abolition of beggary as well as provision for social security against unemployment if any, old age, sickness, invalidity (disability), maternity, orphanhood, (c) socialisation and secularisation of all secular institutions and provision for free education for all, (d) freedom of conscience and worship, (e) cultural autonomy, (f) removal of all traces of untouchability and similar caste distinctions, racial prejudices, equal rights for all, (g) complete equality of sexes and (h) civil liberties for all.

The first beginnings of the USOI were thus promising enough, and the Provisional General Council established at the Conference met under the stewardship of Sarat at 1 Woodburn Park for three days from 4 to 6 December 1949. The structures for coordination of the programme of work both national and provincial were discussed and put in place, and the programme itself launched in earnest. The organisation of workers and peasants, the protection of civil liberties and freedom of the press received early attention.

* * *

Meanwhile, Sarat's grand vision of a socialist democratic India and its place in Asia and the wider world had led inexorably on his part to a focus on how a fully sovereign state of India might conduct its international relations. Even before the cataclysmic disaster of partition, Sarat had begun to think of ways in which the nations of the subcontinent and their immediate neighbours might be encouraged to work towards shared objectives in matters of regional and international concern and avoid becoming pawns in the hands of the powers of the new world order dominated by the United States and the Soviet Union. After the Transfer of Powers in August 1947, Sarat remained concerned that India under Prime Minister Nehru (and Pakistan) had chosen Dominion status under the British Commonwealth and was thus in his view still under British thrall.

Sarat's thinking on this matter of regional unity and protection from the hegemony of the big powers, began to gravitate towards the concept of a United Nations of South Asia (UNSA), and he chose the occasion of Burmese Independence Day on 4 January 1948 to articulate and otherwise give expression to his evolving vision[11]:

Today is a red letter day in the history of Burma. It marks the consummation of Burma's struggle for freedom, a struggle in which Indians under the leadership of Netaji played no inconsiderable part. Today we recall with pride Netaji's association with that brave and gallant son of Burma, General Aung San, now unfortunately no more, and the fighters for Burma's freedom.

...We wish and we hope that Burma's newly-constituted Republic, will make for peace, for alliances, military and otherwise, with her neighbouring countries, for commerce not merely in the limited sense in which that word is generally used, but also intellectual and cultural commerce—and for enlightenment.

...We desire to cooperate with the people of Burma in all matters of common concern and in all that vitally affects and will affect the future of our respective countries and adjoining countries of South Asia. We shall, among other things, endeavour to make our humble contribution to the shaping of the foreign policies of the countries I have just referred to. India intends to be friendly with the powers of the East and of the West, and I have no doubt, so does Burma. But it will not do for us merely to declare a policy of friendship and neutrality towards the powers which are competing for the mastery of the world.

In the context of the present world situation, neutrality will undoubtedly be the wisest policy for our country and may I venture to say, it will also be the wisest policy for yours. But we have to prepare our countries for such a neutral position. A policy of neutrality has to be backed up by requisite action in our country as well as in yours. There are groups of people in India who have been and are advocating India's participation in the Anglo-American Bloc. There are other groups in our country who believe that in the third World War which is already in the offing, India should line up with the Soviet Union. As far as I am aware, there are similar groups in your country as well...

...If we are to maintain our neutrality we have to endeavour from now to bring all those countries on a common platform as

[11] *Sarat Chandra Bose Commemoration Volume*, 399–401.

far as foreign policy is concerned and to set up an International Organisation in South Asia on a regional basis which may be described as the 'United Nations of South Asia' with India, Pakistan, Nepal, Burma and Ceylon as its constituent members. The United Nations of South Asia will have to function as a Neutral Bloc and should not have any military alliance either with the Anglo-American Bloc or the Soviet Bloc. It will, of course, be necessary for the constituent members of the UNSA to have military alliances with one another, but they will have to decide also that no single member of the UNSA is to be permitted to enter into military alliances with any outside power or powers.

It will also be necessary for the UNSA to enunciate a doctrine somewhat similar to the Monroe Doctrine for the Indian Ocean and to see to it that no power other than a member of the UNSA is permitted to possess or control any naval or military base in the countries of its constituent members. It will also help the policy of neutrality if we are able to establish a Customs Union on the basis of the regional grouping I have just referred to. It ought to be our endeavour and our aim to encourage foreign trade and commerce among the members of the UNSA so that the UNSA may increasingly become an economically self-sufficient unit.

What I have indicated in outline does not, to my mind, conflict with the rights and duties of our countries as members of the UNO [United Nations Organisation] I feel that a regional international organisation on the lines suggested by me will pave the way to peace and progress and will be able to implement to a large extent and in an effective manner the declared policy of the UNO.

If we are left free, our way will be the way of peace, of thinking not in terms of selfish interest or of petty power, but of human beings living as they have a right to live for the best that their own energies and their states can give, and contribute at the same time to the world the best that is in us. I feel that other States of South Asia can face the task in a similar spirit and with equal hope and because of that conviction and of the mutual help I know we can render to one another.

One year later on 3 January 1949 while passing through London, on his way back from a European tour with his wife

Bivabati and two younger daughters (Roma and Chitra), Sarat had informed a gathering of British and foreign journalists in London of his ambition to see all the leftist political organisations in India combine, so that the strength of the opposition could properly be measured against the incumbent Congress Government of India. Sarat also told the attending pressmen that in his opinion the formation of a UNSA was vital, and that India, Pakistan, Nepal, Burma and Ceylon should form such an organisation immediately as the foundation of an ultimate United Nations of Asia. This did not mean that he advocated India's withdrawal from the existing United Nations Organisation, adding that the United Nations of South Asia should work side by side with the UNO to ensure world peace. Only a strong, virile, powerful Asian bloc can prevent the UNO from being an instrument of power politics—as it has been so far (as reported in *The Nation*).

Sarat developed a particular affection during this period for newly independent Burma and its pre-independence Prime Minister and nationalist leader Dr Ba Maw, now away from the centre of politics in Burma. Dr Ba Maw and Subhas had themselves been good friends during Subhas's war-time stay in Burma and had represented their countries at the Greater East Asia Conference held in Tokyo in November 1943, hosted by Japanese Prime Minister General Hideki Tojo. Dr Ba Maw gave unstinting support to Subhas, and subsequently named one of his children Neta (from Netaji) in his honour.[12]

In letters of 17 May 1949 from Dr Ba Maw to Sarat and 16 November 1949 from Sarat to Dr Ba Maw, they exchanged impressions on the impact and significance of Sarat's newspaper *The Nation*, and informed each other of developments of interest in their respective countries, including the United Socialist Conference of October 1949 in Calcutta and the birth of the USO of India. They also discussed how they might help each other with sharing of news information and views, including through Dr Ba Maw's efforts to arrange for the publication of a periodical in English to be known as *Padauk* (a Burmese tree).[13]

---

[12] Edward M. Law-Yone, 'Dr Ba Maw of Burma—*An Appreciation*', *Contributions to Asian Studies*, Vol. XVI (1981), 7.

[13] Anjana Bera, *Interpreting a Nation*, xlii–xliii.

Sarat's vision of a UNSA failed to gain traction in his lifetime and indeed for several decades after. It is true that the Non-Aligned Movement was formed in 1955 with the active leadership and participation of India and Burma, together with Indonesia, Ghana and Yugoslavia; but the concept of regional blocs of cooperation and even integration did not fire the imagination of the leaders and peoples of South Asia, to the extent that it perhaps did elsewhere in other regions in Africa and Latin America.

On the contrary, the relationship between India and Pakistan has been characterised by tension and bouts of armed conflict, including the period of insurgency in East Pakistan which led in 1971 to the creation of Bangladesh. The South Asian Association for Regional Cooperation (SAARC) formed later in December 1985, involving Bangladesh, Bhutan, India, Maldives, Nepal, Pakistan and Sri Lanka, has its value but falls well short of what Sarat had envisaged.

Amiya himself propagated the concept of regional cooperation in his talks and lectures, and in 1976/77 established contact with Lord Mountbatten, now retired in England at his home in Broadlands in Hampshire. After a personal call on Mountbatten at his London flat sometime in October 1976, Amiya wrote to him on 2 December 1976 and received the following reply:

BROADLANDS
ROMSEY
HAMPSHIRE
SO5 9ZD

3 January 1977

Dear Mr Amiya Nath Bose

Thank you so much for your letter of 2nd December and for so kindly sending me a copy of the speech delivered by your father, the late Sarat Chandra Bose on Burma Independence Day in Calcutta on 4th January 1948. I remember the occasion well and took part in the celebrations in Delhi on the same day. I have read what your father said with the greatest of interest and am glad you are proposing to do some work on the lines suggested by your father.

As I mentioned to you in discussion, I was instrumental in setting up the original Joint Defence Council between India and

Pakistan with the Governor-General of one of the two Dominions (as they then were) taking the Chair as appropriate. As it happens, Mr Jinnah insisted on my taking the Chair on each occasion that we met, even when the meeting took place in Pakistan.

All was going rather well with this Joint Defence Council which was basically set up to ensure that the Indian Sub-Continent after Partition should not drift apart on matters of defence and foreign policy, but it broke down when the mass migrations, riots and massacres got out of hand and when the tribesmen invaded Kashmir.

My own view has been persistent that a revival of the Joint Defence Council system would be the best way of re-approaching the problems as this would introduce Bangladesh into the Joint Defence Council, making a Council of the three Nations which occupy the former British Indian territories. One thing is certain. It is a tragedy if the Sub-Continent continues to be broken into three separate Nations who have no close contact and understanding with each other.

I do hope you will keep in touch with me in developing your own thoughts and meanwhile send you my very best wishes for 1977 and thank you for your Greeting Card.

Yours sincerely
Mountbatten of Burma

For his part the indefatigable Sarat continued to fight a rear guard action for the unity and integrity of his beloved Bengal, and harmony between the two communities Muslim and Hindu, even beyond independence until the day he died over two years later on 20 February 1950. At that time in early 1950, against the background of outbursts of communal violence in East Pakistan against minority Hindu communities, Sarat had again been engaged in negotiations with Bengali Muslim colleagues Abul Hashim and Fazlul Haque, this time with a view to bringing East Pakistan into the Indian Union as a separate state.

It had been agreed among them that Sarat would start the ball rolling with coverage in *The Nation*. So it happened that just 30 minutes before he passed away close to midnight at home in 1 Woodburn Park, he signed off on an editorial for the following day's issue of *The Nation*, entitled: 'An Appeal to India and Pakistan.' The pain of the division of India and of

Bengal was thus with him until his last breath, and it was seen as hugely symbolic that the last written words from this great son of Bengal and India should have been a final attempt on his part to salvage something from the wreckage of partition. The editorial read as follows:

Writing on Saturday before last, the 11th instant, under the shadow of a great personal bereavement [death of a dear brother], I appealed to my brother Bengalis in East and West Bengal for peace, for peace with honour—honour to prudence, honour to sobriety, honour to sanity. I appealed to them in the name of all that was sacred, in the name of Bengal's past, in the name of the comradeship that was and will remain, in the name of humanity, to abjure the cult of violence, restore sobriety and sanity and to re-establish communal peace and harmony. I asked them not to look either Delhi way or Karachi way, for light would not come from there. I asked them to be guided by the light that was within them.

During the last eleven days I have been thinking deeply as to what is the real solution for the present state of things. I have considered in turns the suggestions offered from different quarters, namely, mass evacuation of Hindus from East Bengal or exchange of population between the two Bengals. As a result of deep thinking and mature consideration, I have been forced to the conclusion that neither of them is the solution. I need only remind the people of India and Pakistan that compulsory mass evacuation in and from the Punjab has left behind numerous problems each of which has defied solution up till now.

The solution that I offer for the acceptance of the people of India and Pakistan is that East Bengal as a distinct and separate State should join the Indian Union and that the people of India and Pakistan should bring pressure to bear upon their respective Governments to bring it about as soon as possible. I have been saying repeatedly during the last three years, that to my mind, a division of provinces on the religious basis was and is no solution of the communal problem, that even if the provinces were so divided. Hindus and Muslims would still have to live side by side and that communal segregation or religious quarantine was neither desirable nor feasible.

That being my political opinion, I have never made any distinction at any time of my life between Hindu or Muslim in undivided

Bengal or in divided Bengal. The population in both the Bengals remains as composite in character as before. I do not want to disturb the partition of Bengal which has already taken place. I am well aware that there was in the recent past a sense of frustration among the people of East Bengal, which was one of the reasons which gave rise to the demand for partition.

The solution which I am offering will mean the least possible interference in the present state of things. Let East Bengal live and flourish as a distinct and separate State, but in the interests of the future well-being of the communities living in the two Bengals which, as I have said before, are integral to each other, which are each other's bone of bone and flesh of flesh, let East Bengal live and flourish under the fostering care of the Indian Union.

In the name and on behalf of my colleagues in 'The Nation' as well on my own behalf I offer this solution for the consideration of and acceptance by the people of India and Pakistan. 'The Nation' believes that this solution will conduce to the peace and prosperity not only of the two Bengals, but also to the peace and prosperity of India and Pakistan and it will dedicate itself to the task of speeding up the solution by all peaceful and legitimate means.

With the sudden and untimely death of Sarat, the idea for East Pakistan to become a state of the Indian Union was still-born. At the same time, as predicted by many including Sarat and even Mountbatten, and as feared by Jinnah, East Pakistan proved not to be a viable proposition for a host of reasons. Less than a quarter of a century later in 1971, a new sovereign state of Bangladesh emerged out of bloody revolution and mayhem with, it should be noted, the intervention and armed assistance of the State of India.

The USOI survived Sarat's passing for a while, but the considerable momentum generated by his charismatic leadership could not be sustained. Efforts continue to this day to bring together the many leftist entities of India, to forge an effective political fighting force. It is perhaps symbolic that the Indian state of West Bengal is one of the few states of India to have hosted a leftist coalition government, with CPI (Marxist) leader Jyoti Basu as Chief Minister in league with Forward Bloc for more than three decades.

It is also noteworthy that West Bengal since independence has not figured prominently in the national political discourse, as Bengal once did in pre-independent India. Virtually since Sarat's death in 1950, there has been no prominent Bengali national politician who could even begin to match the influence, impact and charisma of C. R. Das, of Subhas and of Sarat. That time is still to come.

Epilogue

Subhas

As the afternoon shadows lengthened on a crisp Calcutta winter's day on 16 January 1941, the 'Prince of Vagabonds' (a sobriquet ascribed to Subhas by Sarat) was making his final preparations to escape from his Elgin Road home and self-imposed isolation in his bedroom. In the early hours of 17 January 1941, Subhas slipped away by car, train and on foot, and made his way from eastern through north and north-west India to Kabul in Afghanisthan. From Kabul he travelled by car and train to Moscow. He eventually arrived in Berlin in early April 1941 by air from Moscow.

A carefully planned scheme in league with brother Sarat, and involving a handful of other close family members, enabled Subhas to deceive the cordon of watching British agents, and embark on what he saw as the next and final phase of the Indian struggle, this time by force of arms from outside India.

We now know that from the time of his arrival in Berlin, Subhas spent his time seeking to build and empower an Indian Legion, which would fight alongside German troops to prepare for an eventual attack on British India from the West. We know too of his growing disillusionment with the Hitler-led German regime and their reluctance to declare in support of Indian independence. Subhas was not impressed with the Aryan race theories of Hitler and his supporters. He demanded on several occasions, including during his brief meeting with Hitler himself, that certain objectionable remarks about India in 'Mein Kampf' be removed. This did not happen.

Subhas was particularly disappointed and dismayed when in June 1941, Germany turned against its erstwhile ally the Soviet Union. Subhas had always been favourably disposed towards the Soviets to whom he had hoped to turn for assistance in an armed struggle against British imperialism. On 15 August 1941, Subhas, residing in Berlin in the heart of the Third Reich, wrote to the German Foreign Minister J. von Ribbentrop that 'The march of the German troops towards the East will be regarded as the approach not of a friend, but of an enemy'. Nevertheless, Subhas managed to convince the German authorities to allow him to broadcast his anti-British and anti-imperialist messages from Berlin, after publicly surfacing with the first of his open broadcasts on 19 February 1942. Until then he had been using his pseudonym Orlando Mazzotta.

Amiya in London was requested by the BBC to visit their studios to authenticate the voice issuing forth over the airways from the continent. Amiya had no difficulty in recognising the voice and confirming that it was none other than Subhas Chandra Bose speaking on Azad Hind Radio (Free India Radio). Amiya in fact had kept a radio in his room mainly to listen to the broadcasts of his Uncle Subhas. British surveillance reports also claim that Amiya had a large photo of Subhas in his room!

By early 1943 with the juggernaut of Japanese conquest in full swing throughout most of south-east Asia and parts of the western Pacific, Subhas had managed to persuade the German authorities that it made more sense for him to play a lead role in the Indian independence effort by force of arms in Asia and in alliance with the Japanese. It helped that by this time messages were reaching the authorities in Germany from counterparts in Japan, of the desirability for Subhas to be in the Asia/Pacific theatre of war. He was being called upon to lead efforts for the rejuvenation of an INA formed earlier by Tokyo-based Indian revolutionary Rash Behari Bose, but now floundering.

Thus, it transpired that from 8 February 1943, Subhas under-took a particularly perilous voyage, this time from Europe to south-east Asia by submarine in the midst of a world war. He travelled first with the Germans in a U-Boat accompanied by his aide Abid Hasan to near Madagascar in the Indian Ocean, there to be transferred on the high seas to a Japanese submarine which took him on to Saban, Sumatra in present-day Indonesia. From there he was flown by Japanese military aircraft to Tokyo.

Thereafter, he proceeded to Singapore. With the support of the Government of Japan, he was able in an amazingly short span of time to form the Provisional Government of Azad Hind on 21 October 1943, launched at the landmark Cathay Building in Singapore; lead as Supreme Commander a rejuvenated and re-motivated INA as an effective fighting force alongside the Japanese Army; and, for very brief moments to once again touch the soil of his beloved India.

The clarion calls for independence and freedom now boomed out, not from Europe but from Singapore, Tokyo and Rangoon, and from the jungles of south-east Asia: to the British—an uncompromising demand to leave India; to his countrymen and women—stay united, freedom is coming; and to the soldiers of the INA—Chalo Delhi!

The INA under Subhas was to prove a revelation in its own right, defeated in battle by circumstance and superior forces, but destined to be a critical factor in Britain's final realisation—even after victory in a world war—that India could no longer be the 'Jewel in the Crown' of their Empire. The British were forced to recognise that they had lost the allegiance of the British Indian Armed Forces and could no longer hold on to India. Remarkably, the British were gone from the subcontinent within a year or two of the conclusion in August 1945, of a world war in which they were one of the most prominent victors.

Where the INA itself was concerned, the Indian people throughout the cities, towns and villages of imperial India were stunned and immensely moved to learn that their kinfolk from the British Indian Army and from the Indian expatriate populations of Malaya, Singapore, Burma and Thailand, both men and women, had broken the imperial hoodoo and had fought for them—for their rights, for their freedom and for their independence. They were astounded to learn also that this Indian revolutionary army had been completely and deliberately non-communal, with a senior strategic command under Subhas that was Hindu, Muslim and Sikh.

When the three senior commanders, Prem Sahgal (Hindu), Shah Nawaz Khan (Muslim) and G. S. Dhillon (Sikh), were put on trial by the British in the Red Fort in Delhi in early 1946, it seemed for one glorious interlude that the shining example of non-communalism put into practice by Subhas, might point the way to the vision of the Bose Brothers of a new, united India. Sadly, as events proved, it was not to be, too late to prevent the emergence of a truncated India and a disjointed Pakistan, and tragically too late to prevent the monstrous bloodbath of Partition.

It is and will remain one of the great unknowns of history, what might have happened if Subhas himself had been able to fulfil his vision of leading the INA back to India whether in victory or defeat. To be certain, he would have continued the fight against vivisection of the subcontinent, and his reappearance may have given new life to the 'tired old men' who accepted partition as the price for power. Perhaps Subhas may have been able to deal more constructively with Jinnah, who had been increasingly mauled and humiliated by the Congress leadership from the early 1930s onwards. Certainly, Subhas would have firmly resisted the blandishments of Mountbatten, assuming that the latter would even have deigned to deal seriously with someone whom he, Mountbatten, regarded as a traitor. Circumstances would have in all probability forced his hand.

With the effective disappearance of Subhas from the political and strategic landscape from 18 August 1945, just a few days after the end of the war in the Pacific, sadly none of this was to be. It is alleged that late in the afternoon of that day, Subhas died in a crash on take-off of a Manchuria-bound Japanese bomber aircraft, which had stopped for re-fuelling at an airfield in Formosa (now Taiwan). With the assistance of the Japanese military, Subhas had on 16 August 1945 begun the journey by air from Singapore to Bangkok, where he spent the night. The following day, 17 August 1945, he had flown on to Saigon (now Ho Chi Minh City) and spent the night there, departing the following day for Formosa.

The story of the air crash is contested to this day. It is hardly surprising that many believe that it was yet another ruse for him to slip away once again, this time to link up with the forces of the victorious Soviet Union in Manchuria. There have been no less than three official enquiries ordered by the central government of India.

The Congress Party in particular has for its own reasons clearly demonstrated over time a determination to bring closure to the fate of Subhas through acceptance of the air crash story. If further clarity is to be brought to the matter, then the answers will need to be found in as yet un-released archival material in Britain, Russia, the United States, Japan, and India itself.

In the meantime, the persistence of doubt around the air crash story has only added to the aura of mystery surrounding this legendary figure of Indian and Asian independence struggles. The theories surrounding his disappearance wax and wane: he managed to reach Russia and met an as yet unknown fate; he was reported to have reached Mao Tse Tung's China, and a wistful Sarat thought he saw the hand of Subhas in a reply of the Chinese leader to Sarat's message of congratulation on the former's assumption of power on 1 October 1949; he returned quietly to India and became a sadhu; he has been spotted numerous times on trains, in ashrams and elsewhere.

There is one certainty of which the reader can be sure, namely, that the flame of Subhas has not died and will not die. He will continue to fire the imagination and inspire the generations to come.

Sarat

Sarat was not to see his beloved younger brother Subhas again, after the latter melted away under cover of darkness from Calcutta on 17 January 1941. As part of the subterfuge and to avoid provoking any suspicions on the part of the watching police agents, Sarat and wife Biva travelled out of Calcutta on the day following the night-time escape, to their up-river retreat at Rishra on the Hooghly River. They then returned home to 1 Woodburn Park to join innocently in the hue and cry. In a private letter which was expected to be read by the authorities, Amiya in London was informed by his father Sarat that his Uncle Subhas had gone 'missing'. Subhas himself had sent a telegram to Amiya a few days before his escape from Calcutta—'Recovering slowly. Don't worry. Subhas.'

By this time, Sarat and Subhas had been suspended from the Congress governance bodies in the wake of the events of Tripuri in 1939 and following. Congress Ministers in both provincial and central legislatures had resigned from office positions across British India, and the Muslim League under the astute and increasingly aggressive leadership of Jinnah was moving with the British authorities to fill the vacuum. The seeds of

Gandhi's Quit India movement of August 1942, which seemed to belatedly recognise the broad position of the Bose Brothers, were being sown. While Subhas was settling temporarily in Berlin from early April 1941, Sarat was turning his attention to the politics of Bengal and the dark spectre of communalism which was once again beginning to rear its ugly head. As we have seen, Sarat and Subhas had failed in 1937 to persuade Gandhi and the CWC of the desirability of Congress entering governing coalitions both in Bengal and elsewhere. The inevitable result was that from 1937 to 1941, a Muslim League-dominated ministry ruled over Bengal and communal tensions were re-emerging.

Thus, it was that in concert with his old sparring partner and sometime ally Fazlul Haque, now much disaffected with Jinnah and the League, Sarat, himself under suspension from the Congress, was able to stitch together a new Progressive Coalition for Bengal with Haque as its leader. By the end of 1941, with a new non-communal ministry set to take over in Bengal welcomed by Hindus and Muslims alike, the attacks by Japan on both British and American forces in south-east Asia and the Pacific came as a thunderclap.

Within days of immediate declarations of war on Japan by the British and the Americans on 7–8 December 1941, Sarat was arrested on 11 December 1941 by the British, citing his close contacts with the Japanese and the threat which he posed to British war interests. While these were undoubtedly contributing factors the prospect of the 'troublesome' Sarat Bose as an influential minister in the new, Haque-led coalition ministry in Bengal, clearly displeased and unnerved the British, as reflected in their records.

Sarat was to spend almost the next four years in British-controlled jails in India, much the greater part of it in Coonoor, Tamil Nadu, in the hot and humid south of India far from Bengal. By the time of his release on 14 September 1945, one month after the capitulation of Japan on 14 August 1945 and the hammer blow of the disappearance of Subhas on 18 August 1945, his physical health had been compromised but clearly not his indomitable spirit.

Immediately upon his release from jail, Sarat set to work on all fronts. The most immediate demand was the resumption of his work as a barrister to support his large family and other dependents, as well as pay off debts accumulated while in prison.

For the last few months of his imprisonment, Sarat had been urged by Gandhi to return to the Congress fold. As noted earlier, Gandhi had done so largely through the good offices of Amiya, who had returned from Britain in December 1944. Amiya notes in his unpublished memoirs that Gandhi had invited him to Poona in May 1945 where Gandhi was staying at the 'Nature Cure Clinic'. Amiya remained in Poona for one week with Gandhi and others. During this time, Gandhi dictated a letter to Sarat requesting him to rejoin the Congress on the grounds that all of the nationalist forces needed to be combined in a resumption of the political and constitutional fight to oust the British.

Sarat did rejoin the Congress, but Amiya was later to rue his own role in deflecting his father from the more radical and even revolutionary alternatives which were bubbling just beneath the surface at the time, and which if acted upon, just might have prevented the epic tragedy of the partition of the subcontinent and led to a united, independent India.

In any case, with his son Amiya now firmly by his side as adviser and confidante, Sarat embarked upon this next and final phase of his remarkable life. He began immediately after his release with the challenge of re-absorption of the erstwhile Subhas-led INA into Indian life and politics and propagation of their hitherto blacked-out exploits.

There followed Sarat's election in December 1945 from a Calcutta constituency to the Central Legislative Assembly in Delhi, where from mid-January 1946 he was Leader of the Congress Parliamentary Party, in effect Leader of the Opposition in the Assembly. On 2 September 1946 and against the backdrop of the 'Great Calcutta Killings' of the previous month, Sarat was confirmed as a member of the Viceroy-initiated Interim Government and named Minister of Works, Mines and Power (Viceroy Wavell reportedly had qualms about the inclusion of Sarat but Congress insisted). Sarat's term of office was to last only a matter of weeks when he felt obliged to resign to make way for the recalcitrant Muslim League to offer its own representatives to the Interim Government, which then became effectively paralysed.

Sarat remained in the 15-member CWC for a time, but by the end of 1946 was so disillusioned with the course of events and the evolving Congress position towards partition, that he resigned from the Committee on 6 January 1947. On 1 August 1947, with the dreaded prospect of partition, both of India and Bengal, now virtually a fait accompli, Sarat formally resigned from the Congress which he had served for more than 40 years.

There were no celebrations in the Bose household on that day, nor two weeks later on 15 August 1947 when India and Pakistan were born and Bengal cleaved into East and West, the one a part of the new Pakistan and the other a part of India.

Now out of Congress, heavily defeated on Partition, and increasingly isolated in the politics of the new, Congress-dominated Indian province of West Bengal, Sarat might have been forgiven for withdrawing from the field of battle. For one thing, he had to continue to provide for his own and a large extended family through his legal practice; and from early 1946, he had become immersed in the relief and welfare of erstwhile INA soldiers returning to India as British prisoners-of-war and released. While he had been instrumental in the establishment of India-wide support for the ex-soldiers under Congress auspices, he was particularly involved in Bengal where with the close assistance of Amiya, he led the relief campaign.

Both father and son were extremely active in ensuring that all manner of support was provided to INA personnel and their families, including educational and employment opportunities. For the years around and immediately following independence in August 1947, they were also increasingly embroiled with the rising and formidable challenge of coping with the flood of Hindu refugees pouring out of East Bengal/East Pakistan, as well as with the agonies of Hindu communities remaining in East Pakistan.

As addressed in Chapter 6, on 1 August 1947 when he renounced the Congress, Sarat announced the formation of his Socialist Republican Party on the same day. Just over one year later on 1 September 1948, he launched his daily newspaper *The Nation* to give voice to the leftist, socialist forces in the new India. On 14 June 1949, while he was absent in Europe for medical treatment but with Amiya at home helping to coordinate his campaign in a bye-election for the South Calcutta constituency of the West Bengal Legislative Assembly, he won with an overwhelming majority over the Congress candidate.

No doubt buoyed by a huge public reception for him on return to Calcutta a little over two months later on 20 August 1949, on 28 October 1949 Sarat was instrumental in the formation of the USOI. This was at that time the latest in a long line of initiatives over the years to unite the so-called leftist forces in the Indian political arena. The USOI did not long survive Sarat's passing but it was not through want of effort, imagination and commitment on his part.

* * *

Life was no less active and challenging for Sarat on personal family matters. Emilie Schenkl, an Austrian by birth who had worked for Subhas in Europe on and off since mid-1934 as his secretary, had written to Sarat on 12 March 1946. She sought to explain that she and Subhas had married in Berlin in January 1942, and that a daughter Anita had been born to them in November of that year:

Dear Sir,

You will be surprised to get a letter from a person unknown to you. I had for a long time hesitated till I decided to write to you in a matter regarding your family as well as mine. In the following I am going to explain matters to you.

I started working with your late brother, Sjt Subhas Chandra Bose in 1934, when he wrote his book "The Indian Struggle" as his secretary. You might perhaps have known that when ever (sic) he was in Europe, I worked with him.

Your brother has come to Europe again in 1941 and asked me, if I could come and join him in Berlin to work with him. I agreed and joined him in April 1941 and we worked together till autumn 1942.

Your brother asked me when I was in Berlin if I would accept his proposal to marry him. Knowing him since years as a man of good character and since there was a mutual understanding and we were very fond of each other, I agreed. The only difficulty was to get the necessary marriage permission from the German Government. Though Austrian by birth, I had at that time been

German subject and, therefore, to obey German laws. And it was very difficult for a German to get the permission to marry a foreigner. And since we both did not want to beg for a favour and wanted also to avoid making an affair of the whole matter, we decided to settle it between ourselves and got, therefore, married according to Hindu fashion in January 1942. The whole thing was kept a secret, only two friends knowing about it.

On November 29, 1942, a daughter was born to us. I had returned to Vienna in September already, in order to avoid unnecessary talking and difficulties with the German authorities. I have kept my maiden name and nationality therefore.

Our daughter's name is ANITA-BRIGITTE. She should actually bear the name of AMITA, but the German authorities would have certainly objected to such an unusual name so we chose the name Anita which is almost sounding like Amita. Brigitte was chosen by me because its short form in German is Gita.

Your brother had unfortunately only once seen his daughter when she was four weeks old. Shortly before he left Europe in 1943 he wanted again to come down to Vienna to see his child once more but due to his sudden departure he had to leave without seeing her again. I had been with him three weeks before he left Europe but could not bring Anita with me.

The day before he left for the East he wrote a letter to you which he asked me to have photo-copied [a photograph of the letter] and sent to you in case anything should happen to him. This letter is written in Bengali and he informed you about his marriage and the birth of his daughter. Unfortunately one cannot at present send any photos or documents to foreign countries, so the only thing I could do, was to write to you personally about the whole matter. Later on, when it is permitted again to send photos, I shall let you have a photo-copy of the above-mentioned letter as well as some pictures of the child so that at least you might have an idea how she is looking.

Allow me to explain my way of living to you so that you might be informed how the child of your brother is brought up. Anyhow, I want to emphasise that I am n o t demanding any financial help from you or your family. My object in writing this letter was to inform you about the existence of the child so that she might have a help later on, in case anything should happen to me. But I do earnestly hope that I will live and be able to earn my living till Anita is grown up and can look after herself.

I am working at present as clerk in the Trunk Office of Vienna holding the position of interpreter for English and French. I am earning about 200 Shillings (Austrian) a month. I am staying with my mother who is drawing a pension from the municipality after my late father. Therefore, we have no financial difficulties. Other difficulties re: food and clothing are only due to the all-round shortage in the world. Anita is not yet old enough to attend school. When she is six she will have to enter primary school. Later on I shall try my level best to give her as good an education as might be possible for me. She is quite a clever child and I hope to be able to help her so that she might later have an easy way in life.

According to your brother's wish she has not been christianed [sic], because he had been hoping to take us both to India one day and then she would have been brought up as a Hindu girl. I shall perhaps have her christianed [sic] later on when she begins with school since most probably she will always stay in Europe and not having a religion might prove to be a handicap for her later on.

It might perhaps interest you to hear that Anita is absolutely resembling her father. She has got his eyes, his mouth and his nose. Only the colour of the eyes is a little lighter than her father's and her hair is brunette (you would call it blonde). Also her complexion is lighter than her father's but one can at once see that she is not European.

As far as one can speak of the character of a child of three, I must say she is a very good soul. Very soft-hearted, helpful and affectionate. But at the same time very will-strong (sic). I should say that even in character she is resembling her father completely. She is also very pious and likes to pray, since she has been taught from the very beginning that there is a God. She has, of course, also her faults. But who in this world is without faults? I would be thankful if you could drop me a few lines to acknowledge this letter. Could you also let me know how your family and yourself are getting on? Is your respected mother still alive? If you think you can do it, please give the lady my and my daughter's pranams. How is your son Amiya? Is he in India or England?

We read in the papers and hear in the wireless a lot about the present conditions in India. It naturally interests me very much but at the same time I am very sorry that also this country has to suffer so much from post-war difficulties like Austria. I hope conditions for your family and yourself are not too bad, since one hears that the country is starving.

I would like to add that, when I heard the news of your brother's death, I was very much shocked and grieved. Because through his death I have lost the only person in this world whom I really loved and respected. Unfortunately I cannot live like an Indian woman should after the death of her husband, because I am bound to live in Europe and due to the fact that I must earn my living I am forced to mix with people and cannot make a show because they would not understand my feelings here. Besides the whole thing is still a secret. But in my memory I have put up a shrine for him and through his child he will always be alive for me.

Should you want to make any suggestions regarding the child or have any questions to put, please let me know and I shall gladly answer you or give you any information wanted. May I in this connection ask you to send me later on some family photos so that I might keep them for Anita till she is grown up and then give her an idea about her father and his family.

Please accept my best wishes for your family and yourself as well as my best regards,

Yours sincerely,
Emilie Schenkl

In the absence of a response from Sarat, Emilie re-sent copies of the letter on 15 May and 1 August 1946, again with no word from Sarat, who as it later transpired had received none of them.

In the meantime, an Indian doctor residing in Vienna Dr Akmat, who together with his wife had known Emilie and Anita, took it upon himself around mid-1947 to draw to the attention of Nehru and Sardar Patel the existence in Vienna of the wife and daughter of Subhas, claiming that they were living in hard circumstances. On 11 and 13 August 1947—virtually on the eve of independence—Sarat received from Nehru and Sardar Patel, respectively, copies of Dr Akmat's missive. Sarat responded somewhat acerbically that if the information were true, he Sarat was quite capable of looking after Subhas's family in the absence of Subhas.

Thus, it was that in August 1947 when he was contending with the catastrophe of Partition and the tragedy of divided Bengal, Sarat came to learn from those who were now his political enemies, of the possibility that Subhas had left a wife and child in Europe. Sarat would have been acutely aware too that those who feared a return of Subhas at this time to the Indian political landscape would miss no opportunity to denigrate him. Clearly, the matter continued to fester in Indian political circles and on 10 April 1948, Sarat, still oblivious of Emilie's letter to him of 12 March 1946, wrote to her as follows:

Dear Madame Schenkl,

This letter will probably come upon you as a surprise. We have never met but, I am sure, we are not complete strangers to each other.

On the 11th August 1947, I received a letter from Pandit Jawaharlal Nehru forwarding to me a statement from one Dr. Abdul Hafiz Akmat regarding you. Two days after that, I got a letter from Sardar Vallabhbhai Patel enclosing a copy of the same statement. I wrote to both on the 14th August 1947 saying that it seemed rather strange that although Dr. Akmat had sent copies of his statement to them, and possibly to others, he had not sent me a copy.

In his said letter to me, Sardar Vallabhbhai Patel said: 'I am sending herewith some information which has come to me about Subhas. I am writing to Nathalal who is in Belgium to make enquiries and to assist the family if the information is correct'. In my letter to Sardar Vallabhbhai Patel dated 14 August 1947, I said: 'I have read the enclosure to your letter very carefully. I wish you had referred the matter to me before writing to Nathalal. I do not think Nathalal has the training necessary to make enquiries of this nature and he may do more harm than good. After all, if Subhas left a family, it is up to me and not to Nathalal to assist the family'.

Sardar Vallabhbhai Patel replied to my letter of the 14th August on the 18th and in it he said: 'I am sorry if I have committed an indiscretion in referring the matter to Nathalal. I confess I was carried away by the story of sufferings of the alleged widow and the child and I thought, as Nathalal was near, it will be better to render immediate assistance if the story was true'.

On the 22nd August, 1947, Pandit Jawharlal Nehru wrote to me again and along with his letter enclosed a statement from Mr. A. C. N. Nambiar. After that, I asked my son Amiya, whom you know, to correspond with Nambiar and I also put into the former's hands some money for sending a remittance to Nambiar meant both for you and him. Unfortunately, on account of certain restrictions imposed by the Government the money was returned by the Bank and could not be sent.

On or about the 15th November 1947, I received a letter from Mr. Nathalal Parikh enclosing therewith a photographic copy of a letter purporting to be written by my brother and addressed to me. Thereafter, I had some further correspondence with Nathalal and he told me in one of his letters that you had got the photographic copy made by a local photographer at Vienna and that he had sent another photographic copy of that letter to Sardar Vallabhbhai Patel. Since then, I have been thinking of writing to you but for some reason or other I could not write earlier. I hope you will not mind the delay.

I have a desire to come to Europe some time towards the end of this year and if I am able to come, I shall certainly come to Vienna and meet you. In the meantime, if there is anything you would like to let me know, or if there is anything I can do at this end, please write to me.

It is difficult these days to trust many people here. Most of the eminent Congress leaders were political enemies of my brother and tried their best to run him down. Their attitude does not seem to have changed much, even after all that has happened since 1941. Nathalal Parikh used to be my brother's host when the latter visited Bombay from time to time, but he joined the other camp in 1945. I would, therefore, prefer to correspond directly with you.

With all good wishes,
Yours sincerely,
(Sarat Chandra Bose)

Emilie's reply to Sarat of 17 May 1948 was received by him on 27 May 1948, and his second letter of 8 July 1948 in response finally resolved the confusion caused by the failure of her original correspondence to reach Sarat for more than two years. With the puzzle now solved, Sarat welcomed Emilie and daughter Anita into the Bose family, together with a note of caution about false propaganda continuing to be spread by 'eminent Congress leaders who were political enemies of my brother':

Dear Madame Schenkl,

Your kind letter of the 17th May last was delivered here on the 27th May and was most welcome. In 1946 up to the month of October, I was mostly away from Calcutta and was also moving from place to place. My wife and daughters were with me. I had no secretary then in Calcutta and I would not be surprised if the letters you wrote to me in 1946 fell into the hands of people who opened them and pocketed them. I need hardly say that anything that concerned and concerns my brother always had and has the greatest significance for me. Possibly you heard from him several times of the relations between him and me.

I heard from Colonel Habib-ur-Rehman in August 1946 all about the air-crash story; but, though I have not had any facts to the contrary, I ought to tell you that the air-crash story left me unconvinced about its truth. I have always had and am still having the feeling in me—it is no more than a <u>feeling</u>—that my brother is alive.

I did not reply to your letter of 17th May earlier as I had intended to go to Bombay and find out for myself the nature of the propaganda that was being carried on there against my brother and to communicate to you something about it. By the time your letter came, I had heard from friends in Bombay who had come to Calcutta something about that propaganda. My wife and I went to Bombay last month and returned to Calcutta on the 4th of this month. The propaganda that is being carried on in Bombay is subtle. The suggestion is that my brother had committed a sin and had left you stranded. It is also being circulated in Bombay that Sardar Patel came to your rescue and that he has paid you rupees 18,000. I know that it is altogether false propaganda; still I felt that I owed it to you to give you some information about it. Of course I did not expect anything better from eminent Congress leaders who were political enemies of my brother, or from Nathalal Parikh who joined them in September, 1945.

Dr. Akmat's conduct was strange. He may have meant well; but he certainly ought to have written to me before writing to Nehru and Sardar.

I fully appreciate all that you have written about yourself and also the reasons for your unwillingness to receive any support or help at the moment. I was very much relieved and assured to learn that you were earning enough to manage your living.

My nephew Aurabindo has not yet handed over to me copies of the snaps he took when he was there, though I was told in Bombay last month that he had shown them to some people there. Will you kindly send me photos of yourself and the child at your convenience?

There is one information I would like to have. In 1938, I sent my brother some of the letters he wrote to me from Cambridge in the year 1920, which I had preserved. He used some of the letters in his Autobiography but, subsequently, the original letters could not be traced. He left them in Europe. Will it be possible for you to trace them? If you are able to do so, please keep them with you until I come to Europe. My wife and I intend to come in September or October this year. If our intention materialises, we shall certainly come to Vienna and see you and the child. There will be plenty of opportunities then to talk about matters that concern you and me. In the meantime, we shall correspond with each other.

Is Professor Demel in Vienna? If you meet him, please convey to him my kind regards.

Nambiar arrived in Calcutta yesterday. At the moment he is in this house. He will be leaving Calcutta in a day or two but intends to come back here again before he leaves for Europe.

I trust this will find you all in good health and spirits. With all good wishes,

Yours sincerely
(Sarat Chandra Bose)

As he had promised in his correspondence with Emilie, Sarat resolved to go to Europe with wife Bivabati as soon as possible to meet Emilie and daughter Anita. Later that year in the autumn of 1948, Sarat and Biva with three of their children (Sisir, Roma and Chitra) met with Emilie and Anita in Vienna in an emotional coming together of family. The bonding was spontaneous and immediate, and Emilie was finally able to hand over to Sarat the original handwritten letter in Bengali of 8 February 1943 to him from his beloved brother Subhas. Emilie stayed in close touch with Sarat for the few years left to him, and thereafter with Sarat's children and their families until her death on 13 March 1996, more than 50 years after the disappearance of Subhas.

* * *

For Sarat, it appeared that bouts of recuperation and medical attention in Europe in 1948 and again for several months in 1949, may have restored his health. His London heart specialist was said to have told him that he was as fit as a young man! Sadly, the disappearance of his beloved younger brother, the heavy toll of two long periods in jail, the crushing disappointments of Indian political life, and his own frantic work schedule, pushed him towards an early and untimely death at the relatively young age of sixty.

It is symptomatic of the man that on the day of his passing on 20 February 1950, he had spent a good part of the day in the High Court, with son Amiya incidentally appearing for the other side. He had spent much of the evening writing an editorial for *The Nation* calling for the reunification of Bengal, if necessary by Indian force of arms. He passed away just before midnight after signing off on the editorial, with Bivabati and a few members of his immediate family by his side. Amiya recalled his father's last day:

On 20 February 1950 father woke up in the morning at his usual time. Although he was not in the best of health after several heart attacks, he was as ever fully engaged in both his professional and public activities. Indeed he was in the midst of his final major effort to mitigate the disastrous consequences of the vivisection of Bengal.

On that day he had two matters in the High Court—an appeal in the court presided over by Chief Justice Trevor Harris and an application in the court of Mr Justice S R Dasgupta. The matter before Chief Justice Harris was taken up in the morning and he was engaged in that court for almost the whole day. In the application before Justice Dasgupta I was opposing him. Mr S. K. Basu was his junior in that matter. After completing his work in the Chief Justice's Appeal Court, he came to the Court of Justice Dasgupta at about 3.30 p.m. Our matter was concluded before the Court rose for the day.

During our journey back home to 1 Woodburn Park, father told me that he must take the step the same evening towards realisation of the plan over which he had had numerous discussions with Fazlul Haque and Abul Hashim. Father said that it was agreed that efforts would be made by both Fazlul Haque and Abul Hashim with the support of their followers to set up a Provisional Government in East Pakistan, and then seek its accession to India. It was understood that such a Provisional Government would not survive long unless India accepted their proposal for accession and gave immediate armed assistance to the Provisional Government.

It had been further agreed among them that East Bengal would then join the Indian Union as a distinct and separate state. Father said that Fazlul Haque and Abul Hashim had asked him to make an appeal to the people of both West and East Bengal through his newspaper The Nation to accept this new plan as a solution to the intractable communal problem.

On reaching home father requested Mohit Kumar Moitra, the Editor of The Nation, to come to Woodburn Park at around 9 p.m. After dinner father started to dictate his article to his personal secretary E. Bhaskaran. Mohit Moitra arrived at Woodburn Park as agreed and the typed article was brought to my father for his corrections and approval. While we were working on the draft in his office on the first floor, my father started to have breathing difficulties. He made some corrections on the draft and asked Bhaskaran to re-type the article.

By the time the corrected draft was brought to father he was having acute breathing difficulties. I realised with dread that he was having another heart attack. I told my mother, and my uncle Dr Sunil Bose who was a renowned cardiologist was alerted and called to the house. Father waited for the final draft, signed the editorial and asked Mohitbabu to take it to the office of The Nation for publication the following morning. Mother and I pressed him to go to the bedroom without delay, and with mother and I supporting him he somehow managed to walk to his room.

To our dismay on reaching the bedroom father insisted on returning to his office again, which he did, only to lock the drawer of his desk in which he kept his confidential papers. Attention to detail and responsible to the very end! Mother and I then almost had to carry him to his bed where he collapsed soon after. His brother the doctor tried his best to revive him. But father was gone. Strangely, at about the same time, my eight months old baby son suddenly cried out loudly. For a few moments it seemed I had gone blind—there was only darkness around me. I felt drained of all strength and energy.

On 24 February 1950, Amiya wrote to Prime Minister Nehru:

You may have seen in the papers father's last editorial for The Nation which he wrote just half an hour before he passed away. At the time he was dictating the article, father told us that he

intended to write to you and Sardarji the next day and to suggest to you that Indian troops should immediately enter Eastern
Pakistan and take over the administration of East Bengal. Father
did not live to convey to you his ideas on the subject. I, therefore,
consider it my duty to let you know what he was thinking during the last few hours of his life. He felt that it is only after East
Bengal had been brought within the Indian Union that any nego-
tiation with the Pakistan Government should be started. You are
aware of father's views on Kashmir. It is true that he had always
been opposed to a division of Kashmir. But he felt that for the
incorporation of East Bengal into the Indian Union as a distinct
and separate state, India might have to make some concessions
regarding Kashmir. I am conveying this to you in the hope that
father's last wishes will receive your earnest consideration.

Nehru responded soon. In his missive dated 28 February 1950
the Prime Minister rejected the proposal saying that, 'anything
that your father wrote must, of course, be given the best consideration. As you know, we are deeply exercised about developments
in Eastern Pakistan. But the suggestion made by your father
appears to me to be fraught with grave danger and difficulty.'

Amiya

At the time of his father's death, Amiya had been married to
Jyotsna for a little under two years and they were the parents
of a baby boy Surya. Amiya himself was still only 34 and had
been pursuing his law practice while also teaching economics
at university level since his return from England in December
1944. Much in the image of his father, Amiya had been thrust
into multiple roles while seeking to make his mark as a lawyer
at the High Court of Calcutta. He was drawn into the vortex of
the tumultuous political events which unfolded almost immediately after Sarat's release from prison in September 1945, and
he remained his father's close confidant and aide until the end.

The most immediate and pressing challenge facing Amiya
from 21 February 1950 onwards was the inevitable but potentially ruinous one of financial solvency. Sarat had passed away

at a time when his newspaper *The Nation* had indeed proved successful as a voice for the Left but was still considerably in debt. To Amiya fell the responsibility first of all of meeting those and other debts. At the same time he was called upon to play the major role in maintaining and supporting, in addition to his own nuclear family and mother Bivabati, the relatively large extended family (older and younger siblings, including spouse and children) at 1 Woodburn Park.

A part of the debts were recovered by the sale of land and property from Sarat's estate, and the rest by an arrangement under which a portion of Amiya's private legal earnings were sequestered each month by creditors. The debts were eventually paid and Amiya strived to keep *The Nation* alive, but by year's end the newspaper had to close.

Amiya and his young wife Jyotsna accepted, without demur, the responsibilities thrust upon them by the untimely death of father Sarat. This support for members of the wider family was to endure for more than a decade after Sarat's death, with the major household expenses continuing to be met from Amiya's legal practice earnings.

Somehow Amiya also managed to maintain for the use of the extended family, the hill sanctuary at Giddhapahar in Kurseong which Sarat had acquired in 1922, and where both Sarat and Subhas had also spent various periods under house arrest. Amiya assumed the sole responsibility of upkeep of the Giddapahar house well into the 1970s and usually spent a few weeks of his annual vacation there. In later years with no support forthcoming from the other inheritors of the property the cottage fell into a state of disrepair and was eventually taken over in the mid-1990s by the Government of West Bengal. Today the property has been rehabilitated and is administered under the umbrella of the Netaji Institute for Asian Studies based at 1 Woodburn Park. The latter, with the agreement of Amiya and his three brothers and with token compensation, had earlier been taken over in the early 1970s by governmental authorities, to be administered by the West Bengal Government.

It was widely noted among friends and colleagues that Amiya and Jyotsna bore the responsibilities towards the extended family and accompanying expenses without second thoughts. That there was little or no acknowledgement and even enmity for no obvious reason from certain extended family members who benefitted from the generosity and sense of duty of both Amiya and his wife did not deter them.

At the same time such stoicism could not conceal a sense of betrayal felt towards those kin who had easily enough accepted Amiya's generosity but who had later orchestrated his expulsion from the Netaji Research Bureau (NRB) and the Netaji Hall Society, institutions whose establishment and growth owed much to his personal efforts, initiative and drive.

Soon after Sarat's passing, Amiya moved naturally to reinforce the familial bonds with Emilie and Anita, which had been nurtured by Sarat and Biva from the time that contact had been established with them from April 1948. Amiya and Jyotsna visited Vienna during October–November 1950, where Jyotsna remembered with fondness the time spent with Emilie. They enjoyed their visits to the iconic Viennese cafes and restaurants. On her part, Emilie used to recall with pleasure anecdotes, including Jyotsna's delight at seeing snowfall up on the hills overlooking Vienna.

Amiya had of course met Emilie long before in December 1937. As a student at Cambridge University in England, he had been asked by his Uncle Subhas to travel to Badgastein in Austria to join him for the Christmas period, where Emilie was also present as Subhas's secretarial assistant in the preparation of his autobiography *An Indian Pilgrim*. As recalled by Amiya, by the time he arrived in Badgastein to be met at the train station by Subhas and Emilie, Subhas had already begun writing (in two exercise books) and Emilie was transcribing two copies from the manuscript, as she had done earlier in Vienna in 1934 with *The Indian Struggle*.

Subhas had told Amiya that he intended to round off the book with three chapters entitled: My Faith (Philosophical); My Faith (Economic); and My Faith (Political). As it transpired Subhas was only able to complete the first of these three proposed concluding chapters. According to Amiya, Subhas drew heavily on the writings of Frederic Engels, who as Amiya also noted was to inform aspects of Subhas's landmark Presidential Address at the Haripura Congress in February of the following year 1938.

Subhas may have been helped in his autobiographical quest by the presence in Badgastein over that exceptionally cold wintry Christmas of 1937, of an eclectic collection of friends. They would all have contributed to animated fireside discussions on India's freedom struggle and the shape of Indian society to come.

Amiya noted that the day after his own arrival A. C. N. Nambiar came in from Prague where Subhas had helped him to open up contact with the then President of Czechoslovakia. Hungarian opera star Frau Hedy Fullop-Miller, the estranged wife of renowned Austrian author Rene Fullop-Miller (*The Mind and Face of Bolshevism*) was also there, together with a Doctor and Mrs Richter from Rome.

Subhas wanted Amiya with him in Badgastein for another purpose, and that was to entrust to his nephew the preparations and arrangements for his proposed visit to England the following month January 1938. Some days after Christmas, Amiya returned to London to put the programme in place, in cautious collaboration with the redoubtable Mr Krishna Menon and his India League.

Amiya reported that a large crowd was on hand at London's Victoria Station to receive Subhas when he arrived by train on 9 January 1938. For the following 10 days until his departure for India, Subhas embarked upon a frenetic tour de force. He met with Labour and Liberal Party political leaders such as Clement Attlee, Arthur Greenwood, Aneurin Bevin, Sir Stafford Cripps and Sir Harold Laski. He addressed large gatherings of the Indian community in London, and gave lectures in London, Cambridge and Oxford. He also addressed a meeting at Chatham House in London.

Amiya recorded that during his final public meeting, presided over by Labour Party luminary Arthur Greenwood at Caxton Hall in London, Subhas was handed a telegram from Pandit Nehru in India, to the effect that he Subhas had been unanimously elected—and thus confirmed—to succeed Nehru as the next President of the Indian National Congress, to take effect in the following month of February 1938 in Haripura.

Subhas's final meeting in London, perhaps fittingly, was with visiting Irish President Eamon de Valera during the evening of 18–19 January 1938 at the Piccadilly Hotel, where De Valera was staying. Subhas had gone earlier in the evening to the residence of Sir Stafford Cripps for dinner and had left Amiya with instructions to fix an appointment later in the evening with De Valera, as he Subhas was leaving for India the next day. In the event, Amiya on arrival at the Piccadilly Hotel just before 8 pm found himself invited personally by De Valera to join him while they waited for Subhas to return from his dinner engagement with Sir Stafford. Subhas duly arrived around 11 pm and spent almost a further five hours of one-on-one discussions with the Irish President. There could have been no doubt left in the mind of the President as to the views and intentions of the Boses!

Subhas emerged from the President's suite at around 4 am on 19 January 1938, returned with Amiya to his nearby rented apartment at Artillery Mansions to pack and check out, and proceeded to Croydon in south London to catch the flight to India.

Just before boarding the aircraft, Subhas handed over to Amiya the two exercise books containing the manuscript of his unfinished autobiography written at Badgastein the month before, with a parting comment: 'Ami, complete this work if I die in an air crash.'

Subhas never did get around to finishing his autobiography, either before or after his disappearance in August 1945. Two years later, the autobiography began to be serialised in the first issue on 21 October 1947 of a weekly journal *The Socialist Republican*, the acknowledged mouthpiece of the Socialist Republican Party, and edited by Sarat's close friend Satya Ranjan Bakshi.

In the light of the growing uncertainty of the air crash story and the strong urge to believe that Subhas was still alive, great care was exercised to make it clear that the series was a 'yet-to-be finished Autobiography of Netaji'. The manuscript carried by Amiya was eventually entrusted by him to the Netaji Bhawan Museum and Archives established in 1946 by Sarat, at the ancestral house at 38/2 Elgin Road.

Further publication of *An Indian Pilgrim* came about on 23 January 1948, the birth anniversary of Subhas, as Part I of a series entitled *Netaji's Life and Writings,* through another branch of the large Bose family. Aurobindo and Kalyan Bose, sons of Subhas's older brother Suresh, had reportedly managed in 1947, to obtain a copy of the manuscript of *An Indian Pilgrim*, and formed the Netaji Publication Society as the 'authority' for publication by Thacker, Spink and Co. (1933) Ltd., Calcutta. INA luminaries Shah Nawaz Khan and Lakshmi Sahgal were included as members of the Society. Publication of Part 2 of *Netaji's Life and Writings* which comprised *The Indian Struggle 1920–1934*, hitherto published only outside of India by Lawrence and Wishart UK in January 1935 but banned in India by the British, followed on 2 July 1948.

In the meantime Amiya with the full endorsement of Sarat and also Emilie had arranged for the original manuscript of *An Indian Pilgrim* entrusted to him by Subhas, to be translated into Bengali and published by Signet Press in Calcutta. The first edition appeared in June 1948, with the cover page designed by fellow Bengali Satyajit Ray, who was to become a film producer and director of international renown. Amiya retained full copyright for this. Signet Press was also instructed by him in March 1948 to bring out a Bengali translation of *The Indian Struggle 1920–1934*.

A few years later, in 1952, Amiya arranged for publication in English by Chuckervertty Chatterjee & Co. Ltd. Calcutta, of the second part of *The Indian Struggle 1935–1942*, written by Subhas in January 1943 immediately prior to his leaving Germany for the Far East and left as a manuscript with Emilie. The following year, again on the birth anniversary of Subhas on 23 January 1953, Amiya oversaw its publication in Bengali, complete with Foreword from Sarat's widow Bivabati.

Thus for the first time, the unfinished autobiography of Subhas and the two chronological parts of *The Indian Struggle* covering the combined period from 1920 to 1942, were readily available in Bengali to complement what was already there in English. Most importantly this enabled outreach to a much broader base of Bengali readership. Prices were kept at very reasonable levels to enable such broad-based access.

Further publication and dissemination of the writings, speeches and statements of the Bose Brothers, together with relevant correspondence between them, friends, political colleagues and family members, were undertaken by The Sarat Bose Academy (established in 1952 in Netaji Bhawan) under the overall guidance of Amiya as General Secretary. A permanent photographic gallery depicting the life and work of the Bose Brothers designed and developed by the Sarat Bose Academy became a feature of the Museum at Netaji Bhawan. A combined edition of Subhas's *The Indian Struggle 1920–1942* covering both chronological periods was brought out in 1964 by the Bombay-based Asia Publishing House. Much later, the NRB, formally registered in Netaji Bhawan in 1961 and complementing the already-established Netaji Museum and Archives and the Sarat Bose Academy, was given particular responsibility for continuing with the research on and publication of writings pertaining to Subhas.

Over the decades other organisations such as Jayasree Prakashan have published key writings of Subhas. Also Forward Bloc, the political party founded by Subhas, has for its part recognised the challenge of reaching mass readership and awareness among the people of India as to the message of Subhas and has also been publishing and distributing Subhas's works at a reasonable cost.

* * *

Netaji Bhawan

The institutional architecture at the Netaji Bhawan ancestral home at 38/2 Elgin Road had its beginnings with Sarat's release from jail in September 1945. He decided shortly after that the ancestral house built by father Janakinath in 1909 should henceforth be used in memory of his missing brother, for research, analysis and propagation of the ideals and principles for which Subhas—and, it should be added, Sarat himself—stood. Thus during the course of 1946, after in effect acquiring the property from the four brothers (Subhas was one among them though absent) who had inherited from their father Janakinath, Sarat inaugurated 'Netaji Bhawan' at 38/2 Elgin Road, and laid the foundations for a Netaji Museum and Archives as a centre for research in honour of his brother.

It was Sarat's wish that above all the Bose house should be available to the people of India and be used for 'public and charitable purposes'. The Azad Hind Ambulance Corps began to provide a much needed medical service out of Netaji Bhawan, including for the victims of the then rampant communal riots and for the refugees beginning to flood Calcutta from all directions.

With the passing of Sarat only a few years later in 1950, Amiya played a key role in an initiative supported by friends of Sarat, eminent historians, journalists, judges and lawyers to establish The Sarat Bose Academy at Netaji Bhawan in 1952. The Academy had as its primary objective an ambitious programme to develop Netaji Bhawan as a centre of excellence for research and information exchange on matters of national and international importance, as a beacon for the promotion of the arts, music and languages, and as a provider of public services. At the same time it was envisaged that Netaji Bhawan would become the repository for the vision and works of Sarat and Subhas, and for all manner of documentation and records relating to them including their publication.

As General Secretary of The Sarat Bose Academy, Amiya presided over the intensive effort which began almost immediately towards the collection both at home and abroad of key documents, recordings, films and photographs on the lives and activities of the two brothers. Amiya led the way in this quest, and the following years found him far afield in Japan, Germany, the UK, Italy and elsewhere in Europe. A mass of exploratory and follow-up correspondence bears witness to his dedicated leadership in and personal commitment to the assembly of the archival materials.

The Academy over time attracted many young enthusiasts and committed volunteers including Sibabrata Ghosh, Sushil Kumar Roy, Sadhan Neogy, Santimoy Ganguly and Suprakash Mazumdar who gave their time and energy to realise the objectives of The Sarat Bose Academy and of Netaji Bhawan as a whole.

The decade of the 1950s was thus a time of energy and growth for the Netaji Museum and Archives and The Sarat Bose Academy. Many key documents including the writings, speeches and statements of Sarat and Subhas, and their political and private correspondence were collected and published under the auspices of the Academy.

Towards the end of the 1950s, progress in the collection of archival materials of all types was such that the idea began to take shape of the creation of a separate entity 'to undertake a systematic study of Netaji's life and mission'. Thus in 1957, the third arm of a triumvirate of entities housed in Netaji Bhawan came into being as the NRB. A younger sister of Amiya, Gita Biswas, who was a graduate in English and who had once acted as her father Sarat's private secretary, began to organise the work of the new office. Other siblings of Amiya including Chitra Ghosh and Subrata also became active in the development of the rapidly growing centre.

Later in mid-1961, the NRB was formally registered with long-time colleague and friend of Sarat and Subhas, Satya Ranjan Bakshi, as the inaugural Chairman. Renowned historian Dr Ramesh Chandra Majumdar and Amiya, as well as other luminaries were appointed as members of the first Council. Amiya's younger brother Sisir, who had been away in the United States from 1957 to 1960 for further paediatric studies, was appointed as General Secretary on his return.

Earlier in the year on 23 January 1961, the expanded Netaji Museum had formally been opened to the public in the presence of a large and distinguished gathering. Amiya welcomed the guests on behalf of the Bureau and eminent historian Dr Ramesh Chandra Majumdar inaugurated the Museum.

The three pillars namely the Museum and Archives, The Sarat Bose Academy and the NRB, henceforth were meant to act as a vanguard in preserving and promoting the legacy of the Bose Brothers, and helping to realise their most cherished dreams and aspirations.

The stage was now set for the realisation of Sarat's vision of Netaji Bhawan not just as a museum-cum-monument, but as a beating heart for the social, educational and cultural life of Calcutta, Bengal and beyond. By 1964, Amiya, with the firm support of eminent Indian personalities both from Calcutta and elsewhere, was instrumental in constituting the Netaji Hall Society. The first President of the Society was a former Chief Justice of India, Justice Sudhi Ranjan Das, and Amiya was the first General Secretary and a Life Member of the Society.

It was foreseen that the Society would be an umbrella organisation to oversee the ambitious development of Netaji Bhawan and an adjoining plot of land—the latter also previously acquired by Sarat for future family accommodation for his four sons—into an amalgam of auditorium, exhibition halls, lecture theatres, seminar and conference rooms, public reading areas and canteen. The initiative involved the proposed construction of a multi-storied building on the plot now belonging to the four brothers on condition that the building was erected within five years. Otherwise the land would revert to the possession of the four brothers.

At Amiya's invitation, Prime Minister Nehru visited Netaji Bhawan in December 1961, where Amiya had seized the opportunity to flag the then-embryonic plans for expansion. Nehru in response had offered financial support from the Government of India. When fund-raising efforts began in earnest upon the launch of the Society in 1964, Nehru wrote again to express his support in principle, although making no mention of an earlier commitment of Rupees 10 lakhs. It was unfortunate for the financial viability of the project that Nehru died shortly after on 27 May 1964.

By the mid-1960s, Amiya felt that over the 20 years since 1946, a solid foundation had been laid to sustain the momentum of preserving the Bose legacy, including through the multi-faceted institutional framework at Netaji Bhawan. Sadly, over the following crucial years this framework began to unravel.

In 1967, Amiya realised an ambition to serve in the central parliament of India the Lok Sabha, when in a general election he won the rural-based Arambagh constituency with a massive majority. In the process, as an independent candidate supported by the Left, he unseated the Congress Central Government Finance Minister Sachin Chaudhury, also a senior barrister colleague and friend.

Amiya was to serve in the Lok Sabha for the next several years. As remuneration for members was at that time modest, he also had to continue with his private legal practice both at the Supreme Court in Delhi and the High Court in Calcutta. In his role as parliamentarian Amiya continued to propagate the ideology of the Bose Brothers, and their vision of an independent India rooted in socialistic principles, equality, justice and communal harmony.

Sometime over this period in 1967/1968, The Sarat Bose Academy found itself without a home. When office-bearers of the Academy arrived one morning at the premises of Netaji Bhawan, they found a large padlock barring the way to their offices. Subsequently, an open confrontation between the office-bearers of The Sarat Bose Academy and the then Director of NRB Dr Sisir Kumar Bose, forced the relocation of the Academy to the residence of one its members. Over this period, the Azad Hind Ambulance Service also faded away.

This ouster of The Sarat Bose Academy from Netaji Bhawan, the emerging exclusivity of the Netaji Research Bureau and the departure in disillusionment of many of the personalities who were the founders and supporters of the Netaji Hall Society, effectively put an end to the grand vision for Netaji Bhawan and the Society.

For Amiya the end of the dream came suddenly and unexpectedly on 8 October 1977, just a few months prior to his appointment as the Ambassador of India to Burma. On that day, at a meeting of the Netaji Hall Society called by his brother Sisir as a member, he Amiya was expelled in his absence from the Society that he had done so much to create.

* * *

Amiya then turned to other ways to uphold and spread the message of the Bose Brothers. As Indian Ambassador to Burma from 1978 to 1980, he was credited with strengthening India's relations with a country which had played a crucial role in India's struggle for freedom. He revived the folk memories of Subhas's time in Rangoon and Burma, and of the close relationship between Sarat and Subhas on the one hand, and legendary Burmese nationalist leader and revolutionary General Aung San and Burmese war-time Prime Minister Dr Ba Maw, on the other.

The otherwise closed and secretive military regime of General Ne Win enabled Amiya and Jyostna to travel widely throughout Burma, including to Mandalay Jail where Subhas had been incarcerated and to the Burmese-style cottage at the hill station of Maymyo just above Mandalay, from where Subhas had once commanded the INA. Happy times were spent in Rangoon with the widow of Aung San, then living in retirement in her lakeside home in Rangoon.

While in Burma, Amiya continued with his quest to gather materials and other information. He was able to track down local residents who had served with the INA and its Supreme Commander Netaji, and thus obtain first-hand accounts from survivors about the exploits of the Indian soldiers who had lived and died fighting in the final battles for the independence of India. Various items of memorabilia such as INA military insignia, soldiers' pay books, a copy of *The Indian Struggle* published in Malaya, and even a chair used by Subhas as Head of the Provisional Government of Free India which now rests formally in the Red Fort in Delhi, were entrusted to Amiya.

On his return from Burma, Amiya embarked upon an intensive programme of lectures both at home and overseas, now without the hitherto supporting structures at Netaji Bhawan. From his position as an observer of and participant in many of the momentous events of the final struggle for Indian independence, Amiya continued his long campaign to place the efforts and achievements of the Bose Brothers in their historical context, and to do everything he could to ensure their legacy.

Amiya went on an extended lecture tour in Europe during 1980 and again during 1989–1990. In 1980, he was invited to speak on 'Burma Today in the Light of its Colonial History' at the Wien International Centre in Vienna. He also spoke both on India and Burma at the Heidelberg and Stuttgart Universities in Germany. On an invitation from Professor Hugh Tinker of the London School of Oriental and African Studies (SOAS), Amiya gave an extended lecture on the 'Partition of India and Its Consequences'. During a later visit to Europe in 1990, Amiya spoke at the Asian Centre of The Graduate Institute of International Studies in Geneva.

Amiya passed away peacefully at home in Tollygunge Calcutta during the early hours of the morning of 27 January 1996. Only three days before he had delivered a lecture at Presidency College Calcutta entitled 'My Uncle Subhas', yet another presentation in his ceaseless efforts to keep alive for succeeding generations the flame of the Bose Brothers—his father Sarat and uncle Subhas—and to cement their legacy for the future of India.

Amiya himself had made no small contribution to this enterprise, as a highly respected practitioner of law, as an elected representative in the halls of government, as an ambassador abroad for his country and as a devoted family man. Family, friends and colleagues knew him as impeccably honest, principled, generous to a fault and always with the courage of his convictions.

Speaking on 30 January 1996, the Advocate-General of West Bengal the Hon N. N. Gooptu, in remembrance of Amiya, said:

> In one year's time we would be celebrating 50 years of our independence from the shackles of colonialism. But today when our country is passing through a critical phase, the absence of public figures such as Amiya Nath Bose, who had an abiding commitment to democracy and secularism, will be deeply felt. An effective way of paying our tributes to this great personality is to dedicate ourselves to complete his unfinished task. Amiya Nath Bose has left behind a rich legacy of devotion to public cause and we need to enrich this spirit further.

Glossary

Asuric and Sattwic Force	Hindu philosophical concepts
Baisakh	Indian calendar month (April/May)
Bande Mataram	Hymn to the motherland
Brahmacharya	Virtuous lifestyle including celibacy
Braho Samaj	Reform movement of Hinduism
Chotodada	Older but not the oldest brother
Dadabhai	Bose family sobriquet for paternal grandfather
Jethababu	Senior uncle
Khaddar	Hand-spun cloth
Khuro	Uncle
Ma-Janani	Bose family sobriquet for paternal grandmother
Mam	Short form for maternal uncle
Mejdada	Older second brother
Mejobowdidi	Second sister-in-law
Mejomami	Second maternal aunt
Mofussil	Rural districts
Sannyasis	Hindu ascetics
Satygraha	Allegiance to truth
Swadeshi	National self-reliance movement
Swaraj	Independence

Index

About the Author

Madhuri Bose was born and grew up in Kolkata. She is the daughter and second child of Amiya Nath and Jyostna Bose, granddaughter of Sarat Chandra Bose and grandniece of his younger brother Subhas Chandra Bose. Reminiscences from her father Amiya of the immense contributions of the iconic Bose Brothers to the Indian freedom struggle were the stuff of her childhood and the genesis of this book.

After graduate and post-graduate studies in the University of Calcutta and Jadavpur University, Madhuri undertook post-graduate research at the Graduate Institute of International Studies in Geneva, Switzerland. She has pursued her professional career as a human rights advocate for over more than three decades with the International Labour Organisation, Geneva; the United Nations Development Programme, East Africa; and the Commonwealth Secretariat in London. In her professional capacity, Madhuri has written extensively on human rights issues and has travelled widely in Africa, Asia and Europe.